MW00674587

THE EUROPEAN UNION AND THE ACCOMMODATION OF BASQUE DIFFERENCE IN SPAIN

Manchester University Press

SERIES EDITORS: THOMAS CHRISTIANSEN AND EMIL KIRCHNER

Angela K. Bourne

THE EUROPEAN UNION AND THE ACCOMMODATION OF BASQUE DIFFERNCE IN SPAIN

MANCHESTER UNIVERSITY PRESS
Manchester and New York

distributed exclusively in the USA by Palgrave

The right of Angela K. Bourne to be identified as the author of this work has been asserted by her in accordance with the Copyright, Designs and Patents Act 1988.

Published by Manchester University Press
Oxford Road, Manchester M13 9NR, UK
and Room 400, 175 Fifth Avenue, New York, NY 10010, USA
www.manchesteruniversitypress.co.uk

Distributed exclusively in the USA by
Palgrave, 175 Fifth Avenue, New York,
NY 10010, USA

Distributed exclusively in Canada by
UBC Press, University of British Columbia, 2029 West Mall,
Vancouver, BC, Canada V6T 1Z2

British Library Cataloguing-in-Publication Data
A catalogue record for this book is available from the British Library

Library of Congress Cataloging-in-Publication Data applied for

ISBN 978 0 7190 6750 1 *hardback*

First published 2008

17 16 15 14 13 12 11 10 09 08   10 9 8 7 6 5 4 3 2 1

Typeset in Minion with Lithos
by Action Publishing Technology Ltd, Gloucester
Printed in Great Britain
by Biddles Ltd, King's Lynn

To Anthony

CONTENTS

$\mathcal{M}$APS

*T*ABLES

ACKNOWLEDGEMENTS

Many people helped me with this book, far too many to name. The patience of the publishers, the advice of many colleagues and the help of librarians, officials and administrators from around the world – Aberystwyth, Bristol, Bilbao, Brussels, Dundee, Madrid and Reno – have been indispensable. I am grateful for grants from the University of Bristol, the University of Dundee, The Carnegie Trust for the Universities of Scotland and the Centre for Basque Studies, the University of Nevada, Reno. More than anyone else, thanks should go to Michelle Cini for helping me through the ups and downs of my PhD and to Anthony Gómez, whose patience and support were of incalculable value.

BNG	*Bloque Nacionalista Galego* (Galician Nationalist Block)
BOCG	*Boletín Oficial de las Cortes Generales* (Official Bulletin of the Spanish Parliament)
BOE	*Boletín Oficial del Estado* (Official Bulletin of the State)
BOPV	*Boletín Oficial del Parlamento Vasco* (Official Bulletin of the Basque Parliament)
CARCE	*Conferencia para Asuntos Relacionados con las Comunidades Europeas* (Conference for Affairs Related to the European Communities)
CC	*Coalición Canaria* (Canary Islands Coalition)
CFI	Court of First Instance
CiU	*Convergència i Unió* (Convergence and Union)
CoR	Committee of the Regions
COREPER	Committee of Permanent Representatives
CPMR	Conference of Peripheral Maritime Regions
CSEA	Conference of the regions of the Southern European Atlantic
DSCG	*Diario de Sesiones de las Cortes Generales* (Record of Proceedings of the Spanish Parliament)
DSPV	*Diario de Sesiones del Parlamento Vasco* (Record of Proceedings of the Basque Parliament)
EA	*Eusko Alkartasuna* (Basque Nationalists)
EC	European Community
ECJ	European Court of Justice
EE	*Euskadiko Ezkerra* (Basque Left)
EH	*Euskal Herritarrok* (Basque Citizens)
EP	European Parliament
ERC	*Esquerra Republicana de Catalunya* (Republican Left of Catalonia)
ESC	Economic and Social Committee
ETA	*Euskadi Ta Askatasuna* (Basque Homeland and Freedom)
ETAm	ETA *militar* (ETA military)
ETApm	ETA *político-militar* (ETA political-military)
EU	European Union
FEVE	*Ferrocarriles Españoles de Vía Estrecha* (Spanish Narrow-Gauge Railways)
GAL	*Grupos Antiterroristas de Liberación* (Antiterrorist Liberation Groups)

HB	*Herri Batasuna* (Popular Unity)
HST	high-speed train
IU	*Izquierda Unida* (United Left)
IU-ICV	*Izquierda Unida, Iniciativa per Catalunya–Els Verds* (United Left, Initiative for Catalonia–Greens)
LOAPA	*Ley Orgánica de Armonización del Proceso Autonómico* (Organic Law on Harmonisation of the Autonomy Process)
MAP	*Ministerio de Administraciones Públicas* (Ministry of Public Administration)
MEP	Member of the European Parliament
MLNV	*Movimiento de Liberación Nacional Vasco* (Basque National Liberation Movement)
MOPTMA	*Ministerio de Obras Públicas, Transportes y Medio Ambiente* (Ministry for Public Works, Transport and the Environment)
MTTC	*Ministerio de Transportes, Turismo y Comunicaciones* (Ministry of Transport, Tourism and Communications)
OJ	Official Journal of the European Communities
PCTV	*Partido Comunista de las Tierras Vascas* (Communist Party of the Basque Lands)
PNV	*Partido Nacionalista Vasco* (Basque Nationalist Party)
PP	*Partido Popular* (Popular Party)
PSE-EE-PSOE	*Partido Socialista de Euskadi – Euskadiko Ezquerra – Partido Socialista Obrero Español* (Basque Socialist Party – Basque Left – Spanish Socialist Workers Party)
PSE-PSOE	*Partido Socialista de Euskadi – Partido Socialista Obrero Español* (Basque Socialist Party – Spanish Socialist Workers Party)
PSOE	*Partido Socialista Obrero Español* (Spanish Socialist Workers Party)
RENFE	*Red Nacional de los Ferrocarriles Españoles* (Spanish National Rail Network)
REPER	Permanent Representation to the EU
SPRI	*Sociedad para la Promoción y Reconversión Industrial* (Association for Promotion and Industrial Reconversion)
UA	*Unidad Alavesa* (Alavan Unity)

Introduction

By accident and by design, the European Union (EU) has touched nationalist politics in many parts of Europe. After nationalist excesses of World War Two, the founding organisation of today's EU, the European Coal and Steel Community, sought to make war between France and Germany 'not merely unthinkable, but materially impossible'. The market integration policies of the European Economic Community helped break down economic and physical barriers between states, including those dividing national communities which straddled state borders. Enlargement policy sought to dampen nationalist tensions by promoting the rights of national and other minority groups in applicant states. It was even used for goals as ambitious as the reunification of Cyprus. Likewise, nationalist conflict in the Balkans has been a major testing ground for the EU's common foreign and security policy. In this book, I examine the relevance of the EU for nationalist politics in a further case – the impact of the EU's institutions, practices and policy regimes on politics in the Basque Country.

The Basque Country covers just over twenty thousand square kilometres of the western Pyrenees on both its French and Spanish sides. Basque nationalist geography identifies seven Basque provinces.[1] Four of these – *Álava, Guipúzcoa, Vizcaya* and *Navarra* – correspond to current provincial structures in Spain. Three – *Labourd, Basse-Navarre* and *Soule* – lack distinctive administrative structures and form part of the French department, *Pyréneés-Atlantiques*. While markers of Basque identity, such as use of the Basque language (*Euskera* or *Euskara*), or selfidentification as Basque, can be found in all seven provinces, language use and identification patterns vary significantly among the provinces. So do levels of sympathy for Basque nationalism. Spain's 1978 constitutional settlement, negotiated after four decades of rule by the dictator General Francisco Franco, produced partial unification. It led to creation of the *Comunidad Autónoma del País Vasco* (Autonomous Community of the Basque Country), encompassing all Basque provinces in Spain except Navarre, which was governed by the separate *Comunidad Foral de Navarra* (Foral Community of Navarre). Although it does not encompass the entirety of Basque social and political life, the Autonomous Community of the Basque Country is a focal point. Its institutions provide a platform for managing political conflict and for conducting relations with Spanish and EU authorities. For this reason, politics within the Autonomous Community of the Basque Country (henceforth the shorter, Basque autonomous community) will be the principal focus of this study.

Ideally, a study of the EU and its incidence in Basque politics deserves an approach as complex and intricate as its subject. There are many potentially insightful avenues of enquiry. One might examine, for instance, the impact of European integration on the values, methods and constitutional horizons of Basque nationalists or the Spanish governing class (Keating 2001). There is profit in exploring the impact of specific EU policies, including the signifi-cance of EU counterterrorism policies targeting militant Basque nationalists or EU funds promoting economic, social and cultural contacts between Basques on either side of the French–Spanish border (Bourne 2004; Letamendia 1997a). One might explore the limits and possibilities of propos-als sometimes made in the Basque Country for an EU role in peace talks involving *Euskadi Ta Askatasuna* (ETA, Basque Homeland and Freedom). However, considerations of time and space inevitably put limits on the scope of research and in this book I focus on the impact of European integration on the dynamics of Basque devolution.

The topic picks up on a theme of EU scholarship which specifically exam-ines the relationship between the EU and regional governance.[2] This theme, often identified with the concept of multilevel governance, explores implica-tions of regional authorities' increasing interest and mobilisation in the EU sphere, something which emerged as a general phenomenon from around the mid-1980s (see, for instance, Hooghe and Marks 2001; Keating 1998a; Loughlin 1996). It also acknowledges changes at the EU level in the 1990s, such as creation of a specialised Committee of the Regions and authorisation for regional ministers to participate in the EU's key lawmaking body, the Council. The changing role of regions in the EU may be explained by many factors, including augmentation of EU regional policy instruments like the structural funds, emergence of new policy paradigms advocating local 'endogenous' economic development and internal institutional dynamics of the EU (see Kohler Koch 1996; Tömmel 1998). But it also grew from regions' concerns that progressive treaty reforms transferring state competencies to the EU increasingly impinged on regional responsibilities and limited the scope of their decisionmaking powers (Jeffery 1997a and 2004; Börzel 2002; Pérez Tremps *et al.* 1998).

One clear implication is that these developments altered the nature and practices of regional autonomy in Europe. The emergence of new policy arenas in Brussels, incentives for regional mobilisation beyond the state, the new regions' (and local authorities') body in Brussels and new rules legit-imising an EU role for regions fortify external or European dimensions of regional selfgovernment. Despite many years of study, however, the broader implications of this complex phenomenon are less clear. Some have seen opportunities for regional empowerment, including empowerment vis-à-vis central state authorities (Loughlin 1993; Marks *et al.* 1996; Bullman 1997). Others draw contrary conclusions, lamenting the largely unforeseen effects of EU memberships on the internal distribution of territorial power at home

(Bullain 1998; Pérez Tremps *et al.* 1998; Roig 2002). Some consider EU developments a boost for the emergence of cooperative relationships among regional and state authorities (Börzel 2002). Others still consider these developments of rather limited significance overall, given the preponderance of central government decisionmaking prerogatives in the EU, their resources and gatekeeping abilities (Anderson 1990; Pollack 1995; Bache 1998).

Such debates are of particular interest for the study of nationalist politics in the Basque Country due to the centrality of devolution as an instrument for the accommodation of national differences in Spain. The 1978 constitution laid foundations for Spain's 'state of autonomies' by authorising devolution of political power to what eventually became seventeen autonomous communities. In so doing, political elite pursued a variety of objectives, including the desire to modernise and democratise the highly centralised state apparatus inherited from the dictatorship. However, the strength of demands for political autonomy and cultural recognition in the Basque Country, Catalonia and (to a lesser extent) Galicia generated intense pressure and indeed the impetus for devolution.

I do not claim that the devolution of power to Basque institutions has been a panacea. Basque society remains polarised; there is still significant electoral support for radical nationalist, antisystem parties and significant sectors of the Basque political class consider current arrangements insufficient. ETA has yet to definitively abandon armed struggle, despite two ceasefire declarations in the last decade or so. Nevertheless, many consider devolution a crucial ingredient for managing conflict in the Basque Country. It provides historically unprecedented resources for Basque nationbuilding and Basque institutions serve as a meeting point for negotiation of conflicting political projects in Basque society. Furthermore, devolution is an integral element of an institutional framework, sustained by the rules and procedures of liberal democratic politics, for mediating disputes with state authorities. My argument here does not necessarily imply that current arrangements or even more extensive devolution are the best way to give form to Basque desires for selfgovernment; this is an issue beyond the scope of the research. My point is that devolution has been an important – if imperfect – instrument for political coexistence up to now and this makes examination of the EU's impact on Basque devolution pertinent.

Regional power, conflict and cooperation

I investigate this topic by addressing two questions reflecting rationales for Basque devolution and key debates in EU scholarship about regional governance:

* Does European integration alter the way Basque institutions of selfgovernment exercise political power?

- Has Spain's EU membership been a source of conflict or provided new incentives for cooperation between Basque and central governments?

Beginning with the first question, one must acknowledge that political power is notoriously difficult to define, even if most understand it intuitively. For this research, I adapt Steven Lukes' (1986) definition to conceptualise Basque political power – or regional power more generally – as regional authorities' ability to influence public policy decisions in their favour and their ability to control, or escape the control, of other political actors. If regional autonomy is conceived as 'the right of communities defined by territory, language, culture or religion to govern themselves in a way which protects and promotes their distinguishing features' and interests (Loughlin 1998: 110), the link between regional autonomy and regional power is clear. To be able to promote and protect distinguishing features, to formulate distinctive policies and defend diverging preferences, regional authorities must be able to influence decisions in their favour, control, and escape the control of, other political actors, at least some of the time.

As mentioned earlier, existing EU scholarship does not provide a simple answer to questions about the EU's impact on regional power. There are arguments that European integration may empower regions, disempower them or have 'no effect'. Rather than an obstacle for research, however, this ambiguity provides, in the first instance, a varied source of propositions about how European integration may affect regional, and thus Basque, political power. More specifically, it directs the researcher to consider three further clusters of research questions, namely:

- Does the EU's institutional design alter the territorial balance of power within member states to the detriment of regions? Or, do domestic institutional adaptations allow central and regional authorities to share power in EU decisionmaking?
- Does EU decisionmaking resemble a multilevel process of interest aggregation, where regional authorities, perhaps in alliance with EU authorities, can be influential? How relevant are domestic processes of interest aggregation by comparison?
- And finally, do the actions of, or ideas promoted by, EU authorities affect the legitimacy of regions as authoritative decisionmakers?

By examining this range of propositions – which beyond my own work (Bourne 2003) have not, to my knowledge, been examined together in a single study – it is possible to systematically probe ambiguity about the impact of European integration on regional power. In this way, the research makes both a theoretical and an empirical contribution to the broader literature on the EU and regional governance.

Turning to the book's second main research question on the EU, conflict and cooperation within Spain, one confronts the thorny problem of defining the nature of the Basque conflict. This is problematic because divergent views on causes of – and thus appropriate solutions for – nationalist conflict are part of what is at issue. A full discussion of such a complex issue cannot take place here, but it is appropriate to describe key features, even at the risk of oversimplification (for more nuanced, authoritative discussions see Clarke 1984; Jáuregui 1996; de la Granja 2003; Mees 2003). There are both 'internal' and 'external' dimensions to the Basque conflict. Internal dimensions involve differences among Basques. There are differences over what being 'Basque' means in a social and political sense, encompassing questions such as: *To be Basque must one be a Basque nationalist? Can one be Basque but also feel Spanish or French to some degree?* There are differences over constitutional forms, embracing questions such as: *Is an independent Basque state, in or out of the EU, most desirable? Is Basque autonomy within the Spanish and French states preferable?* And finally, although differences have diminished very considerably since the 1970s, Basques may hold contrasting views about appropriate forms of political action, including views about the appropriateness of violence relative to standard instruments of liberal democracy.

External dimensions of the conflict are not always easy to separate from internal dimensions, but the distinction is useful for analytical purposes. In particular, it helps identify the limits of my enquiry, which is mostly confined to examination of external dimensions of the Basque conflict. In essence, external dimensions of the conflict are about relationships between Basques, on the one hand, and the Spanish and French states, on the other. It includes both institutional relations of governing elite and relations between minority and majority national communities, even if boundaries between such communities are fluid. At stake in these relationships are both the routine, daily management of differing ideological preferences and material interests, but also more fundamental questions such as: *To what extent, and in what ways, should the state recognise Basque difference? What is the most appropriate strategy for combating Basque nationalist terrorism? What form should institutions of Basque selfgovernment take? What are the limits and possibilities for autonomous action by Basque institutions?*

Once Spain joined the EU in 1986, and especially as the Basque autonomous community sought to establish a role for itself in EU decision-making, many of these issues acquired a European dimension. It became necessary, for instance, to contemplate institutional reforms to manage state and autonomous community relations with the EU, and to negotiate new codes of appropriateness for their EU actions. Given the sensitivity of questions about the scope of Basque autonomy and configuration of Basque relations with the Spanish state, one could expect these issues to excite controversy. However, some studies suggest EU membership provides new incentives for state territorial actors to share political power and promotes the evolution of 'cooperative' political cultures (Kerremans and Beyers 1996;

Börzel 2002). Indeed, in a study of the EU and intergovernmental relations in Spain, Tanja Börzel argues that autonomous communities initially adopted competitive and confrontational strategies with the central government, but eventually opted for a cooperation modelled on the German experiences of cooperative federalism (2002: 5–6). This intriguing possibility underlies the book's second main research question; namely, whether Spain's EU membership has been a new source of conflict between Basque and central authorities, or whether it has provided incentives for cooperation.

Content and structure of the book

I begin by exploring theoretical puzzles broached in the research. In chapter one I examine arguments about European integration and regional power and why they tend to contradict one another. I then present a theoretical framework designed to explore a range of propositions about European integration and regional power and to permit more general conclusions about the effect of European integration. As a prelude to later chapters, the second chapter examines primary rationales and arrangements for Basque devolution; identifies principal actors, pertinent issues and disputes in Basque politics; and highlights characteristics of Basque relations with central state authorities.

Guided by the theoretical framework and research questions identified above, I then examine the evolution of state and EU level arrangements for Basque participation in EU decisionmaking, and present two case studies analysing Basque experience of European integration. Chapters three and four explore responses to the observed institutional bias of the EU against regions and, more specifically, whether institutional reforms recalibrate territorial power in Spain. Chapter three examines adaptations within Spain and the effectiveness of channels for Basque participation in state decisions on EU matters. It explores Basque involvement in state parliamentary and intergovernmental bodies and the significance of informal links between political parties governing in multiple territorial arenas. Chapter four examines Basque participation in EU decision bodies, such as the Committee of the Regions, the Council, European Commission advisory committees and Community courts. These chapters do not only address the territorial distribution of power within Spain, the evolution of state mechanisms for interterritorial collaboration and prospects for Basque autonomy beyond the state. They also provide a fitting case for examining how Basque and central governments negotiated their way through challenges posed by EU membership.

Moving beyond institutional arrangements for Basque participation in EU decisionmaking, chapter five picks up on questions about regional influence in the EU, regional alliances with supranational authorities, relative importance of domestic interest aggregation and, ultimately, whether there is a multilevel process of interest aggregation in the EU. It does so by examining Basque government campaigns to influence EU blueprints for high-speed train networks, decisions highly relevant for Basque transport priorities. The chapter focuses on alliance strategies employed; responses from state and supranational authorities; the utility of different channels for Basque participation in EU decisions; and territorial relations in more routine EU policy processes.

The last chapter explores the effect of ideas and doctrines promoted by supranational institutions on political autonomy in the Basque Country. A long running dispute, where various EU institutions have questioned the compatibility of Basque taxation measures with common market goals, provides the setting in which this matter is examined. The chapter investigates normative preferences and legal doctrine developed by the European Commission and Community courts and implications for Basque taxation devolution. The dynamics of territorial relations is particularly salient because the dispute affects politically sensitive prerogatives, provides incentives for collaboration between Basque and central authorities, but was closely related to broader domestic disputes about Basque taxation powers.

Much of the research made use of a large pool of academic material and official documents from Basque, Spanish and EU government sources. Case studies, selected after a preliminary survey of available data, also drew on newspaper articles, parliamentary debates and interviews with politicians and officials from all levels of government studied. Most material was collected during field trips to the Basque Country from August to September 1999, July to August 2005 and in December 2006. Newspaper articles were drawn from both statewide (*El País* and *El Mundo*) and local Basque newspapers (*El Correo* and *Deia*). Interviews were used early in the research as an exploratory tool to facilitate case selection and later to confirm findings obtained from other sources.[3] Episodes examined in the book received considerable attention in the media, political commentary and parliamentary debates, suggesting that they were more than just trivial incidents.

In research of this nature, informality and lack of transparency present unavoidable obstacles which inevitably prevent a complete reconstruction of policy processes. Analysis of Basque and central government involvement in the interministerial Sectoral Conferences and related bilateral instruments, for instance, was hampered by the absence of publicly available minutes of meetings or verbatim reports, although some gaps could be filled by government reports and academic commentary. Similarly, largely informal cooperation between Basque and statewide political parties had to be approximated through newspaper and academic commentary. Considerable care was taken to systematically collect and evaluate a wide range of publicly available material. Nevertheless, I do not claim to have captured every detail of policy processes examined in the book.

I conclude that Spain's EU membership has been much more than a trivial or incidental aspect of Basque experiences of selfgovernment. Many Basque and EU competencies overlap, including some of the most politically sensitive Basque prerogatives. EU decisions condition public policymaking in the Basque Country and provide incentives for complex lobbying strategies in multiple territorial arenas.

Furthermore, I argue that EU membership has shaped the territorial distribution of power in Spain. For many years, the central government was able to dominate the state's EU relations, which limited autonomous community influence over policy with European dimensions, including policy affecting autonomous community competencies. However, the central government gradually overcame its reluctance to share power with autonomous communities, making it much more difficult to detect territorial imbalances caused by EU membership. Adaptations within Spain and EU reforms have permitted a more significant Basque presence in Brussels and other seats of the EU.

I found no evidence that collaboration between Basque and supranational authorities could undermine central government positions or provide alternative means for Basque authorities to influence EU decisions in their favour. Indeed, the study provides a counterpoint to perceptions that EU regions and supranational authorities are natural allies. Studies of supranational responses to Basque EU campaigns identified obstacles to alliance formation and when market integration and Basque autonomy appeared incompatible, supranational authorities supported the former.

And, finally, the research provides evidence supporting the view that EU membership provides incentives for collaboration between territorial entities within member states. There were many instances of collaboration between Basque and central authorities in EU matters and over time Basque authorities involved themselves more fully in state institutions. However, in the Basque case, this collaboration does not amount to a more cooperative political culture in territorial relations. There have been many high-profile disputes about the form of Basque participation in EU politics. These disputes merged with, and became integral to, broader disputes about the permissible scope of Basque autonomy and appropriate means of recognising Basque difference in Spain.

These experiences undoubtedly affect the way Basque authorities exercise political power in the contemporary period. However, they provide more evidence that European integration has limited the scope of Basque political power than enhanced it; and little evidence that European integration has played a role in the resolution of nationalist conflict in Spain.

Notes

1   Place names in Castilian (and where applicable French) will be used in this book

because they are more likely to be familiar to English-speaking readers. The names of these provinces in the Basque language are, respectively, *Araba, Gipuzkoa, Bizkaia, Nafarroa, Lapurdi, Behe Nafarroa* and *Zuberoa.*

2   I use the term 'region' in a generic sense and in a way that need not contradict chacterisation of Basques as a national community. Minority or stateless nations form a distinctive, but nevertheless integral subcategory of the regional experience in Europe, especially when they possess their own political institutions.

3   Overall, twenty-eight interviews were conducted during field trips in the Basque Country (August and September 1999 and December 2006); in Madrid (September 2000 and December 2006); and Brussels (September 2000 and February 2004). Interviewees were: representatives from all main Basque and statewide political parties; officials from the Basque government, Basque Historic Territories (Álava, Vizcaya and Guipúzcoa), Spanish central government, and Basque delegation in Brussels; and officials in the European Commission's directorates-general for competition and regional policy.

1

The impact of European integration on regional power

This chapter explores the key theoretical puzzles of the book: firstly, why is it that existing studies present such contradictory conclusions about the impact of European integration on regional power? Some see European integration as a source of empowerment for regions, while others argue that it may undermine regional power. Others still do not think the EU affects regional power at all. The second theoretical puzzle concerns the problems this theoretical ambiguity presents for empirical research and how they might be overcome.

I begin with a brief exploration of the concept 'regional power'. I then examine arguments about the impact of European integration on regional power found in three interrelated fields of study: the constitutional implications of European integration for regions; the origins and nature of regionalism in Europe; and debates about multilevel governance. From this discussion it becomes apparent that evidence and arguments sustaining the different empowerment, disempowerment and 'no effect' conclusions are built on analysis of different dimensions of the EU-regions problematic. As Table 1.1 illustrates, different conclusions tend to focus on arguments about different *means* by which European integration affects regional power. Some focus on the EU's institutional bias against regions, while others focus on the emergence of a more inclusive multilevel process of interest aggregation, the potential for EU institutional-regional alliances, ideas promoted by EU institutions or central government dominance. They may also focus on the effect of European integration on different *sources* of regional power. Some focus on legal-constitutional powers, but others develop arguments about relational sources of regions' power, their resources and legitimacy. I use this insight as a foundation for developing a new theoretical framework, outlined at the end of the chapter, and then applied empirically in chapters that follow.

Table 1.1 Impact of European integration on regional power: summary of arguments

Impact	How integration affects regional power	Source of regional power affected
Disempowerment	Bias of the EU's decision-system against regions	Legal-constitutional
Empowerment	Supranational institutions are potential allies for regional governments	Relational
	Emergence of multilevel process of interest aggregation where others may depend on regions' resources	Possession of valued resources
	Supranational institutions promote ideas that affect legitimacy of regional actors	Legitimacy
No effect	Domestic processes of interest aggregation are more salient for regional influence and central governments can dominate state relations with the EU	Relational

Defining regional power

The simplest way of identifying a region is to observe the existence of formal institutions, or to use the Assembly of European Regions' formulation:

> [Regions are] that territorial authority situated directly below the central state level which has its own elected political representation.

A region may be more or less than a political space, however (Keating 1998b: 20). For instance, a region may be a functional space, with institutions responsible for planning and the implementation of regional policies but lacking directly elected regional bodies. A region can also be a cultural space, especially where a particular territory is inhabited by a distinctive ethnic group. Furthermore, a region can be defined with reference to the context within which its political institutions operate or, as Michael Keating put it, as 'systems of social and economic exchange underpinned by institutions and a system of action' (Keating 1998b: 11). It is important to reiterate that I use the term 'region' in a generic sense and in a way that need not contradict characterisation of the Basque Country as a national community. Minority or stateless nations form a distinctive but nevertheless integral subcategory of the regional experience in Europe, especially when they exercise some form of political autonomy.

In an adaptation of Steven Lukes' conception of political power, I define 'regional power' as a region's ability to influence decisions about public policy in its favour or its ability to control or escape the control of other political actors (Lukes 1986: 4 and 9–10). As mentioned in the introduction, the relationship between this conception of regional power and regional autonomy is clear: To be able to promote and protect the distinctive political, cultural and material attributes of the region, and to be able to formulate policies and preferences that differ from those of other territorial entities, regional authorities must have some capacity to influence decisions in their favour and to escape the control of other territorial actors, at least some of the time.

There are many sources of regional power, or means by which regions are able to influence decisions in their favour, control or escape the control of other political actors (Loughlin 1998: 146–56; Keating 1998b: 25–8). Of these, *legal-constitutional* sources of power are the most fundamental. These are the formal rules that may guarantee a region's right to exist, endow it with decisionmaking prerogatives, regulate its institutional forms and establish its rights in relation to other territorial entities. Another source of regional power is *relational*. Cooperation or strategic alliances with other more powerful political entities, including other regions, central governments and EU institutions, can help a region to promote and protect their goals and interests.

A region's *resources* can be another source of political power. Financial resources are needed to run regional governments and implement their policies. If a region has tax-levying powers and/or a significant degree of freedom to decide how its budget will be spent, the region will be much less dependent upon, and therefore less subject to control by, other political entities. Physical resources, such as energy, infrastructure, valuable factors of production, or informational resources, such as local knowledge or expertise, may give a region significant political leverage, especially when others are dependent upon such resources. Institutional resources, such as organisational efficiency, may enable a region to pursue its goals more effectively. Other sources of power may derive from a region's internal characteristics such as its political cohesion or stability, characteristics that may improve the ability of its governing institutions to legitimately define and pursue regional interests.

In what ways, then, does European integration affect the political powers of regions? As the following discussion will show, this is a question that can be examined from a variety of perspectives, one of which involves examining the constitutional implications European integration raises for regional autonomy.

Disempowerment and the EU's institutional bias against regions

The role of institutions and their impact on power relationships has been an enduring theme in the study of politics. Under the rubric of 'new institutionalism' this theme has received renewed attention in recent years in both the field of EU studies (Cini and Bourne 2006; Wiener and Diez 2004) and political science more generally (Hall and Taylor 1996). One key insight of this literature is that organisational resources, rules, procedures and cultures can help promote and perpetuate particular beliefs, values, interests and political projects through time (March and Olsen 1989 and 1996; DiMaggio and Powell 1991; Goldstein and Keohane 1993; Aspinwall and Schneider 2000). They may also affect power structures if, for instance, institutional resources and rules systematically benefit one group over another. This relationship between institutions and political power is well captured by the concept of 'institutional bias' developed many decades ago by Peter Bachrach and Morton Baratz. Institutional bias occurs, according to these authors, when 'a set of predominant values, beliefs, rituals and institutional procedures ("rules of the game") operate systematically and consistently to the benefit of certain persons or groups at the expense of others' (1970: 43).

Together with the insights of new institutionalism, the concept of institutional bias helps capture key arguments about negative effects of the EU on regions' legal-constitutional powers. At the heart of this argument is the observation that the EU is designed in the first place as a 'union of states', secondarily as a 'union of peoples' and only as a 'union of regions' in a very minimal sense. As such, the EU's institutional design puts significant limits on the representation of regions' interests at the European level and provides opportunities and justifications for central governments to assume responsibility for competencies which would otherwise belong to regions. Given the focus of these arguments on constitutional issues, it is not surprising that this perspective has largely come from legal scholars in federal and regionalised states (see Jáuregui 1986; Fernández Monje 1989; Bullain 1990 and 1998; Pérez González *et al.* 1994; Bustos 1996; Albertí 1998; Jiménez 1999; Roig 2002; Lucas 2000; Biglino 2003; but also see Kerremans and Beyers 1996; Jeffery 1997a and Börzel 2002 for political science perspectives).

The EU is probably the best illustration of an international organisation that has moved beyond the exclusive use of intergovernmental principles, but a series of EU rules and political practices nevertheless aim to ensure that the EU remains, in large part, a union of states. Major decisions are taken or must be endorsed by the European Council and the Council, the EU bodies representing member states. Important powers have also been delegated to supranational institutions designed to represent the collective interests of the member states. The European Commission exercises important policy initiation, administrative and executive functions; the European Court of Justice (ECJ) performs a range of interpretative and dispute resolution roles; and the European Central Bank is responsible for setting monetary policy for Eurozone states.

In addition to EU rules and institutions serving member states' individual and collective interests, there have been attempts to give substance to idea of the EU as a 'union of peoples'. The European Parliament (EP), whose members have been directly elected by citizens of the member states since 1979, has become more influential in the last two decades and may now, under certain conditions, veto decisions that member states might otherwise want to adopt. The Maastricht Treaty's creation of 'EU citizenship', encapsulating a series of rights for member state nationals, attempts to enact a 'Treaty Establishing a Constitution for Europe' (henceforth Constitutional Treaty), and the EU Charter of Fundamental Rights are further attempts to 'bring Europe closer to the citizen'.

In response to demands from regional authorities, the Maastricht Treaty also established a Committee of the Regions (CoR). While creation of the CoR was a significant symbolic recognition of the regional (and local authority) levels in EU decisionmaking, the CoR was only given very weak decision powers. It must be consulted when the EU legislates on a variety of issues of relevance to regions, but its opinions are not binding. If it comes into force, the Constitutional Treaty will enhance the CoR's role but gives no guarantee that regions' collective or individual views will be taken into account.

In addition to an institutional design which gives regions only very limited formal status in the EU, member state central governments may benefit – at the expense of regions – from a series of international conventions and rules embedded in the EU decision system. In both international and EU law, the state is conceived as a unitary actor in relation to its formal representation in key decision bodies, the presentation of negotiating positions in such bodies, and state responsibility for compliance with agreements made (Mangas 1998; Aja 2003: 164). These principles tend to privilege central authorities in regionalised and federal states because central authorities usually assume responsibility for the states' international relations, even where regions may simultaneously possess some powers with international dimensions (such as treatymaking powers) (Pérez Tremps *et al.* 1998). Central governments in Germany and Spain have sought to justify restrictions on regional participation in EU decisions with reference to these central government responsibilities, although these have, in the Spanish case, been successfully challenged in the Constitutional Court, and in Germany been overtaken by agreements allowing extensive regional participation in EU decisions (Mangas and Liñán, 2004: 516–7; 524–5; Aja 2003: 165; Börzel 2002: 104–6, 60–6, 77; Hrbek 1999: 289).

It is also important to be aware that conceptions of the state as a unitary actor in international affairs must sit alongside the principle of internal autonomy, which supposes that a state's system of government and the distribution of power among regional and central authorities is a purely internal matter (Mangas 1998; Jiménez 1999: 172). Together, these principles mean that there need not be an obstacle to regional or local authorities playing a part in the implementation of EU obligations, even if the state as a whole retains ultimate responsibility (Peréz Tremps 1987; Jiménez 1999: 172).

Furthermore, conceptions of the state as a unitary actor and the principle of internal autonomy mean that each state is responsible for designating who will represent the state in its international and EU delegations (Mangas 1998), which has in practice allowed regional representatives to form part of state delegations in bodies like the Council. However, because of the requirement that states present a single negotiating position in EU bodies, a region's presence in state delegations does not provide an opportunity for the representation of an individual region's views on the matter at stake (Mangas 1998). Moreover, where there are no specific domestic arrangements for regions and central authorities to share responsibility for the state's EU decisions and representation, the central government will usually assumes these responsibilities.

Of particular interest here are arguments that all of this has a direct bearing on regions' legal-constitutional powers. Many scholars have argued that as progressive treaty reforms have transferred state powers to the EU level, regions have seen the EU assume responsibility for a significant number of their policy competencies but have lost out because they have no way of guaranteeing their views would be heard in the EU (Fernández Monge 1989: 96–7; Bustos 1996: 488; Bullain 1998: 348; Pérez González *et al.* 1994: 328; Albertí 1998: 488–9; Roig 2002: 29; Börzel 2002: 54). Moreover, these authors argue that, facing a situation in which EU rules allowed central authorities more say than regions in decisions affecting transferred competencies, regions could loose out as the balance of power tips in favour of central governments. In other words, by virtue of their EU prerogatives, central governments could find themselves involved in decisions affecting policy areas allocated exclusively to regional authorities in domestic constitutional arrangements, or be the only territorial level involved in decisions which were shared with regional authorities in those domestic arrangements.[1]

Especially since the mid-1980s, a lively political and academic debate has ensued covering both the significance and the appropriateness of possible responses to the challenges posed by EU membership. In many of the EU's federal and regionalised states new rules were established allowing central and regional authorities to share responsibility for the state's EU decisionmaking and representation. However, both the sufficiency and effectiveness of these mechanisms for powersharing remain an issue. Many EU regions – including those from states with the more robust domestic arrangements for power-sharing in EU matters – have continued to call for various EU level reforms (Keating 2004). There have also been calls to enhance 'protections' against EU incursions into regional powers through a strengthening of the EU principles of 'subsidiarity' and 'proportionality', which are essentially principles of restraint (Jiménez 1999; Jeffery 2004).

Evaluations of Spanish institutional responses are mixed. On the one hand, Tanja Börzel, for instance, argues that central authorities now share the state's EU decision powers with autonomous communities, who have meaningful input (2002: 134–47). In an argument of particular relevance to this study's focus on conflict and cooperation in the Basque case, Börzel conceptualises EU challenges to regional powers as new incentives for territorial cooperation. Once autonomous communities 'learnt' that they could not 'redress the institutional balance of power' through their limited direct access to EU decisionmakers, autonomous communities turned their back on the traditional political culture of competitive regionalism and 'embraced a cooperative strategy' in the domestic arena (2002: 5–6). Against Börzel's optimistic conclusions, however, range many critical evaluations identifying deep problems with the way Spain's institutions for territorial cooperation work in practice (Roig 1998, 1999a, 2000, 2001 and 2002; Albertí 1998; Aja 2003; Rey 2003). Evidently, evaluations of the effectiveness of responses designed to meet the challenges of European integration will determine whether, and to what degree, the EU continues to affect the exercise of regional competencies and the territorial distribution of power in federal and regionalised states.

Regionalism, alliances and the empowerment of regions

A very different set of conclusions about the impact of European integration on regional power can be found in studies of regionalism in Europe. They suggest that European integration has changed the nature and strategies of regions in a way which could have positive consequences for regional power.

As John Loughlin defines it, regionalism is 'an ideology and a political movement advocating greater control by regions over the political, economic and social affairs of their regions, usually by setting up political and administrative institutions with legislative powers' (Loughlin 1996: 148). Regionalism has a long history. It emerged in the nineteenth century as a conservative and traditionalist political movement reacting to the emergence of the liberal state (Loughlin 1996: 141). Regionalism re-emerged in the 1960s and 1970s, a phenomena which was variously described as 'new regionalism' (Keating 1998a), the 'renaissance of the regional' (M. Rhodes 1995: 1), the 'rise of mesogovernment' (Sharpe 1993) and the 'new territorial politics' (Keating 1996: 43–64). One important manifestation of the phenomenon was an upsurge in minority nationalism in many European states (Rokkan and Unwin: 1982). Another was a new dynamic of regional economic 'entrepreneurialism', where regional actors more aggressively 'took charge' of their own economic development (M. Rhodes 1995; Leonardi 1993). An important consequence of the growing significance of regionalism was an increasing tendency for Western European states to regionalise their state structure and devolve more political power to substate entities (Sharpe 1993).

Analysts suggest a range of explanations for the regionalist revival, including a number specifically relating to European integration. Some points to changing ideas, such as a stronger identification between democracy and decentralisation (Sharpe 1993: 14–15; Keating 1988: 171), or the increased legitimacy of 'selfdetermination', the doctrine that 'any selfdifferentiating people, simply because it *is* a people, has the right, should it so desire, to rule itself' (Connor 1972: 331). Other arguments have focused on the effects of globalisation, which may simultaneously encourage competitive regional entrepreneurialism in the economic domain (Parkinson and Harding 1995: 67; M. Rhodes 1995; Leonardi 1993) and fuel the perception that minority cultures need defending from the growing diffusion of 'global' messages, ideas and cultures (Connor 1972: 331; Rokkan and Urwin 1982: 3). Others still focus upon some central governments' desire to 'off-load' troublesome policy responsibilities to regional administrations, or the implications of central government policies to improve the plight of economically deprived areas through regional development policies (Sharpe 1993: 12–13; Keating 1988).

Explanations specifically relating to the impact of European integration on regionalism include the argument that the EU provided a new and seemingly less radical constitutional horizon for minority nationalist parties. The call for 'independence in Europe (or the EU)', rather than independence *per se*, appeared to considerably reduce the political and economic costs of separation from existing states, a development which some have argued helped improve the popularity of minority nationalism (Lynch 1996; Keating and Jones 1995: 6). Furthermore, European economic integration is thought to have intensified more economically developed regions' impulse for regional economic entrepreneurialism because it intensifies competition between regions in their search for investment and economic opportunities in the EU's single market (Leonardi 1993; M. Rhodes 1995; Parkinson and Harding 1995; Cheshire 1995).

In addition in the argument that European integration contributed to the revival of regionalism in the last few decades, many argue that the EU has added a European dimension to the governing experiences of regional governments and that this provides opportunities for regional empowerment (Mazey 1995: 78; Loughlin 1993: 14; Loughlin 1996: 157; Bullman 1997: 4; Keating 1998a: 163). They point to the emergence of regional lobbying in Brussels; an activity which the growth of regional information offices in the Belgian capital indicates is now a permanent and regular one. Attention is drawn to formation of organisations representing regions from all over the EU to provide a collective regions' lobby on a wide range of EU issues and to facilitate other forms of cooperation. Treaty reforms creating the CoR or reforms to EU regional policy arrangements which introduced the 'partnership principle' have been held up as signs of the growing significance of regions in the EU. Partnership required 'close consultation' between the European Commission, central governments and competent local and regional authorities during key regional policy implementation phases.

In such developments, some have seen opportunities for regional empowerment, although this prospect is raised more often as a possibility that has yet to be fully demonstrated (Bullman 1997: 17; Loughlin 1993: 15, Keating 1998a: 163). However, in contrast to arguments about the disem-powering effects of European integration on *legal-constitutional* sources of regional power, arguments about empowerment focus on *relational* sources. This source of regional power, it will be recalled, is derived from cooperation or strategic alliances with other political entities that could help a region to promote and protect its goals and interests. A crucial aspect of the argument that European integration might empower regions is that new possibilities for cooperation between regions and EU institutions might strengthen both regional and EU institutions' positions when bargaining with member state central governments (Bullman 1997: 17; Loughlin 1993: 15; Keating 1998a: 163). There is also the suggestion that, in some instances, these alliances might help regions to escape the control of their central governments (Keating 1998a: 163).

Another difference between analysis supporting empowerment and disempowerment conclusions are arguments about the means by which European integration may produce these effects. While the argument under-pinning the disempowerment option is that the EU's institutional design may induce alterations in the domestic distribution of power, the possibility that European integration might empower them is supported by the argument that some form of triangular relationship between regions, states and EU institutions has emerged (Loughlin 1996; Keating 1998a: 164; Keating 1998b: 24). Arguments about the nature of such triangular relationships – also called multilevel governance – have been more fully developed in debates about the evolution of the EU. It is to this debate that I now turn.

Multilevel governance and the empowerment of regions

Key themes underpinning debate about multilevel governance are questions about the changing nature of the state in Europe and the relative power of state central governments. This theme is often presented as debate about whether the state's political authority and capacity to act are being eroded 'from below' by the demands of territorially-based regional groups and 'from above' by the logic of economic and political integration among European states (Kolinsky 1984; Bullman 1997: 3).

The two main 'classical' schools of European integration – neofunction-alism and intergovermentalism – have long addressed challenges to the state from 'above' (Haas 1961, 1968 and 1970; Lindberg 1963; Lindberg and Scheingold 1970; Hoffman 1966; Taylor 1975). In the 1980s, however, the Europeanisation of the regionalist movement prompted many analysts of European integration to adapt old and develop new concepts and models to theorise challenges 'from below' as well. From these debates about the impact of both regionalism and European integration on the power of the state, a number of theoretical propositions about the impact of European integration on regional power can be drawn.

The theory of multilevel governance, developed principally by Gary Marks and Leisbet Hooghe, and drawing on important elements of neofunctionalism, issued some of the most challenging propositions (Marks 1992 and 1997; Hooghe 1995b and 1996; Marks and Hooghe, 1996; Hooghe and Marks, 2001; Marks *et al.* 1996). The principal claim of multilevel governance is that 'the state no longer monopolises European-level policymaking or the aggregation of domestic interests (Marks *et al.* 1996: 346). Marks and Hooghe accept the intergovernmentalist argument that central governments remain the most important players in EU politics. But alongside this argument they bring in the neofunctionalist idea that EU supranational institutions like the European Commission, the ECJ and European Parliament 'have independent influence in policymaking that cannot be derived from their role as agents of state executives' (Marks *et al.* 1996: 346). Importantly, they also argue that regional actors may have a role in EU-level decisionmaking that does not always involve the mediation of central governments. These changes suggest the emergence of multilevel governance, or a new multilevel EU polity, where regions and EU authorities, among others, become important actors alongside central state governments.

There are several key features of this multilevel polity (Marks *et al.* 1996: 346–7). It is a polity

- where regional, state and supranational actors 'share ... control over many activities that take place in their respective territories';
- where states are 'one among a variety of actors contesting decisions that are made at a variety of levels';
- where 'complex interrelationships in domestic politics do not stop at the nation state but extend to the European level';
- where 'subnational actors operate in both national and supranational arenas';
- where there are transnational linkages between actors located in and representing different-level political arenas;
- whose features are discernable but not yet fully defined; and
- whose structure is variegated in the sense that the above-mentioned features will be observable in some EU policy areas but not others, and that some regional actors will be more able (and inclined) to participate in multilevel politics than others.

Marks and Hooghe are not the only analysts to develop a model of the EU as a multilevel polity. Peter John (1996) and Elizabeth Bomberg and John Peterson (1998), for example, have developed similar models.

The argument that the EU is developing into a multilevel polity with these features provides an important explanation of how European integration may empower regions. In the first place, the development of a multilevel process of interest aggregation, where regions and EU actors become more important policy participants at the EU level, provides a setting in which regional-EU institutional alliances can flourish. As mentioned in the previous section, these regional-EU institutional alliances have been highlighted as a possible means by which regional actors can enhance relational sources of power. They could help strengthen regions' positions in bargains with central governments and could even allow regions to influence EU decisions in a way that did not subordinate their interests to those of the state's central government or the state as a whole.

Furthermore, a central argument of multilevel governance, and indeed other multilevel polity approaches, is that decisions in some policy areas are becoming interest aggregation processes conceptualised as 'policy networks' (Marks 1996; John 1996). Interest aggregation is a core rational choice concept which models collective choice as a bargaining process where selfinterested actors manage to reach agreements satisfying each actor's interests. 'Policy networks' is one way of modelling such a process. It emphasises the dependence of selfinterested actors on each others' resources – legal, organisational, political and informational – and the need for actors to agree to exchange their resources in order to reach mutually acceptable policy decisions and to achieve policy goals (R. Rhodes and Marsh 1992; R. Rhodes, Bache and George 1996: 368).

The policy networks concept is particularly attractive for multilevel polity approaches because it enables analysis to move beyond policy participants' formal decisionmaking powers – which for EU institutions, and especially regions, are relatively weak in EU decisionmaking – to consider power derived from the dependence of political actors on each others' financial, informational and other resources (Marks 1996: 417–19; John 1996: 298). In addition to its control over the management of EU finances, for instance, the European Commission has resources like expertise, its supranational perspective and 'technocratic objectivity', which can make it a more powerful policy participant (Marks 1996: 419). Similarly, regions' local knowledge may be a resource enhancing central governments and EU authorities' dependence, especially if that local knowledge can enhance the effectiveness of policy implementation. In other words, even where institutional rules do not require the incorporation of regional or EU authorities' interests into an EU decision outcome, the emergence of a multilevel process of interest aggregation may nevertheless empower regions when they possess resources valued by other policy participants.

Work on multilevel governance has evolved into a broad church so that rational choice-inspired policy network approaches coexist with those drawing attention to the role of norms and ideas. These generate a further set of proposals about the impact of European integration on regional power;

namely, the argument that institutional actors created in the course of European integration have promoted ideas and concepts that increase the legitimacy of regions as policy actors.

In the 1980s, the European Commission championed a new approach for conducting EU regional policy (Kohler Koch 1996: 373–6; Tömmel 1998: 57–61). The new method involved orientating EU regional policy instruments towards developing regions' endogenous economic potential and creating new decisionmaking and implementation procedures. Previously, EU regional policy had been largely dominated by central governments, but the new approach gave regions (and local authorities) a much more important role in policy implementation. While the European Commission initially met some resistance from member state central governments, it eventually succeeded in institutionalising its new regional policy approach with enactment of the 'partnership' principle outlined above.

By pushing for this new approach the European Commission was, in Beate Kohler Koch's formulation, propagating the idea that the best way of conducting EU regional policy was 'cooperative problem solving', an integral component of which was the idea that regional actors ought to be involved alongside private and public actors from different territorial levels in this policy domain (1996: 372–3). Thus, propagation, acceptance and institutionalisation of this idea in the EU created a new rule, or norm, of appropriate behaviour which legitimised and therefore empowered regions as more important policy participants (Kohler Koch 1996: 373–4).

Multilevel policy approaches are not without critics. Patrick Le Gales and Christian Lequesne, for example, argue that optimism about regions becoming more important players in EU politics have not materialised and that regions, therefore, remain minor actors in European governance (1998: 8). Others criticise a tendency to confuse regional participation or involvement in EU decisions with an ability to influence them, a tendency that they argue shows significant weaknesses in the descriptive accuracy and explanatory power of such approaches (R. Rhodes, Bache and George 1996: 370; Kohler Koch 1996: 375). Another set of criticisms relates to the tendency to underestimate the significance of domestic relationships. As Charlie Jeffery argues, rather than an opening up of possibilities for regional participation in EU institutions, some of the most important changes in regions' capacity to influence EU decisionmaking have taken place in the domestic arena (1997a and 2000).

In other critiques and counterarguments confronting multilevel governance approaches, however, it is possible to discern a set of arguments that give a very different answer to the question under examination here: The argument that central government control means European integration has 'no significant effect' on regional power.

Central government control and the 'no effect' argument

A key distinguishing feature of intergovernmentalist accounts of the EU is an emphasis on central government abilities to control politics 'beyond the state'. EU decisionmaking is modelled as a process where central government bargains determine outcomes. Supranational institutions are conceived as 'agents' of the member states with very limited scope for autonomous action. These propositions form the foundations for a sustained critique of multilevel governance approaches. From arguments about the limited autonomy of supranational actors, it follows that regions' alliances with EU authorities will not give them significant influence in EU decisions. Central government dominance also means, as Mark Pollack argues, that regional and EU authorities are little more than actors in an 'intergovernmental play' because it is central governments who 'establish the institutional context within which both the Commission and regional governments act' (1995: 362).

A similar argument can be found in work by Jeffrey Anderson (1990) and Ian Bache (1998 and 1999) who argue that central governments still enjoy ample statutory and other resources at home which enable them to insist that they remain the principal intermediaries between regions and EU authorities. This gives central governments important 'gatekeeping' powers, allowing them to block actions by EU institutions or regions which may significantly affect the interests of the central government or the state as a whole.

It should also be emphasised that such positions need not imply that regions have absolutely no influence over EU decisionmaking. Regions may still be able to influence EU policymaking if their views can be subsumed into the negotiating position that their state's central government defends in EU decision fora. This argument is essentially an application of Robert Putnam's (1988) 'two-level' game model of international decisionmaking to the context of EU politics, an application exemplified in Andrew Moravcsik's work (1993 and 1998). Moravcsik models EU decisionmaking as a two-level game where domestic political actors – like regions – articulate preferences through 'domestic institutions and practices of political representation' which eventually become 'a set of national interests or goals that the state brings to international negotiations' (1993: 483–5). Armed with a set of preferences sensitive to the concerns of domestic interest groups, central governments then engage in a process of interest aggregation at the European level. However, it is important to realise that from this viewpoint, regions' influence is attributable to domestic variables rather than EU variables and cannot, therefore, form part of an argument about EU effects on regional power.

Taken together, intergovernmentalist arguments about the dominance of central governments in EU decisionmaking and the central government 'gatekeeper' thesis provide grounds for concluding that European integration has 'no effect' on regional power: Central governments can block regional–supranational alliances which might otherwise allow regions to promote their interests and escape central government control. Insofar as these arguments serve as critiques and counterarguments to multilevel governance approaches, it is not surprising that they also focus on the EU's impact on relational sources of regional power, which emphasise the effects of cooperation and strategic alliances.

Unravelling ambiguity: a new theoretical approach

From the foregoing discussion, it should be clear that there is considerable ambiguity about the impact of European integration on regional power in the findings of existing studies. The substance of this observation is summarised in Table 1.1, presented at the beginning of the chapter. It shows the principal underpinnings for conclusions that the EU disempowers, empowers and has no effect on regional power. Table 1.1 also identifies important differences in arguments sustaining these conclusions, particularly different views about how European integration has its effect on regional power and about the sources of regional power affected.

It may be that there is truth in more than one of these options and, as some argue, that ambiguity and paradox is an inevitable feature of the regional experience in contemporary Europe (Wright 1998; Christiansen 1999). However, it is possible that ambiguity might be a result of theoretical failings that can be observed in the way this topic has been dealt with so far. It may be that the effect of European integration on regional power looks so ambiguous and contradictory because these different options have not been integrated into a single approach where evidence for each of the three conclusions can be weighed against evidence for the others. Table 1.2 presents a theoretical framework that will allow the researcher to explore this possibility.

The research questions in Table 1.2 are divided into three sections. This signifies the need to employ different approaches and techniques to address different questions or clusters of questions. The task of identifying exactly which regional competencies may be diminished by EU membership, an objective implicit in the first set of questions, is not as simple as it may at first seem. The interpretation and daily implementation of constitutionally entrenched lists of competencies are, in practice, open to varying interpretations due to imprecision or ambiguity in legal texts; ideological or normative preferences; and changing political, economic and social circumstances (Peréz Tremps 1987: 86–90). It is possible to appreciate something of the range of regional competencies affected by the EU by examining areas where EU bodies must consult the CoR: economic and social cohesion (focusing on regional economic development); transEuropean infrastructure networks (including public works); health; education; culture; employment policy; social policy; environment; vocational training and transport. Even this long

Table 1.2 Impact of European integration on regional power: theoretical framework

Research questions	Findings
Does the EU's institutional design alter the territorial balance of power within the member state to the detriment of regions? Or do domestic institutional adaptations allow central and regional authorities to share power in EU decisionmaking?	Empowerment, disempowerment or no effect?
Do alliances between supranational and regional authorities help regions to influence EU decisions? Is this evidence of a multilevel process of interest aggregation? How relevant are domestic processes of interest aggregation?	Empowerment, disempowerment or no effect?
Do ideas promoted by supranational actors affect the legitimacy of regions as authoritative decisionmakers?	Empowerment, disempowerment or no effect?

list is not exhaustive. Inventories of overlapping Basque autonomous community and EU competencies also include fisheries, industry, consumer affairs, research and development, youth affairs, taxation, policing and communications media (Gobierno Vasco 1996a: 41–2; Fernández Monge 1989: 109). Indeed, by one calculation, around 80 per cent of Basque competencies have been affected by EU policies to a greater or lesser degree since the Maastricht Treaty entered into force (Diego Casals 1995: 1028).

For all but specialised legal scholars, the complexity of interpreting competence distribution makes it difficult to analyse the effects of the EU on regional competencies with absolute precision. However, it is possible to make judgements about the impact of the EU on the territorial distribution of power within a member state on the basis of generalisations about broad changes in the location of responsibility for public policy. This can be deduced from observations about the adequacy of state-level adaptations to EU membership and, more specifically, observations about the extent to which central and regional authorities share power in EU decisionmaking. In this book, these tasks are undertaken in chapters three and four. Such a focus on the evolution of institutions and practices for powersharing within member states has the advantage of recognising two integral features of the contemporary EU: Firstly, that EU membership involves a commitment to share or pool sovereignty in many policy areas; and, secondly, that the complexity of the EU decision-system leaves little scope for 'compensating' each individual region for transferred competencies by giving them participation rights equivalent to a member state.

In order to address the second set of research questions one can employ process-tracing techniques. Once a region's preferences, lobbying and alliance strategies in relation to a specific EU decision are known, it is possible to assess whether the region was able to find support from supranational actors by examining the evolution of those actors' preferences through different stages of the policy process. If a region's EU campaign provides evidence that the region has been able to benefit from such alliances, especially if the region's preferences differ from those of central authorities, this will provide evidence of a multilevel process of interest aggregation. Furthermore, by examining the formulation of central government preferences in response to the region's EU campaign and preferences defended in the EU, it should also be possible to assess central authorities' ability to dominate state involvement in EU decisions and the relative importance of domestic interest aggregation processes. This approach is employed in a study of a Basque government EU campaign presented in chapter five.

To address the third research question outlined in Table 1.2 it is possible to use a variety of approaches. One could, for instance, follow the lead of existing studies and examine the impact of the EU's partnership principle on the role of regions in the implementation of regional policy (see Bourne 2003). However, the role of ideas can be explored in other ways too. It can be explored through case studies in other EU policy areas where supranational authorities – be it the European Commission, the ECJ or the European Parliament – may develop policy paradigms, doctrine or normative positions that affect the legitimacy of regions as authoritative decisionmakers. This is the approach I employ in this book, whose sixth chapter examines EU controversy over special Basque taxation prerogatives.

The central idea of the theoretical framework is that it may be possible to unravel ambiguity by examining all of these propositions in each of a series of single-region case studies. For each region, results from empirical studies examining each proposition can be compared to determine whether, overall, European integration: 1) mainly empowers the region; 2) mainly disempowers the region; or 3) mainly has no effect on the region's political power. A fourth possibility is that evidence from the study will confirm the ambiguity expectation in existing studies. This would occur if there is evidence supporting each or most of the empowerment, disempowerment and no-effect options. Conclusions for individual regional studies can then be compared to develop more general conclusions about the overall impact of the EU on regional power.

Ideally, this procedure should be used to examine a number of single-region case studies simultaneously. The advantage of employing the comparative method is that theoretical propositions can be tested in a variety of settings and, on the basis of similarities or differences observed, generalisations can be drawn which would help characterise the experience of all EU regions (Mackie and Marsh 1995; Landman 2000). One of the problems with this method, however, is that there is always a tradeoff between generalisability and detail (Mackie and Marsh 1995; Landman 2000). In this research, generalisability is sacrificed for a detailed examination of the effect of European integration on the political power of a single EU region – that of the

Basque autonomous community. This is justifiable given the exploratory nature of the theoretical framework and primary focus on the issue of political accommodation and Basque difference in contemporary Spain. Nevertheless, the theoretical framework does provide a model for future research and my findings provide a first case study that could be compared with studies of other regions in that future research.

Note

1   It is also relevant to note some other effects of the EU on regions' legal constitutional powers, even though they will not be dealt with in any detail in this research. These include the more intensive use of certain types of EU laws which may limit the scope of regional authorities' discretion; particularly Regulations (a form of EU law which does not need to be transposed domestically) and the enactment of more detailed Directives (laws which do need domestic transposition) (Jiménez 1999; Börzel 2002: 54).

2

Devolution and the accommodation of Basque difference in Spain

The statute of Gernika ... constitutes a point of encounter for the will of the majority of Basques and the legal framework which Basque society endowed itself, in a specific historical moment, to accede to selfgovernment and regulate peaceful coexistence, representing, as a consequence, an expression of their own will ... and a historic achievement without precedent in the contemporary history of the Basque people, even if it does not encompass ... all and each of the demands of the diverse sectors ... of society. (Preamble, 'Pact of Ajuria Enea', Vitoria-Gasteiz, 12 January 1988, my translation)

It is necessary to articulate a new political pact that adjusts our framework of self-government to the desire of the majority of Basque society today. ... the solution to the problem of political normalization resides in accepting that the Basque people are not a subordinate part of the State, but a people with their own identity, with capacity to establish their own framework of internal relations and for incorporating themselves by free association into a truly plurinational state. (Speech by Juan José Ibarretxe, president of the Basque autonomous community government, on a 'New Political Pact for Coexistence', 27 September 2002. (my translation)

The profile of 'Basque difference', invoked in the book's title, is captured by the strength and institutional dominance of Basque nationalism in many spheres of Basque political and social life. Basque nationalism has a long history rooted in medieval and later experiences of political autonomy, the social dislocation of industrialisation and resistance to the homogenising effects of Spanish state- and nation-building drives (Caro Baroja 1985; Letamendia 1994; de la Granja 1995 and 2003; de la Cierva 1997; Conversi 1997). It had institutional form from the late nineteenth century, when the party still dominating the nationalist movement, the Basque Nationalist Party (PNV, *Partido Nacionalista Vasco*), was formed. This party initially provided a platform for the ideological pioneer, Sabino Arana Goiri (1865–1903), who defined many of the movement's core values and symbolic artefacts. Ideological divisions later produced other Basque nationalist parties, which competed with the PNV for leadership. However, Basque nationalism has never been hegemonic. It has always competed with other political movements, including a strong, largely immigrant-based, labour movement. These circumstances define a complex political conflict involving multiple fronts: Battles to achieve nationalist goals against the preferences of a sometimes hostile, but sometimes accommodating, state elite; and domestic struggles to win allegiance in Basque territories.

In this chapter, I examine the founding assumption of the research; namely that devolution has been an important instrument for the accommodation of Basque difference in Spain and for dealing with some of its key political consequences. Basque nationalism gained strength through the twentieth century, but until Spain's transition to democracy in the 1970s it won a role in parliamentary and governing bodies only intermittently. The most important exception was a Basque autonomy statute granted by Spain's democratic second republic in 1936, just months after the Francoist rebellion launched the Spanish civil war (1936–39). Civil war gave the Basque government of 1936–37 a chance to lead what José Luis de la Granja calls a 'semi-independent Basque state', but defeat cut its life short after just nine months (2003: 35–6). After the death of the dictator Francisco Franco in 1975, Basque nationalists obtained their first enduring foothold in the state apparatus and the unification of three Basque provinces within a single political framework. Earlier forms of Basque selfgovernment have been almost exclusively provincial; in contrast to Catalonia, which emerged as an identifiable territory and jurisdiction with its own language in the middle ages (Keating 1996: 115).

In the rest of the chapter, I explore the nature of contemporary devolution and its implications for political conflict in the Basque Country, beginning with constitutional arrangements and key rationales for devolution. I then examine evidence that devolution promotes Basque nationalist goals and helps manage diversity within the Basque Country; but also acknowledge shortcomings including the persistence of ETA and deep divisions about appropriate forms of selfgovernment. The passages opening the chapter express this duality: the first, from a political declaration signed in 1988 by all main Basque parties except the political wing of ETA, emphasises the historic significance, popular legitimacy and integrative potential of devolution. The second, by the Basque president in 2002, articulates the more recent, but controversial and divisive, preference of mainstream Basque nationalism for alternatives forms of selfgovernment. In the final part, I introduce a theme explored more fully in subsequent chapters, namely the impact of devolution on relations between Basque and central authorities.

Constitutional debates and construction of the 'state of autonomies'

In the 1970s, the strength of minority nationalist feeling in Spain had crucial political ramifications (Carr and Fusi 1981: 234–5; Martínez-Herrera 2002: 427–6). Opposition to the dictatorship was intense where minority nationalism was strong and calls for democratisation were firmly linked to demands for selfgovernment (Ysás 1998; Gilmour 1985: 213). Like its counterpart in Catalonia, Basque nationalism was a major political force. This became fully apparent in electoral contests: in the first general elections, Basque nationalist parties collectively won 39.3 per cent (in 1977) and 50.6 per cent (in 1979) of the vote in the Basque territories, Álava, Guipúzcoa and Vizcaya (Llera 2003: 18). The Basque Country had become a turbulent place: the dictatorship and transition governments were openly defied; labour militancy and terrorist violence were intense; state security and policing responses were vigorous and sometimes deadly; and effective state control was constantly undermined (Montero 1998; Carr and Fusi 1981).

Under pressure to win over the Basque opposition, Adolfo Suárez's transition governments made (often grudging) concessions, many of which were matched elsewhere. The Basque flag was legalised, political amnesties freed Basque political prisoners (including ETA members) and a Basque General Council was established as a largely symbolic, but important first step to future autonomy (Carr and Fusi 1981: 218 and 234). Most of those who drafted the constitution, including major political parties, supported regional autonomy and some recognition of national differences, despite powerful detractors in the military and disagreement over appropriate political forms (Solé Tura 1985; Gilmour 1985; Núñez 1995). Without devolution, many feared centre-periphery cleavages might undermine the new democracy, especially if significant opposition in the 'peripheries' continued (Martínez-Herrera 2002: 428; Mees 2001: 807–8; Amersfoort and Mansvelt 2000: 455–6).

Despite this basic consensus, constitutional articles defining the national 'reality' of the Spanish state and the devolution framework were among the most controversial. On the nationality question, negotiators eventually settled on an ambiguous formula recognising and guaranteeing autonomy rights for 'nationalities' and 'regions', but insisting on the 'indivisibility of the Spanish nation' and that 'national sovereignty resides in the Spanish people' (articles 1 and 2, Spanish constitution). Similarly, Title VIII, on the 'territorial organisation of the state', postponed decisions on the scope of devolution and territorial reorganisation. Title VIII established basic principles, listed competencies devolved units (called autonomous communities) could assume and competencies ringfenced for central authorities. However, the detail of devolution, including the competencies each autonomous community acquired, would be negotiated case by case once the constitution was ratified. Nor did it map new autonomous community boundaries. Title VIII established procedures whereby existing provinces and island authorities could consensually constitute themselves into what would later become the seventeen autonomous communities pictured in Map 2.1 (below). Case-by-case negotiations, together with further constitutional provisions identifying 'fast' and 'slow' routes by which different autonomous communities could obtain full autonomy, gave devolution a marked asymmetry until the 1990s. According the constitution's second transitory disposition, the Basque Country, Catalonia and Galicia could proceed to full autonomy via the fast route by virtue of autonomy statutes endorsed by referendum in these areas during the second republic in the 1930s.

Between 1979 and 1983, 'autonomy statutes' were negotiated for each autonomous community, including the 1979 'Statute of Gernika' establishing the Basque autonomous community.[1] The conviction that political autonomy was crucial for what many called 'normalisation' and 'pacification' of Basque politics – including an end to political violence and ETA – guided elaboration of the Basque statute (Corcuera 1991, see especially p. 135; Tamayo 1991; Mees 2003: 108). One important manifestation of such priorities was that Spanish and Basque elite allowed the PNV the role of protagonist in statute negotiations. There were, as a result, many concessions to Basque

Map 2.1 Spanish state of autonomies

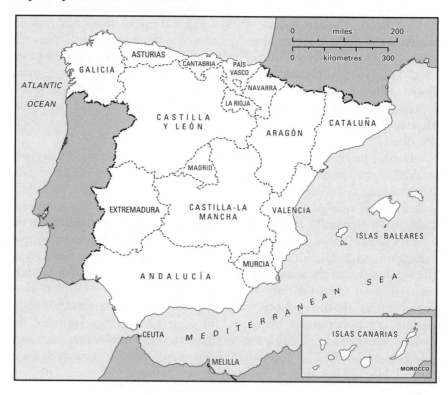

nationalism in institutional design and the allocation of powers. In deference to nationalist sensitivities, a clause even insisted that accepting the statute did not imply 'renunciation of the rights corresponding to the Basque people by virtue of their history' (additional disposition).

In addition to a general framework for devolution, the constitution and autonomy statutes recognised cultural and historical practices of various nationalities and regions. Castilian (or Spanish) was designated official state language, but 'other languages' – such as Basque, Galician and Catalan – soon became coofficial languages in relevant autonomous communities (article 3, Spanish constitution). Where 'other languages' were spoken, autonomy statutes devolved powers to promote and regulate local language use in spheres as important as public administration, education and the media (Aja 2003: 179–82).

Some historically-rooted traditions specific to one, or only some, nationalities and regions were preserved. The most important for the Basque case is a commitment to 'protect and respect historic rights of the foral territories' (first additional disposition, Spanish constitution). This provision refers to historic experiences of Basque selfgovernment codified in foral laws (*fueros*). Foral laws were quasiconstitutional charters, established from the middle ages in many parts of Spain. Foral laws for each Basque province regulated customary practices and institutions within the province, and later their separate relations with the ruling Kingdom of Castile (de la Cierva 1997: 71–6). In the nineteenth century, Basque foral laws were abolished as part of state modernisation and liberalisation drives, and replaced with taxation devolution.

There is intense, politicised debate on the scope of foral autonomy and thus the implication of Spanish constitutional commitments to protect and respect historic rights. These debates cannot be entered into here, except to note that foral laws are part of Basque nationalist claims to political sovereignty; and that constitutional commitments to promote 'historic rights' have taken concrete form in the restoration of Basque provincial institutions and (modernised) taxation powers, among other things (Corcuera 1991).

The democratic transition transformed the Spanish state into a semifederal system, where autonomous communities acquired legislative, executive and judicial institutions and now exercise a wide range of policy competencies. Many now describe Spain as one of the most decentralised states in Europe (for example, Subirats and Gallego 2002: 3; Aja 2003: 14). By 2003, autonomous communities were responsible for 30.9 per cent of state expenditure, with the central government share falling from 91.2 per cent in 1979 to 54.1 per cent (Piedrafita *et al.* 2006: 115). By 2006, autonomous community employees numbered some 1.2 million, around twice equivalent central government figures (Ministry for Public Administration, *ministerio de administraciones públicas*, www.map.es, accessed 12 August 2006). Moreover, autonomous communities are now an established feature of Spanish democracy. They enjoy a separate claim to legitimacy by virtue of regular democratic elections and opinion polls show a high degree of identification with the 'autonomous community' as a form of political association (see Table 2.4 below).

Nationbuilding and political coexistence in the Basque Country

In addition to the historical precedent set by devolution, Basque institutions have provided tools for nationbuilding (Mees 2001 and 2003; Jáuregui 1996: 102). Basque nationalists consistently win a large share of votes in Basque autonomous community elections (see Table 2.1a) and enjoy similar successes at provincial and municipal levels (Llera 2003: 58–61; Gillespie 2000: 119). Moreover, all autonomous community presidents have been Basque nationalists and all autonomous community governments have been run by Basque nationalists, either governing alone or as a major coalition partner (see Table 2.2).

Devolution allowed Basque nationalists to build powerbases from which to pursue various programmatic and symbolic objectives. They influenced construction of new governing institutions and the longterm agenda of

Table 2.1a Basque nationalists in Basque autonomous community elections 1980–2005

Political Party	1980	1984	1986	1990	1994	1998	2001	2005
PNV	38%	42%	23.8%	28.5%	29.8%	28%		
	25 seats	32 seats	17 seats	22 seats	22 seats	21 seats	42.7%[a]	38.7%
EA	–	–	15.8%	11.4%	10.3%	8.7%	33 seats	29 seats
			13 seats	9 seats	8 seats	6 seats		
HB or EH or EHAK	16.6%	14.7%	17.5%	18.3%	16.3%	17.9%	10.1%	12.4%
	11 seats	11 seats	13 seats	13 seats	11 seats	14 seats	7 seats	9 seats
EE[b]	9.8%	8%	10.9%	7.8%	–	–	–	–
	6 seats	6 seats	9 seats	6 seats				
Aralar	–	–	–	–	–	–	–	2.3%
								1 seat
Total Basque nationalist vote	64.6%	64.7%	68%	66%	56.4%	54.6%	52.8%	53.4%
	42 seats	49 seats	52 seats	50 seats	41 seats	41 seats	40 seats	39 seats

Notes: Basque nationalist parties: Aralar; EA – Eusko Alkartasuna (Basque Nationalists); EE – Euskadiko Ezkerra (Basque Left); EH – Euskal Herritarrok (Basque Citizens); – Herri Batasuna (Basque Homeland and Freedom); EHAC – Euskal Herrialdeetako Alderdi Komunista (Communist Party of the Basque Territories); PNV – Partido Nacionalista Vasco (Basque Nationalist Party)
[a]   PNV and EA formed an electoral coalition for the 2001 and 2005 elections
[b]   In the early 1990s one section of EE eventually merged with PSE-PSOE (see Table 2.1b)

Table 2.1b Statewide and regionalist parties in Basque autonomous community elections 1980–2005

Political Party	1980	1984	1986	1990	1994	1998	2001	2005
PSE-PSOE or	14.2%	23.1%	22%	19.9%	17.1%	17.6%	17.9%	22.7%
PSE-PSOE EE	9 seats	19 seats	19 seats	16 seats	12 seats	14 seats	13 seats	18 seats
UCD or CDS	8.5%	–	3.5%	–	–	–	–	–
	6 seats		2 seats					
AP or PPV	4.8%	9.4%	4.9%	8.2%	14.4%	20.1%	23.1%	17.4%
	2 seats	7 seats	2 seats	6 seats	11 seats	16 seats	19 seats	15 seats
PCE or EB-IU	4%	–	–	–	9.2%	5.7%	5.6%	5.4%
	1 seat				6 seats	2 seats	3 seats	3 seats
UA	–	–	–	1.4%	2.7%	1.3%	–	–
				3 seats	5 seats	2 seats		
Total non Basque	22.9%	33.9%	26.9%	29.5%	43.4%	44.7%	46.6%	45.5%
nationalist vote	12 seats	26 seats	21 seats	25 seats	35 seats	34 seats	35 seats	36 seats

Notes: Statewide parties: AP – *Alianza Popular* (Popular Alliance); CDS – *Centro Democrático Social* (Social Democratic Centre); EB-IU – *Izquierda Unida* (United Left); PCE – *Partido Comunista de Euskadi* (Basque Communist Party); PPV – *Partido Popular del País Vasco* (Popular Party of the Basque Country); PSE-PSOE – *Partido Socialists de Euskadi – Partido Socialists Obrero Español* (Basque Socialist Party – Spanish Socialist Workers Party); UCD – *Unión del Centro Democrático* (Union of the Democratic Centre). Regionalist party: UA – *Unidad Alavesa* (Alavan Unity).

Basque politics. Basque institutions promoted Basque language 'normalisa-tion' programmes in education, the media and public administration (Lasagabaster and Lazcano 2004; Agirreazkuenaga 2001). These policies helped end the downturn in Basque language use and increased its social status in public and professional spheres (Mees 2003: 49–50; Agirreazkuenaga 2001: 135). The Basque flag and anthem, invented by the early Basque nation-alist, Sabino Arana Goiri, became official symbols of the autonomous community (Mees 2001: 808). A Basque police force (*Ertzaintza*), responsible to the autonomous community, took over important policing and security responsibilities from central authorities (Greer 1995). The Basque govern-ment, and especially the presidency, became an instrument for Basque 'foreign policy'. It pursues objectives ranging from relations with the Basque diaspora, economic assistance for least developed countries and relations with the EU (Castro and Ugalde 2004).

Some hoped devolution might contribute to 'nationbuilding' in another sense – by providing a meeting point for varying ethnic, class and territorial identities within the Basque Country, or a new framework for constructing pluralistic or civic conceptions of Basque identity (Jáuregui 1996; de la Granja 2003: 37–41; van Amserfoort and Beck 2000: 462). Basque institutions have sometimes provided arenas for bridgebuilding and consociational politics.

The clearest example is formal collaboration between Basque nationalists and the branches of statewide parties in successive Basque government coalitions. As Table 2.2 shows, between 1987 and 1999, the largest Basque nationalist party, the PNV, and the Basque Socialist Party-Spanish Socialist Workers Party (PSE-PSOE, *Partido Socialista de Euskadi-Partido Socialista Obrero Español*), formed the core of successive Basque government coalitions.

Many commentators characterise such periods of coalition government as consensual phases, contrasting them with adversarial styles of earlier and later periods (Llera 2003: 24 and 30; Mees 2003; de la Granja 2003). One notable achievement of PNV and PSE-PSOE cooperation was the Pact of Ajuria-Enea, signed in 1988 by all Basque parties except the radical Basque nationalists of *Herri Batasuna* (HB, Popular Unity). The pact sought to define a joint strategy for the 'normalisation' and 'pacification' of Basque politics. It defined the eradication of terrorism as a fundamental objective of all institutions and democratic forces; called for those using or legitimising violence to abandon arms and participate in institutional politics; and endorsed a negotiated end to violence, involving dialogue between the state and ETA and dialogue among political parties. It articulated the idea, quoted at the chapter's opening, that devolution represented a 'point of encounter' and 'a legal framework that Basque society gave itself' for regulating 'peaceful coexistence', even if it did not satisfy all the demands within Basque society. In political terms, the pact symbolised the unity of democratic parties against those endorsing terrorism.

Moreover, tests of Basque political opinion indicate significant support for devolution in the Basque Country. A 1979 referendum showed strong endorsement of the Basque autonomy statute with 91 per cent of voters (or 53 per cent of the electorate) voting in favour and only 5 per cent of voters (or 3 per cent of the electorate) voting against (Llera 1999: 106). Opinion polls conducted since then show continued support for the autonomy statute, which in 1998 'fully satisfied' 43 per cent and 'partially satisfied' 30 per cent of respondents (Llera 1999: 106). Furthermore, as Francisco Llera argues, democratisation and autonomy processes have changed some Basque preferences on the form of the state and its territorial organisation (Llera 1999: 104–5). Ten per cent more people preferred the state of autonomies model in 1996 than in 1977 and this was the most popular model with 37 per cent support, compared to centralism (4 per cent); federalism (25 per cent); and independence (25 per cent). A 2005 poll commissioned by the Basque government showed that 65 per cent of the population of the Basque autonomous community considered, that overall, twenty-five years of selfgovernment was positive (compared to 7 per cent who considered it negative) and 56 per cent thought the Basque government was the institution that had most contributed to improving the Basque Country (compared to 11 per cent who considered that it was the central government or 7 per cent who considered it was the EU) (Gobierno Vasco 2005a).

Table 2.2 Political parties forming Basque government coalitions

Type of government	Party or parties in government	President
1980–86: Basque nationalist, one party, minority government[a]	PNV	Garaikoetxea (PNV) Ardanza (PNV)
1986–90: Coalition involving Basque nationalists and non-Basque nationalists in minority government	PNV and PSE-PSOE	Ardanza (PNV)
Feb–Sept 1991: Basque nationalist, three-party coalition in minority government	PNV, EA and EE	Ardanza (PNV)
1991–94: Coalition involving Basque nationalists and non-Basque nationalists in majority government	PNV, PSE-PSOE and EE[b]	Ardanza (PNV)
1994–98: Coalition involving Basque nationalists and non-Basque nationalists in majority government	PNV, EA and PSE-EE-PSOE	Ardanza (PNV)
1998–2001: Basque nationalist, two-party minority government coalition	PNV and EA (initially with HB/EH support)	Ibarretxe (PNV)
2001–5: Basque nationalist-dominated three-party minority government coalition	PNV, EA and IU	Ibarretxe (PNV)
2005 to present: Basque nationalist-dominated, three-party minority government coalition	PNV, EA and EB-IU	Ibarretxe (PNV)

Notes: EA = Basque nationalists; EB-IU = Basque branch of United Left; EE = Basque Left; EH = Basque citizens; HB = Basque Homeland and Freedom; PNV = Basque Nationalist Party; PSE-PSOE = Socialist Party of Euskadi-Spanish Socialist Workers Party. [a] 1980 elections contested 60 Basque parliament seats, but this rose to 75 seats from 1984. However, due to its rejection of devolution, the radical nationalist party, HB, did not initially participate in institutional politics and, after the late 1990s, only did so intermittently. This meant that minority governments were frequently majority governments in practice. [b] During this period, one sector of EE merged with PSE-PSOE.

Unresolved issues: polarisation, the 'Plan Ibarretxe' and ETA

Despite the goals of political elite during the transition to democracy, popular support for devolution and the historically significant quota of selfgovernment obtained, the devolution settlement has not resolved some major political problems. Many Basque citizens and party elite are not satisfied with current levels of autonomy; Basque society remains internally divided on key social and political questions and the offer of autonomy rather than statehood has not been enough to convince ETA to abandon violence.

Twenty-five years of devolution, with its platform for Basque nation-building and its attendant opportunities for bridgebuilding, has still left Basque society deeply divided. Opinion surveys show complex patterns of identification in the Basque Country and significant differences over key political questions. According to a 2005 survey (see Table 2.3), the vast majority of respondents in the Basque autonomous community said they felt Basque (83 per cent) and most felt both Basque and Spanish (51 per cent), at least to some degree. Nevertheless, numbers of respondents feeling 'only Basque' was a high 32 per cent, and only a very small minority (8 per cent) felt 'only Spanish'. When these results are compared with a similar survey conducted in the same year across the whole of Spain, it becomes clear that most people (80 per cent) in Spain also express multiple identities and that very few express an exclusively Spanish identity (10.3 per cent). Nevertheless, responses from the Basque Country show much lower than average multiple-identity attachments (51 per cent compared to 80 per cent) and a much higher than average attachment to an exclusive regional/minority national identity (32 per cent compared to 5 per cent).

Table 2.3 Identification as Basque or Spanish, 2005

Survey question: Between Basque and Spanish, how do you define yourself?

Categories	Responses October 2005 (%)
Only Basque	32
More Basque than Spanish	13
Equally Basque and Spanish	34
More Spanish than Basque	4
Only Spanish	8
Don't know	9

Source: Gobierno Vasco, *Sociómetro Vasco 29*, December 2005, p. 84.

The very high numbers of respondents identifying themselves as Basque hides varying conceptions of what 'Basqueness' may mean. According to one study, it is possible to distinguish two very different types of Basque identi-fiers (Davis 1997). On the one hand, there are those who see the Basque language as a defining feature of the national community, but nevertheless see

Table 2.4 Identification as Spanish and attachment to autonomous communities, 2005

Survey question: Which of the following categories do you identify with the most?

Categories	Responses, December 2005 (%)
I feel only Spanish	10.3
I feel more Spanish than an attachment to my autonomous community	10
I feel equally Spanish and an attachment to my autonomous community	57
I feel more of an attachment to my autonomous community than I feel Spanish	13.5
I only feel an attachment to my autonomous community	5
Don't know	3.3

Source: Centro de Investigaciones Sociológicas, Estudio 2610 Barómetro Autonómico, December 2005, question 39.

that language and identity under threat from the modern Spanish state (Davis 1997: 69–72). In these circumstances, participation in active – though not necessarily violent – struggle for the preservation and advancement of the nation is seen as an important marker of Basqueness and selfdetermination is seen as a logical and permissible response to perceived threats (Davis 1997: 72–6). For this type of Basque identifier, being Basque and nationalist are closely intertwined (Davis 1997: 77). On the other hand, the second type of Basque identifier may feel equally Basque and profess an attachment to tangible elements of ethnicity (such as language, family or land), but reject active involvement in the broader nationalist cause because of a perceived association between nationalism and violence and a belief that Spanish citizenship does not constrain Basque identity (Davis 1997: 76–81).

Internal divisions in Basque society are also reflected in the party system and major differences over preferred political forms. As data shown in Tables 2.1a and 2.1b above demonstrates, there is a high degree of fragmentation in the Basque party system (Llera 1999 and 2003). Between 1980 and 2005 seven political parties have won seats in the Basque parliament on average at each election. There are also multiple political cleavages. The largest slice of the vote has gone to three or four Basque nationalist parties, who differ in ideological positions ranging from the revolutionary left, social democratic, centrist and Christian democratic viewpoints, as well as preferred forms of selfgovernment ranging from the pursuit of maximum autonomy within the framework of the Spanish state, to an outright rejection of the state of autonomies in favour of independence. The acceptability of violence as a means to pursue political goals also divides Basque nationalists; governing Basque nationalist parties firmly reject it, while the radical left does not. The rest of the vote in Basque elections is largely divided between Basque branches of the three main statewide political parties – the centre left *Partido Socialista Obrero Español* (PSOE, Spanish Socialist Workers Party); the conservative *Partido Popular* (PP, Popular Party) and the left-wing *Izquierda Unida* (IU, United Left). Significantly, over the last two decades, the political balance between Basque nationalist and statewide parties has gradually approached parity, as Tables 2.1a and 2.1b demonstrate. Internal territorial cleavages spawned Alavan Unity (UA, *Unidad Alavesa*), an anti-Basque nationalist party with a support base in the province of Álava.

Given the salience of support for, or rejection of, Basque nationalism in differing conceptions of 'Basqueness' and as a cleavage in the Basque party system, it is not surprising that identity and party political variables tend to underpin support for different political forms. Table 2.5 shows that around one-third of Basque respondents in a 2005 survey favoured independence, around one-third were against it and another third were undecided. Not surprisingly, the survey also indicated that those who considered themselves 'predominantly Basque' and who voted for Basque nationalist parties were most likely to support independence. In contrast, those who considered themselves equally Basque and Spanish, or predominantly Spanish, were more likely to reject independence, as were supporters of the statewide parties, PSE-PSOE and PP. PNV and IU supporters were something of an exception to these patterns of support; most PNV supporters (42 per cent) and IU supporters (43 per cent) responded that they would be in favour or against independence depending on the circumstances, although a high 37 per cent of PNV supporters did still support independence. Clearly, the experience of selfgovernment over the last twenty-five years has not inspired a large sector of Basque society to abandon aspirations for independence, even if other survey data indicates that most Basques consider this experience a positive one so far.[2]

Table 2.5 Opinions on Basque independence, 2005

Survey question: With respect to the topic of independence for the Basque Country, are you personally ...?

Categories	Responses, October 2005 (%)
In agreement	27
In agreement/disagreement depending on the circumstances	31
Not in agreement	32
Don't know	11

Source: Gobierno Vasco, *Sociómetro Vasco 29,* December 2005, p. 86.

Further doubts about the utility of Basque devolution as an instrument for political accommodation are raised by mainstream Basque nationalists' initial reservations about the statute of autonomy and, by the 1990s, their outright rejection of current arrangements. In the December 1978 referendum on the Spanish constitution, the PNV urged voters to abstain. While the party recognised that the constitution was an advance in the recognition of rights and individual liberties, and voted in favour of provisions recognising 'historic rights of the foral territories', the PNV objected to the fact that the constitution did not fully assume PNV demands for recognition of Basque sovereignty (Fernández and Ruiz 2003: 169–70). In the event, Basque turnout at the statewide referendum on the constitution was exceptionally low, at 45 per cent, compared to the 68 per cent who turned out in Spain as a whole (Llera 2003: 19). This meant that the 69 per cent of Basque voters who endorsed the Spanish constitution only represented around a third (31 per cent) of the Basque electorate; and that the 24 per cent Basque 'no' vote was proportionally higher than its equivalent in Spain overall (8 per cent) (Llera 2003: 19). This result sustained the argument in nationalist circles that Basques had rejected the constitution, although this position has been challenged in both political and academic circles (Llera 2003: 19; Fernández and Ruiz 2003: 167; Moreno del Río 2000: 289).

Until the late 1990s, the PNV had seen the statute as a 'pragmatic' political instrument, valid because it was accepted by a majority of Basque citizens and a useful instrument for political coexistence, even if it was conceived more as a point of departure than an end in itself (Moreno del Río 2000: 190–3).[3] But in a series of controversial moves, the PNV later spearheaded calls for a new political framework for the Basque Country, signalled a new proximity to the independence preference of the radical left, and broke off political relationships with the statewide parties operating in the Basque Country. In July 1998 the PNV signed the Declaration of Barcelona, the first of a series of joint statements with the main Catalan and Galician nationalist parties, which criticised the existing political framework for failing to recognise their respective 'national realities' and called for a 'new phase' of territorial reconstruction founded on a new 'plurinational' state. Much more significant was the Agreement of Lizarra (or Estella) signed a few months later by the PNV, EA, HB and a series of other organisations mostly close to Basque nationalist circles. This document, which contained a reflection on how the Northern Irish peace process might apply to the Basque Country, was largely the fruit of secret agreements between ETA, PNV and EA and was soon followed by ETA's first ceasefire. Lizarra signalled both the birth of a new Basque nationalist front in Basque politics and a new approach to conflict resolution (Mees 2003: 139–64; de la Granja 2003: 315–35). The new nationalist front was apparently designed to spearhead a peace process based on the formula of 'peace for selfdetermination', a formula by which ETA would contemplate abandoning arms in exchange for collaboration with other

Basque nationalists to achieve independence (Mees 2003: 139–64).[4]

The Lizarra Agreement was deeply controversial and reinforced the primary political cleavage between Basque nationalists, promoting a new political framework for the Basque Country, and the main statewide parties, the so-called 'constitutionalists', who favoured the *status quo* or at most reforms permissible within the terms of the 1978 constitution. This new division was reinforced after the 1998 Basque autonomous community elections, which installed a new Basque nationalist-only coalition, initially with the support of the radical nationalists, in place of the decade-long powersharing coalitions centred on the PNV and PSE-PSOE (see Table 2.2). Since then, Basque nationalists have continued to dominate the Basque government, more recently with support of IU. ETA's first ceasefire only lasted fourteen months, but the divisions between Basque nationalists and the 'constitutional' parties lingered much longer. Even as relations between ETA, HB and the mainstream Basque nationalist parties crumbled, the latter continued to call for a new political settlement for the Basque Country. In what became known as the 'Plan Ibarretxe', the president of the Basque autonomous community, Juan José Ibarretxe, called for a new 'pact for coexistence', later elaborated into a formal proposal for a new autonomy statute. The proposal declares the existence of 'the Basque people', which has the 'right to decide its own future' and presents a new confederal model for relations between the Basque Country and the Spanish state based on 'free association'. Among other things, it called for freedom for the Basque autonomous community to establish relations with Navarre and Basque territories in France; many new exclusive competencies in institutional, cultural and economic matters; fuller judicial autonomy; and its 'own voice' in Europe and the world. This proposal, which was just as controversial and divisive as the Lizarra Agreement, found a bare majority of support in the Basque parliament but was decisively rejected in the Spanish parliament in February 2005.

The persistence of ETA remains the most glaring shortfall of Basque devolution. It is also the most tragic, insofar as it failed to prevent the continued loss of life, tallying more than eight hundred to date. ETA began life as a youth group in the early 1950s and soon became dissatisfied with the civil war generation of Basque nationalists and the PNV. From this time, ETA began a long intellectual journey which would take it through my disputes and schisms: disputes about the role of class conflict in nationalist struggle; about the relevance of third world liberation movements, Maoism and various forms of Marxist analysis; and about the role of violence (Jáuregui 2002: 206; Clarke 1985). As the transition to democracy approached, the central conviction that the Basque Country remained an occupied territory of Spain and France and that armed struggle was the ideal means of achieving liberation still held fast. Democratisation and autonomy did lure one faction of ETA away from violence. The faction known as ETA political military (ETApm, *político militar*) formed a political party, Basque Left (EE, *Euskadiko Ezkerra*), which took part in democratic elections, constitutional and Basque autonomy statute debates, and eventually renounced violence (de la Granja 2003: 136).

The other sector, known as ETA military (ETAm, *militar*), continued as today's ETA and chose to pursue armed struggle into the democratic period. Indeed, through a massive escalation of violence, ETA did all it could to destabilise the democratic process.[5] This faction denied the democratic nature of the new political system, refused to support a constitution which did not recognise the right to selfdetermination of the Basque people or an autonomy statute that both fell short of independence and cut off Navarre (Domínguez 2002). At the same time, a series of other organisations supporting ETA's political ideas and military tactics organised and represented what ETA stood for in the democratic sphere. This included the political party *Herri Batasuna* (HB, Popular Unity) and its successor parties *Euskal Herritarrok* (EH, Basque Citizens) and *Batasuna* (Unity) (all of which are now banned), which together with a wide variety of other social groups (cultural, youth, women, environmental etc.) and media outlets formed the Basque National Liberation Movement (MLNV, *Movimiento de Liberación Nacional Vasco*). The electoral successes of the political parties in ETA's circle provide an important indicator of the political significance of this movement. As Table 2.1a shows, HB and its successors have won an average of 15 per cent of the vote in Basque autonomous community elections since 1980.

Despite the continuing political salience of the radical nationalist left in Basque politics, its position has been seriously weakened in the democratic period. In the last two autonomous community elections, radical nationalist parties have seen their share of the vote fall from a high point of 18.3 per cent in 1990 to just 10.1 per cent in 2001, with a slight increase to 12.4 per cent in 2005. More generally, opinion surveys show that favourable attitudes of many Basques in the early transition towards ETA terrorists – who were seen as 'patriots' or 'idealists' – fell dramatically in the years that followed (Llera 1999, 101; Mees 2003: 93 and 98). In the 1990s, a Basque peace movement gathered steam, centring on two mass-mobilising organisations, Coordination Gesture for Peace in the Basque Country (*Coordinadora Gesto por la Paz de Euskal Herria*) and *Elkarri* ('One to the other' or 'Mutually') (Mees 2003: 92–9; Gurrutxaga 2002: 174). And in 1997, a period of active popular mobilisation against ETA was launched when hundreds of thousands of Basques and some six million people across Spain took to the streets to demand ETA abandon its threat to kill the town of Ermua's PP councillor Miguel Ángel Blanco. Blanco was one of a string of ETA kidnap victims and ETA threatened to kill him if the Spanish government did not relocate ETA prisoners to Basque prisons within forty-eight hours. In the end, ETA paid no heed and the councillor was shot, but the event had inspired what was later called the 'spirit of Ermua', a spirit of unity, popular rejection of terrorism and a call for peace (Mees 2003: 75; de la Granja 2003: 313). Many commentators agree that these events, together with the debilitating effects of state security operations, judicial actions dismantling ETA's organisational support networks and the illegalisation of its political wing (including HB, EH and *Batasuna*), significantly contributed to the context in which ETA made its two ceasefire declarations (Mees 2003; de la Granja 2003).

In March 2006, ETA declared its second ceasefire in eight years. Eighteen months earlier, ETA's political wing, the then illegal but still active *Batasuna*, made its Declaration of Anoeta, positioning itself more clearly in favour of dialogue and a negotiated settlement to the conflict. This was later endorsed by ETA itself (*El Mundo*, 16 January 2005), which had not taken a life for nearly three years until the December 2006 Madrid airport bombing that ended the ceasefire. For its part, the PSOE, in government after March 2004, showed a receptiveness to negotiations, held secret contacts with ETA and obtained authorisation from the Spanish parliament for the initiation of talks. The PSOE government also committed itself to the renegotiation of autonomy statutes, which in 2006 culminated in a groundbreaking new autonomy statute for Catalonia. Until the December 2006 Madrid bombings, indications were that a Basque peace process would proceed along two 'tracks', one involving negotiations between ETA and the central government focusing on 'military' matters and another involving all parties present in the Basque political arena, including *Batasuna* (but not the PP who has excluded itself from negotiations). This second track, or roundtable of parties (*mesa de partidos*), was likely to have discussed a new devolution settlement. So far, the devolution formula has not been sufficient to inspire ETA to abandon violence once and for all.

Democratisation, devolution and the new framework for territorial relations

In addition to the institutionalisation of Basque selfgovernment, the state of autonomies provided new possibilities for regulating relations between Basque and Spanish elites. Since democratisation, a series of institutions have been established to channel relations between autonomous communities and state-level authorities. A small portion of the membership of the Senate, the upper chamber of the Spanish parliament, is designated by autonomous communities. A series of policy-specific, interministerial Sectoral Conferences involving representatives from autonomous community and state administrations have been established. More recently an annual summit known as the Conference of Presidents has been established to provide a meeting point for autonomous community and central government leaders. However, as subsequent chapters will spell out more fully, this framework for intergovernmental relations in Spain has taken many years to develop and is still regarded as lacking by most specialists (see for example, Aja 2003; Fernández de Casadevante 2001; Albertí 1998; Roig 2002; Jáuregui 1997; Lucas 2000).

In this context, bilateral contacts, and particularly relations between political parties governing at state and autonomous community levels, provided important informal channels for territorial relations. In the Basque case, relations between political parties have taken two different forms; PNV support for both PSOE (1993–96) and PP (1995–2000) minority governments at state level; and the coincidence of periods of PSOE central government (1982–96) and PSE-PSOE involvement in Basque government coalitions (most of period 1987–98, see Table 2.2 above). The channelling of institutional relations through political pacts has been critiqued and praised. Some, including senior political figures like president Felipe González, have considered the involvement of minority nationalist parties in state-level government a positive step towards fuller integration of the latter into the political life of the Spanish state (Aguilera de Prat 2001: 15; de la Granja 2003: 306–7). On the other hand, the perception that such pacts privileged Basques and Catalans and undermined solidarity among richer and poorer territories in Spain produced tensions between Basques and Catalans, on the one hand, and other autonomous communities (López 2002: 55–7). It also provoked biting criticism from opposition parties.

Since democratisation, this framework has provided a setting for relations that have had their high points and low points. Initially, promises of autonomy in the early transition period appeared to put delicate relations between Basque nationalists and the Francoist reformers on a positive footing. However, relations soon soured with the marginalization of the PNV and some of its key aspirations during constitutional debates and its constant questioning of the constitutional settlement (López 2002: 47).[6] After the constitutional settlement and negotiation of the Basque autonomy statute, new sources of tension emerged. Power struggles over competencies and the constitutionality of Basque and central government actions were played out with great frequency in the Constitutional Court during the 1980s, although slowed down in later years. There have also been long running disputes about transfer of central government resources to Basque authorities, a necessary step for the full assumption of statutory competencies.

Furthermore, major blueprints for the future development of the state of autonomies in the 1980s and early 1990s were made without the support of governing Basque (and Catalan) minority nationalist parties. The most significant of these were the controversial 1982 *Ley Orgánica de Armonización del Proceso Autonómico* (LOAPA, Organic Law on Harmonisation of the Autonomy Process), large parts of which were successfully challenged by Basque and Catalan autonomous communities in the Spanish Constitutional Court, and the 1981 and 1992 *Acuerdos Autonómicos* (Autonomy Agreements) agreed between the major statewide parties. These episodes not only revealed considerable disagreements between governing minority nationalist parties about the desirable scope of autonomous community competencies and the pace of reform. Exclusion of minority nationalist parties produced suspicion and distrust about central government ambitions and further calls for autonomy (López 2002: 52–3). It was not until parties governing in minority at the state level came to rely on Catalan and Basque nationalist parties from 1993 that a period of more cooperative relations developed. The *quid pro quo* for support from minority nationalist parties had been further political decentralisation, providing what some have characterised as an 'autonomist' antidote to 'centralist tendencies' of governing parties prior to 1993 (Fernandéz Manjón 2001: 169, 208–9; López 2002: 55–6).

A final issue dominating Basque and central government relations has been the difficulties defining an appropriate strategy for dealing with ETA. The 1988 Pact of Ajuria Enea can be considered a high point in relations between Basque and state elite. As mentioned above, it represented an alliance of the 'democratic parties' against those undertaking or sympathetic to terrorist strategies. However, even when it was in force, the pact did not eliminate all tensions between Basque and central authorities on the issue of terrorism and, by the late 1990s, it had effectively been disbanded. Disagreements over the appropriateness of the Basque nationalist-led Lizarra process, which focused on 'peace for self-determination', was a deeply divisive issue not only in the Basque Country itself; it eventually provoked serious crisis in relations between the nationalist-dominated Basque government and the PP-led central government of José María Aznar. The illegal, extrajudicial assassinations of suspected ETA members by the state-sponsored *Grupos Antiterroristas de Liberación* (GAL, Antiterrorist Liberation Groups), state prisons policy dispersing ETA prisoners in jails outside the Basque Country and the banning of ETA's political wing, *Batasuna*, have also been damaging for relations between successive Basque and central governments.

Notes

1 Ley Organica 3/1979, *Boletín Oficial del Estado* (*BOE*), 306, 22 December 1979, pp. 29357–63.
2 Overall levels of support for independence do not appear to have changed much since the transition. Basque government data available for 1988–2005 on the question posed in Table 2.5 showed that on average 24 per cent agreed with independence, with support ranging from a low of 21 per cent to a high of 27 per cent (Gobierno Vasco 2005a). During this period, 31 per cent of respondents were, on average, 'in agreement or disagreement depending on the circumstances' and 30 per cent were, on average, in disagreement (Gobierno Vasco 2005a, see also Llera 1999: 104).
3 By way of contrast, it is interesting to note that for PSE-PSOE leaders, the statute was more a point of arrival of autonomy; an instrument permitting the regulation of Basque political and social life; a symbol demonstrating the existence of the Basque community; and a practical integrative tool helping forge the contours of that community (Moreno del Río 2000: 290).

4 It has also been interpreted as an opportunity engineered by ETA to regroup after debilitating successes of the state security forces.

5 ETA was particularly active during the key transition years of 1978 and 1979. It produced twice as many victims during those years than in the previous eighteen (Jáuregui 2000: 151; see also Clark 1985).

6 The PNV was not included in the select circle of parliamentarians who produced a draft constitution, but it did participate in parliamentary debates on the constitution and found other ways of feeding its preferences and favoured concepts into debates (Fernández and Ruiz 2003: 170).

3

Basque participation in the state's EU decisions

The decentralisation process inaugurated during the transition to democracy was soon followed by construction of new institutions to promote cooperation between autonomous community and central state authorities. When Spain joined the EU, these institutions were harnessed for collaboration in EU matters. The state's bicameral parliament housed a 'territorial chamber' – the Senate (*el Senado*) – and subsequent reforms sought to give autonomous communities a say in state EU decisions through their parliamentary representatives. A more comprehensive system of intergovernmental relations was built with Sectoral Conferences (*conferencias sectoriales*), which are interministerial bodies where central and autonomous community governments can coordinate policy portfolios. Informal and bilateral relationships, often channelled through political parties, serve as additional channels for intergovernmental relations.

In this chapter, I examine whether this system of intergovernmental relations serves as a vehicle for powersharing in state EU decisions. An effective system will have allowed autonomous communities to influence the content of EU policy affecting their competencies in a meaningful and consistent manner. If autonomous communities lack meaningful input, however, it will be possible to conclude that EU membership shaped the territorial distribution of power within Spain to the detriment of autonomous communities. Furthermore, an examination of Basque government preferences on, and engagement with, the architecture for intergovernmental relations provides insights about the impact of the EU on conflict and cooperation between Basque and central authorities. The chapter begins by examining parliamentary bodies, the Sectoral Conferences and bilateral intergovernmental relations. It ends by exploring the role of political parties.

The Spanish parliament and representation of territorial interests

The 1978 constitution established a parliamentary framework for the articulation of territorial interests in state decisionmaking. Title III established a bicameral parliament, composed of the directly elected, Congress of Deputies (*El Congreso de los Diputados*), and the Senate. The Senate was designated 'chamber of territorial representation' (article 69.1, Spanish constitution), a role primarily institutionalised through its composition. Around four-fifths (208 senators) are directly elected from provincial constituencies, which, despite vast differences in population size, get an equal share of representatives (with some exceptions for islands and autonomous cities). Autonomous communities' legislative assemblies designate the remaining one-fifth (51 senators). Each autonomous community is allocated at least one senator, with additional representatives allocated in proportion to population. Minority nationalist and regionalist parties, present in both chambers, also articulate territorial interests in state-level politics.

Two parliamentary committees specifically channel territorial interests into state EU decisionmaking: The Senate's General Commission for Autonomous Communities (*La Comisión General de las Comunidades Autónomas*); and the Mixed Commission for the European Union (*La Comisión Mixta para la Unión Europea*).

The General Commission for Autonomous Communities (henceforth General Commission) was established in 1994 to address problems with the Senate's territorial role.[1] A widely acknowledged shortcoming of the Senate is that the small proportion of autonomous community-designated Senators unduly limits representation of increasingly salient autonomous community interests (Gómez 2005: 211–23; Roller 2002; Paniagua 1999; Gutiérrez 1998; Jáuregui 1997). The Senate lacks a role in many 'territorial matters' and decisionmaking tends to obey the logic of party competition rather than territorial politics (Gutiérrez 1998: 81; Aja 2003:163). In the legislative process, and in scrutiny of government action, the Senate is subordinate to the lower house.[2] In short, the Senate tends to duplicate the actions of the lower house, has little autonomous effect on policy and tends to serve the interests of governing parties (Aja 2003: 163; Roller 2002: 79).

The Senate's new General Commission for Autonomous Communities enhanced the territorial role of the Senate (without the politically difficult step of altering the constitutional text).[3] Members of central and autonomous community governments could solicit convocation of the General Commission and intervene in its sessions. It was styled, as some remarked, a 'mini Senate' within the Senate. It was responsible for: informing, evaluating and making proposals relevant to autonomous community competencies and interests in state lawmaking (including the state budget); cooperation among autonomous communities; and relations between autonomous communities and the central government.

Moreover, the General Commission acquired the Senate's first powers specifically relating to the EU. The central government and the Mixed Commission for the EU (see below) would be obliged to inform the General Commission about EU legislation or actions of EU bodies relevant to territorial actors. It could scrutinise the distribution and execution of EU structural funds in Spain and could formulate and present its views on state representation in international bodies permitting regional participation.

Evaluations of the significance of the General Commission's EU activities have been mixed. Cienfuegos (2001: 214–17) argues that the General Commission has been quite active and has acquired a certain importance in EU matters: It has met relatively frequently; received abundant information from the government about EU activity relevant to autonomous communities; held hearings and debates with government ministers and written reports on EU matters. It has served as an important sounding board for autonomous community views, particularly, but not exclusively, in the politically significant but infrequent 'state of autonomies' debates. These have dealt with the topic of autonomous community participation in EU matters at some length and later produced motions with direct repercussions for the development of intergovernmental relations in Spain (Cienfuegos 2001: 217).

On the other hand, Ordóñez argues that the General Commission's attempt to assume a higher profile in EU affairs has been in vain and that the very few sessions held specifically on EU matters confirmed its insignificance (2000: 247–8). Moreover, major parliamentary debates on EU issues of importance to territorial actors have frequently taken place outside the General Commission; sometimes in the Senate plenary, where motions following state of autonomies debates have been discussed (Gutiérrez 1998); sometimes in the Congress of Deputies, where major debates on autonomous community participation in the Council of the EU took place, for instance. Some analysts have argued that the General Commission tends to function more as an instrument for scrutinising government actions than as a forum for collaboration and the resolution of conflicts between autonomous communities and the state government (Roller 2002: 80–1), and even then, the General Commission rarely uses its more effective instruments for government control, such as requiring a minister to attend General Commission sessions.

In accordance with constitutional provisions, the Basque presence in the Senate takes two forms. There are three Basque autonomous community-designated senators. Since 1979, there has always been at least one appointed senator from the party or parties running the Basque government, usually from the PNV, but most other parties, including opposition parties, have appointed Basque autonomous community senators at some point. In addition, there are four senators from each Basque province (Álava, Guipúzcoa and Vizcaya), which again include members of parties running the Basque government and its opposition. Currently, there are no Basque autonomous community-designated senators in the General Commission for Autonomous

Communities, but there is usually a mix of both designated and directly elected senators from the Basque Country.

An examination of the General Commission's activity shows that Basque senators have used this forum for the articulation of Basque interests in a variety of EU matters. Table 3.1 shows numbers of interventions made by Basque senators during General Commission sessions held between 1994 and 2006. This is one important indicator of the relative importance senators and political parties attach to the General Commission. This data makes it clear that senators elected, particularly from minority nationalist parties (PNV and EA), have generally been much more active in the General Commission than the autonomous community-designated senators, which suggests that, like the Senate more generally, the logic of territorial representation gives way to the logic of party politics. Basque nationalists were also more likely to intervene in EU matters, although it is notable that these interventions have focused on general EU issues rather than matters of more specific interest to the Basque autonomous community and that these interventions were a relatively small proportion of total interventions.

Table 3.1 Basque senators' interventions in Senate General Commission for Autonomous Communities' EU debates 1994–2006

Senator and party	Total no. Commission interventions	No. EU debate interventions	Topic
I. Loroño (PNV, elected)	45	7	Structural funds, Convention, CARCE
R. Sanz (PNV, elected)	43	3	Role territorial entities, AC participation, structural funds
I. Boneta y Piedra (EA, designated)	41	4	Structural funds, Convention
J. Gangoiti (PNV, elected)	20	3	Local authorities, structural funds
F. X. Albistur (PNV, elected)	10	0	
M. M. Uriarte (PP, elected)	6	0	
J. M. Martiarena (PNV, designated)	6	0	
M. Onaindía (PSE-EE, elected)	5	1	CARCE
J. M. Barquero (PP, elected)	4	0	
J. Bildarratz (PNV, elected)	4	0	
J. Zubia (PNV, designated)	3	0	
J. A Torrontegui (PNV, designated)	1	0	
G. Zabaleta (PSE-EE, elected)	1	0	
Y. Vicente (PSE-EE, elected)	1	1	Structural funds

Source: www.senado.es, accessed 8 July 2006.

In contrast, Table 3.2 presents a striking illustration of Basque government disengagement with state institutions. Table 3.2 shows that the Basque president or autonomous community ministers have not used opportunities provided by the Senate regulation reform allowing them to participate in, and solicit the convocation of, the General Commission. This includes a Basque government boycott of the high-profile state of autonomies debates held in the Senate. The presence of senators from the same Basque nationalist parties running the Basque government have given it the luxury of being able to use this absence to symbolically register disapproval of Senate reforms without losing the opportunity to articulate its political positions during debates. As Table 3.2 clearly shows, Basque government inaction contrasts with that of all other autonomous community governments which have sent both presidents and regional ministers to participate in General Commission debates, although a similar strategy appears to have been employed by the parties running the Catalan institutions whose attendance has been relatively low until quite recently.

Table 3.2 Interventions by autonomous community governments in Senate General Commission for the Autonomous Communities 1994–2006

Autonomous community	No. interventions by autonomous community president or vice-president	No. interventions by autonomous community ministers	No. interventions per autonomous community
Andalucía	6	46	52
Aragón	7	33	40
Asturias	10	31	41
Islas Baleares	9	28	37
Canarias	9	15	24
Cantabria	8	44	52
Castilla y León	10	37	47
Castilla-La Mancha	12	45	57
Cataluña	7	18	25
Extremadura	20	45	65
Galicia	9	44	53
Madrid	8	43	51
Murcia	10	34	44
Navarra	6	15	21
Valencia	15	36	51
La Rioja	12	43	55
Ceuta	3	27	30
Melilla	3	18	21
AVERAGE	9	32	43
Basque Country	0	0	0

Source: www.senado.es, accessed 7 July 2006.

Many commentators argue that the Senate's problematic composition, its limited role in territorial matters and more general weaknesses may help account for some of the state of autonomy's more general failings (Aja 2003: 163 and 247–56; Lucas 2000: 47; Roller 2002). These commentators argue that the absence of a meaningful autonomous community role in state legislative processes affecting their competencies or interests tends to increase the likelihood of territorial conflict and weakens development of a cooperative political culture. Where competencies are shared by state and autonomous community authorities, limited participation in state lawmaking may undermine policy effectiveness. Some even argue that the weak Senate may compromise the legitimisation of the state of autonomies itself.

All of these critiques have kept the question of Senate reform on the political agenda for many years. Since 1994, a variety of special committees examining proposals for constitutional reform have been set up. A central question in debates about future reform has been the role it might play in state EU policymaking (Roller 2002: 80; Jáuregui 1997). Indeed, the PSOE, currently in government at the state level and in many autonomous communities, have made Senate reform a centrepiece of its agenda for constitutional reform and attempts to make autonomous community participation in EU decisionmaking more effective. Acknowledging the role of the autonomous communities in the execution of EU laws and the impact of the EU on exclusive autonomous community and shared competencies, the PSOE proposes a constitutional reform which would make the Senate a forum for 'deepening relations between autonomous communities, the Spanish government and the EU', to allow the 'aggregation of interests' on EU matters and to 'take on board the principle of subsidiarity' (PSOE 2003: 7–10).

However, so far, debates on Senate reform have revealed significant disagreements among political parties. The PSOE would like to federalise the Senate along the lines of the German *Bundesrat,* replacing direct election of senators from province-based constituencies to autonomous community-based ones and expanding Senate powers to include responsibility for 'first readings' of legislation relevant to autonomous communities (Gómez 2005: 213–15). In more recent years, the PP, with the notable exception of the Galician president, Manuel Fraga, has taken the line that Senate reform is not a priority and, if it must be broached, reform ought to be undertaken within the existing constitutional framework and ensure equality and solidarity among territorial entities (Gómez 2005: 218). For minority nationalists, including the PNV, Senate reform must take into account a variety of cultural, political, constitutional and institutional differences among autonomous communities – the so-called *hecho diferencial* – in order to be acceptable. This would involve creating a special status for historic nationalities and a right to veto Senate legislation affecting the differences just mentioned (Roller 2002: 81–2).

A second parliamentary body with competence in EU matters is the

Mixed Commission for the EU (*La Comisión Mixta para la Unión Europea*). A Mixed Commission with responsibility for European Community matters was created on the eve of Spain's EU accession, but in the postMaastricht context of increasing concern about the democratic deficit and the role of national parliaments in EU decisionmaking, the functions of the Commission were extended. The current Mixed Commission for the EU (henceforth Mixed Commission) is obliged to inform the Senate's General Commission about EU matters of possible interest to autonomous communities, which effectively divests it of responsibility for channelling autonomous community views into its discussions (Cienfuegos 1997a: 29). On the other hand, the Mixed Commission is so called because it includes representatives from both houses of the Spanish parliament. It may, therefore, include autonomous community-designated senators or those representing territorial interests.

The Mixed Commission currently has responsibility for three main tasks: participation in the formulation of state EU policy, holding the government to account for its actions in EU matters and conducting relations with parliaments abroad, including the European Parliament.[4] In order to perform its first function, the Mixed Commission receives the European Commission's legislative proposals and can solicit information from the government and initiate parliamentary debates to discuss these proposals. It may produce reports on general matters of EU interest. To scrutinise government activity on EU matters it has powers to request information from the government, submit oral and written questions and solicit attendance of government personnel to debate EU matters with the Mixed Commission's members.[5] Mixed Commission activities thus give parliamentarians an opportunity to communicate their views on EU policy to the government during debates, by issuing formal proposals and resolutions on EU matters, and through reports.

Studies of the Mixed Commission's activity (Cienfuegos 1997a and 2001; Ordóñez 2000) show that it has been relatively active. It has developed and communicated opinions on a variety of EU matters, including those of general interest and importance – such as enlargement, economic monetary union and the Constitutional Treaty – and more specific legislative decisions. Some of these reports may have been influential (Cienfuegos 1997a: 59), but more generally its influence on government policy is seen as limited. The Mixed Commission's principal activity has centred on obtaining information about the EU and scrutinising government actions. This activity has been pronounced at key moments in the evolution of the EU, such as treaty reforms and Spanish turns at the EU's six-monthly rotating presidency. Like many parliamentary committees, however, the scope, quality and autonomy of its work has been limited by a dependence on the government's willingness to supply meaningful information and the reluctance of parliamentary majorities to challenge governments run by their own party (Cienfuegos 2001).

The forty or so Mixed Commission members are designated at the beginning of each new parliament. The ratio of senators to deputies is roughly in proportion with the relative size of each chamber, which means there are always more deputies than senators. Among the senators serving in the Mixed Commission, there have always been some autonomous community-designated senators, although these have always constituted a very small minority. Initially, there were just one or two autonomous community-designated senators at a single moment in time, but in more recent years there have been closer to half a dozen (www.senado.es, accessed 7 July 2006). A senator designated by the Basque autonomous community has only been a member of the Mixed Commission on one occasion (Joseba Zubia, between May 2000 and January 2004). However, because the Mixed Commission is required to include members of each party group represented in parliament, politicians from a wide variety of minority nationalist and regionalist parties have been members. This means that there has always been a representative from at least one of the parties running the Basque (and indeed Catalan) autonomous community governments in the Mixed Commission. In the Basque case, the PNV has always been represented.

The very small proportion of autonomous community, minority nationalist and regionalist representatives in the Mixed Commission – as well as rules requiring majority support for its decisions – put severe limits on its utility as a forum for territorial actors to influence state EU policy. Nevertheless, the Basque nationalist representatives have used the Mixed Commission to promote Basque government initiatives. A very good illustration of the role Basque nationalist senators and deputies play as representatives of Basque institutions is their work promoting autonomous community participation in the Council. As the next chapter spells out in more detail, Basque authorities have long campaigned for an autonomous community presence in the state's delegation to the Council. At one point, this policy culminated in a 1998 Basque parliament resolution[6] calling on the central government to take necessary steps to allow autonomous community participation in the Council. The Basque parliament resolution was then presented in the Mixed Commission[7] by the PNV Senate spokesperson, who also negotiated a deal with representatives of the central government party (then the PP), to pass a resolution calling on the government to allow autonomous community participation in the Council.[8] Not long afterwards, the plenary of the Congress of Deputies passed a similar motion, on the initiative of a Basque nationalist (EA) deputy.[9]

The Sectoral Conference system

Once the devolution process prefigured in the 1978 constitution began to take form, a series of bilateral and multilateral intergovernmental bodies were established to manage the process of decentralisation and coordinate policy actions of different territorial administrations. After Spain joined the EU, the central government and autonomous communities agreed to give many of these bodies a role in EU decisionmaking.

The Conference for Affairs related to the European Communities (CARCE, *Conferencia para Asuntos Relacionados con las Comunidades Europeas*) met from 1988, initially in the form of unregulated and *ad hoc* encounters (Ortúzar *et al.* 1995: 146–152). The CARCE was given formal footing following negotiation of an 'institutionalisation' agreement in 1992,[10] internal regulations,[11] and finally, in 1997, enactment of Law 2/1997.[12] This law codified previous agreements and set out the composition of the CARCE, its functions and decision rules.

CARCE members are representatives of state and autonomous community governments.[13] The minister for public administration represents the central government, alongside secretaries of state for territorial administration, and for external affairs and the EU. Each autonomous community designates a regional minister (or *consejero*) with responsibility for EU matters to represent it. A Committee of European Community Affairs Coordinators (*Comisión de Coordinadores de Asuntos Comunitarios Europeos*), composed of senior functionaries from state and autonomous community executives, supports the work of the CARCE plenary.

According to Law 2/1997 and its internal regulations, the CARCE is an organ for 'cooperation, consultation and deliberation'. It has three main responsibilities. First and foremost, the CARCE is responsible for designing the architecture for autonomous community participation in EU decisionmaking. It ought to guarantee that this participation is effective. And finally, the CARCE provides a forum where the central government may provide information and debate with autonomous communities on general EU issues (such as treaty reform).

CARCE regulations give the central government preeminence. The minister for public administration presides over and convenes CARCE plenaries, prepares an agenda and performs a series of formal functions, such as inviting guests and signing minutes. Administrative functions are centralised. The ministry of public administration (MAP, *Ministerio de Administraciones Públicas*) supplies a secretary for the Conference, is responsible for minutes and archives, and presides over the Committee of European Community coordinators. The central government must be present for the CARCE to be quorate and the central government must endorse all agreements.

Autonomous community attendance at CARCE meetings is voluntary. Five autonomous communities can call for a meeting of the CARCE, all may propose agenda items and at least fourteen must be present for the CARCE to be quorate. Agreements need the support of at least a majority of autonomous communities, but preferably all those present at relevant meetings. CARCE agreements are only binding on those who sign up to them and do not have legal force.

Since 1990, the CARCE has produced over a dozen agreements, summarised in Table 3.3 below and discussed in more detail throughout this and the following chapter. Agreements now regulate the full range of autonomous community EU activities: involvement in the formation of state EU negotiating positions; the domestic application of EU decisions; participation in state delegations in EU institutions (European Commission committees, the Council and ECJ); and their autonomous presence in Brussels.

Table 3.3 Agreements of the Conference for Affairs Related to the European Communities 1990–2005

Subject of Agreement	Date
1. Autonomous community intervention in state actions relating to European Commission and ECJ proceedings	Nov 1990
2. State aids	Nov 1990
3. Institutionalisation of the CARCE	Oct 1992
4. Extension of thematic scope of CARCE	June 1994
5. Internal CARCE regulations	June 1994
6. Internal participation of autonomous communities in European Affairs through the Sectoral Conferences (1994 Agreement)	Nov 1994
7. Creation of autonomous community representative in Spain's Permanent Representation to the EU	July 1996
8. Transfrontier cooperation	Dec 1996
9. Modification of CARCE internal regulations	June 1997
10. Autonomous community participation in ECJ proceedings	Dec 1997
11. Social security and health assistance for employees of autonomous community delegations in Brussels	Dec 1997
12. Autonomous community participation in European Commission committees 2003–6	March 2003
13. Distribution of European Commission committee representation among autonomous communities 2003–6	March 2003
14. Department of Autonomous [Community] Affairs in Spain's Permanent Representation to the EU and participation in Council working groups	Dec 2004
15. Autonomous community participation in Council formations	Dec 2004

Notes: Text of each agreement can be found, respectively, in: 1. *Boletín Oficial del Estado (BOE)*, 216, 8 September 1992, p. 30853; 2. *BOE*, 216, 8 September 1992, p. 30854; 3. *BOE*, 241, 8 October 1993, p. 33815; 4. *BOE*, 257, 27 October 1994, p. 33815; 5. *BOE*, 269, 10 November 1994, p. 34741; 6. *BOE*, 69, 22 March 1995, p. 10045; 7. *BOE*, 302, 16 December 1996, p. 37314 and *BOE*, 229, 21 September 1996, p. 28394; 8. *BOE*, 207, 29 August 1997, p. 36449 and *BOE*, 297, 12 December 1997, p. 25908; 9. *BOE*, 189, 8 August 1997, p. 24191; 10. *BOE*, 79, 2 April 1998, p. 11352; 11. *BOE*, 79, 2 April 1998, p. 11352; 12. www.map.es; accessed 13 November 2006; 13. www.map.es, accessed 13 November 2006; 14. *BOE*, 64, 16 March 2005, p. 9372; 15. *BOE*, 64, 16 March 2005, p. 9374.

The 1994 CARCE Agreement on the Internal Participation of Autonomous Communities in European Affairs through the Sectoral Conferences (henceforth '1994 Agreement') deserves particular attention. The Agreement delegates responsibility for more routine EU decisions to around a dozen policy-specific Sectoral Conferences with membership regimes and decision rules similar to those of the CARCE. Designated Sectoral Conferences would examine EU presidency programmes and provide opportunities for members to inform one another of, and if so desired coordinate, measures to implement EU policies.

The most noteworthy feature of the 1994 Agreement are procedures permitting central and autonomous community governments to share power in the formation of state positions on prospective EU laws or policies. They were profoundly influenced by German constitutional reforms in 1992, which entrenched *Länder* rights to participate in EU decisions through their representatives in the federal parliament's upper house (*Bundesrat*) and varied *Länder* influence according to the nature of competencies affected by EU decisions (Jeffery 1997: 60; Börzel 2002: 71–2). According to the 1994 CARCE Agreement, Sectoral Conferences would distribute and debate European Commission proposals and monitor the evolution of EU negotiations. The domestic distribution of policy competencies would determine the degree of autonomous community influence over the content of state negotiating positions. Where a prospective EU law affected exclusive autonomous community competencies, the Spanish government was obliged to take a commonly agreed autonomous community view 'decisively' into account when it was involved in EU negotiations. Where competencies were shared, or where EU decisions had financial implications for the state, a common agreement reached by both levels of government would be 'decisive' in determining the state's negotiating position. Where exclusive central government competencies were involved, and autonomous communities demonstrated interest, the former would keep the latter informed. If autonomous communities could not agree common positions, the central government would take views expressed by autonomous communities into account. If possible, new negotiating positions could be agreed throughout the course of EU negotiations. In all cases, the obligation to cooperate could not undermine the state's 'ability to act' or its 'flexibility' in EU negotiations.

Evaluating the effectiveness of CARCE and the EU activities of Sectoral Conferences is not straightforward. Assessments by authoritative sources, including academic specialists, autonomous community spokespersons and official MAP sources, are contradictory. Moreover, there is insufficient documentary evidence available to adjudicate in many of these disputes. MAP has compiled data on the frequency of Sectoral Conference meetings, attendance, summaries of matters discussed and agreements reached (Ortúzar *et al.* 1995; Sanz 1998; MAP 1996, 2001a, 2001b, 2002, 2004 and 2006a). However, these do not provide consistent or sufficiently detailed information to sustain judgements about the quality of collaboration among central and autonomous community administrations.[14]

It is clear that the CARCE and many Sectoral Conferences meet regularly and provide opportunities for autonomous communities and central government ministers to discuss and reach agreements on EU matters. As Table 3.4 shows, some Sectoral Conferences assigned EU responsibilities are more active than others. The CARCE met forty-eight times between 1989 and 2005, an average of three times a year. The Agriculture and Rural Development Sectoral Conference, which has a heavy EU workload, met much more frequently; an average of five times a year, although in some years it met eight (2000), nine (1999) or ten times (2002). From 2000, when it first met, this Conference's special committee for agriculture and EU matters met nine times a year on average. The Fisheries Sectoral Conference, which also deals with many EU issues, and its special committee for EU matters, also met frequently. In contrast, some Sectoral Conferences, such as tourism, transport and culture, only met intermittently.

Table 3.4 Meetings of Sectoral Conferences assigned EU responsibilities 1981–2005

Sectoral Conference or equivalent	Meetings 1981–2005
Agriculture and Rural Development	109
Consultative Council for Agriculture and Community Affairs	54
Fishing	31
Consultative Council for Fishing and Community Affairs	32
Health	73
Fiscal and Financial Policy	54
Education	50
CARCE	48
Social Affairs	36
Environment	34
Labour Affairs	27
Consumer Affairs	20
Tourism	16
Transport	13
Culture	12
Industry and Energy	8
Infrastructure and Territorial Planning	4
Science and Technology	1

Source: Ministry of Public Administration, www.map.es, accessed 20 November 2006.

Note: There is no current data for Civil Protection, International Cooperation and Telecommunications Sectoral Conferences, which were assigned EU responsibilities in the 1994 Agreement.

MAP summaries of matters discussed indicate that EU matters regularly appear on Sectoral Conference agendas (Ortúzar *et al.* 1995; MAP 2001a, 2001b, 2002, 2004 and 2006a). EU matters discussed range from the reform of general policy regimes (such as Common Agricultural Policy), proposals for, and application of, EU laws as well as the management and distribution of EU funds. In addition to agreements listed in Table 3.3, CARCE agendas routinely included EU presidency programmes (including conduct of Spanish EU presidencies) and major developments such as treaty reforms, the single market programme, Agenda 2000, EU enlargements and the Convention on the Future of the EU.

It is much more difficult to characterise the quality of collaboration between autonomous community and central governments in the CARCE and Sectoral Conferences. Many academics and autonomous community spokespersons are critical. Academics specialising in the study of intergovernmental relations in Spain often characterise the Sectoral Conferences as 'irregular', 'precarious' and 'weak' (Aja 2003: 215–38; Roig 1998, 1999a, 2000, 2001 and 2002; Fernández Manjón 2001: 342–48; Rey 2003: 133–46; Albertí 1998; Lasagabaster 1995: 213–17, among others). According to such authors, the Sectoral Conferences are weakened by some combination of the following problems: a tendency for EU discussions to mostly involve information from the central government; a dependence on the political will of presiding central government ministers; limited collaboration among autonomous communities; a disruptive influence of party politics and electoral periods (when Sectoral Conferences tend to become semi-paralysed); inadequate administrative support or technical knowledge available to some members; and limited sensitivity of the foreign affairs ministry – a key player in EU policy-making – to autonomous community demands.

For many of these authors, a near total failure to formally implement provisions of the 1994 Agreement regulating autonomous community participation in the formulation of state EU positions has been an important measure of Sectoral Conference weakness. Before the 1994 Agreement and during Maastricht Treaty negotiations, autonomous communities agreed a common position on the future CoR, which was 'taken into account' by the central government, though not converted into a formal state-autonomous community agreement (Parejo and Betancour 1996: 187–9; Ortúzcar *et al.* 1995: 36–40).[15] A clearer application of the 1994 Agreement was an autonomous community position on the 1996 intergovernmental conference preparing the Amsterdam Treaty. This common position was later discussed in the CARCE and 'taken into account' by the central government during treaty negotiations (Roig 1998: 527; Cienfuegos 1997b: 191; Rey 2003: 116).[16] Autonomous communities were unable to formulate common positions for the Nice Treaty or Constitutional Treaty (Roig 2001: 513; Bourne 2006: 10–11) and until only very recently (see below), there have been very few other examples.[17]

Other evaluations of the CARCE and the Sectoral Conferences' EU role have been more positive (see, for instance, Ortúzcar *et al.* 1995: 152–4; Cienfuegos 1997b: 191–202, 204; Börzel 2002: 103–47). Tanja Börzel argues, for instance, that the Sectoral Conferences generally 'allow for an effective participation of autonomous communities in the formation, decisionmaking and implementation of European policies' (2002: 147); the 'central-state administration regularly informs [autonomous communities] about European issues that affect their competencies and interests, and the [autonomous communities] often make observations that are taken into account by the Spanish government' (2002: 137). These arguments are supported by MAP sources observing that proEuropean leanings of autonomous communities, and the coincidence of many state and autonomous community interests in EU matters, mean there is little disagreement among them in EU matters (MAP 2004: 33, further references to unpublished MAP reports are made in Börzel 2002: 137 and Rey 2003: 142). In short, while the 1994 Agreement is rarely observed formally, autonomous communities nevertheless 'participate *de facto* in the formulation ... of European policies in the Sectoral Conferences' (Börzel 2002: 137).[18] While these observations are difficult to verify with documentary evidence, MAP is an authoritative source and difficult to dismiss.

Since 2005, clearer evidence of more regular and systematic cooperation among autonomous communities and central authorities has emerged. From that year, new rules allowed autonomous communities to participate in state delegations to the Council (see chapter 4). In the first two years, autonomous communities negotiated at least twenty-seven common agreements which, after discussions with the central government, were later presented in the Council (MAP 2005: 11–15; MAP 2006b: 13–19). Autonomous community positions have usually been negotiated in *ad hoc* meetings organised by individual autonomous communities. Collaboration between autonomous community and central government ministries prior to Council meetings has been channelled through Sectoral Conferences, some of which have established new subcommittees to better deal with EU issues (MAP 2005: 12–13; MAP 2006b: 11, 15–16). Texts of autonomous community common positions often provide detailed assessments of EU policies, propose changes to prospective EU laws, and assert a 'regional' perspective. Even though MAP documents do not provide enough detail to satisfactorily evaluate the nature of cooperation among autonomous community and central governments, these new practices provide clear evidence of more regular involvement of autonomous communities in the formation of state EU decisions.

Another important innovation, which may further strengthen intergovernmental relations, was inauguration, in 2004, of a Conference of Presidents. The PSOE promised, in both the run-up to the March 2004 general elections (PSOE 2003: 11) and afterwards,[19] to create a forum for regular political dialogue between autonomous community, autonomous city (Ceuta and

Melilla) and central government presidents. The idea has other high-profile supporters, notably Manuel Fraga, PP president of Galicia between 1990 and 2005 (Aja 2003: 219). At the first meeting, participants agreed to institutionalise the Conference of Presidents as a yearly summit, with few fixed rules of conduct, for the purpose of political debate (rather than formal decision-making) on 'the design of government policy that may affect autonomous community competencies' (MAP 2004: 19–21; Garea, *El Mundo*, 29 October 2004).

Summits were held in October 2004 and September 2005 but let slip for 2006. The first was billed as a historic occasion because it was the first time that all seventeen autonomous community and central government presidents had ever met together (Garea, *El Mundo*, 28 October 2004; *El Mundo*, 29 October 2004). The presence of Basque president Juan José Ibarretxe at both meetings was particularly noteworthy, given that Basque presidents had pointedly shunned multilateral meetings of this type in the past (see Table 3.2). In press statements, Ibarretxe said he attended to promote dialogue; to ask for, and offer, his respect for the decisions of different 'peoples'; but that such multilateral meetings could not substitute preferred 'bilateral dialogue between the Basque Country and Spain' (Cue, *El País*, 29 October 2004).

Certain procedural rigidities may limit the quality of debate in summit meetings. Participants are allocated short time slots to articulate their views and agendas have been deliberately limited to few agenda items, or just one. However, summits have been preceded by much public debate and many preparatory meetings among party leaders and among autonomous community and central government ministers (MAP 2004: 22; Garea, *El Mundo*, 10 September 2005a and 2005b). Sectoral Conferences undertook important preparatory work – especially for the second summit's deal on health-financing reforms – or would put together final details of agreements (Garea, *El Mundo*, 10 September 2005b; Aizpeolea, *El País*, 10 September 2005).

Three issues have dominated formal summit agendas at the two meetings held so far: institutionalisation of the Conference of Presidents itself, reform of health service funding, and participation of autonomous communities in EU matters (Aizpeolea, *El País*, 29 October 2004; Garea, *El Mundo*, 11 September 2005). Spanish president José Luis Zapatero identified EU matters as an important agenda item from the outset,[20] and, following agreement at the first summit, the government promised concrete proposals before the end of the year that were later taken up in the CARCE (see chapter four's discussion on Council participation) (Aizpeolea, *El País*, 29 October 2004). Despite intense pressure from the opposition PP, the central government resisted using the Conference of Presidents to discuss controversial new Catalan and Basque autonomy plans. Evaluations of this new body's salience tend to split along party lines. PSOE autonomous community presidents tend to support it as an initiative promoting dialogue and territorial cohesion (Sánchez, *El Mundo*, 29 October 2004 and 11 September 2005), while the PP tends to reduce its significance to a historic 'photo opportunity', with little meaningful contribution to political dialogue (Ramírez, El Mundo, 29 October 2004 and 11 September 2005).

Basque bilateralism and disagreements over the Sectoral Conference system

In general, the Basque government has not been an enthusiastic participant in the Sectoral Conference system and differences over the appropriate form of autonomous community participation in the formation of the state's EU decisions have often strained relations between Basque and central authorities.

Until 1995 the Basque government formally boycotted the CARCE by refusing to sign up to its 1992 institutionalisation and other agreements. This did not prevent it from participating informally in CARCE activities: Basque representatives were still invited to CARCE meetings and attended with regularity (Ortúzar et al. 1995: 155), albeit with voice but not vote (Castro and Ugalde 2004: 153). Officially, the principal reason for this position was an insistence that Basque involvement in multilateral participation mechanisms be preceded by constitution of a body for bilateral cooperation between Basque and state administrations (Diego Casals 1994: 154; Gobierno Vasco 1993: 80). Insistence that bilateral bodies complement multilateral ones was underpinned by the conviction that the so-called hecho diferencial required bilateral mechanisms for relations between the state and the socially and politically distinctive historic nationalities (Gobierno Vasco 1993: 80; Castro and Ugalde 2004: 154–5). According to this view the hecho diferencial made multilateral mechanisms for autonomous community participation in EU matters unsuitable for dealing with competencies and interests exclusive to one or only some autonomous communities (such as policing, language policy and taxation powers). The official boycott was also underpinned by a harsh critique of the CARCE, which a 1993 Basque government report described as a body that was 'totally unsatisfactory', dominated by the convenience of the presiding central government minister and unwilling to seriously discuss the articulation of an effective EU participation system (Gobierno Vasco 1993: 80; see also Diego 1994: 153; Ortuzar 1998: 15). The report considered the lack of autonomous community pressure, but also the central government's 'lack of will' and its 'enormous interest' in dominating the state's relations with the EU, as major reasons for CARCE failings (Gobierno Vasco 1993: 80; see also Diego 1994: 159; Ortuzar 1998: 15).

Equally conflictual was the process leading to establishment of the Bilateral Commission for Cooperation Administration of the State – Administration of the Autonomous Community of the Basque Country for Affairs related to the European Communities (Comisión Bilateral de Cooperación Administración del Estado – Administración de la Comunidad

Autónoma del País Vasco para Asuntos Relacionados con las Comunidades Europeas) (henceforth 'Bilateral Commission'). Even though Basque and state representatives had agreed to establish such a Bilateral Commission and a constituting act had been on the negotiating table from as early as May 1990, it was not formally constituted until some five years later. In the meantime, the Basque government blamed central government 'intransigence' for the lack of progress (Gobierno Vasco 1993: 81), while the central government argued that the Bilateral Commission had not been convened because proposed agenda items affected other autonomous communities too, or could be dealt with in other bilateral committees (for Basque taxation or policing powers, for instance) (Ortúzar *et al.* 1995: 155–6). The matter remained on the agenda in intervening years, although in accordance with Basque preferences (Ortúzar *et al.*, 1995: 156), the CARCE's 1992 institution-alisation agreement had included provisions for the establishment of bilateral cooperation where European matters affected one autonomous community exclusively or were of particular interest to an autonomous community due to the specific nature of its autonomy. This was later included in the 1997 law regulating the CARCE.

Finally, at the end of 1995, Basque and central authorities formally signed a constituting act for the Bilateral Commission.[21] According to the constituting act, it would involve, on the part of the central government, the minister for public administration, the secretaries of state for the European Communities and for territorial administration, and the director general of territorial cooperation. The Basque government's vicepresident, its secretaries-general for external affairs and for the legal regime and autonomy development, and its director for European affairs would represent the autonomous community. Provisions for equal numbers of state and autonomous community representatives matched other measures to ensure parity, such as the need for 'mutual agreement' on the agenda, for convocation of meetings and for reaching agreements. While the Sectoral Conferences would continue to serve as fora for jointly and multilaterally broaching the participation of autonomous communities in EU decisionmaking, the Bilateral Commission would deal with Basque autonomous community participation in EU decisions exclusively affecting it or, by virtue of the distinctiveness of Basque autonomy, EU matters specifically relevant to it. Significantly, the constituting act included among the particular functions of the Bilateral Commission the prevention of new and the resolution of existing conflicts, and a strengthening of dialogue in the elaboration of measures relating to EU matters. Others functions included studying and analysing matters of mutual interest and fostering relations and institutional coordination between the administrations on EU matters.

Once these arrangements had been agreed, the Bilateral Commission initially met with some regularity – twice in 1996 and once in each of the following three years. However, it did not meet again after June 1999 (Castro and Ugalde 2004: 157),[22] possibly indicating the Bilateral Commission's dependence on the prior existence of good relations between parties governing at state and Basque levels. Data provided by Castro and Ugalde (2004: 157–8) shows that when it did meet, Basque and central government representatives discussed various matters relating to the former's involvement in multilateral mechanisms regulating autonomous community participation in EU decisionmaking, including: Basque accession to the CARCE's 1994 Agreement; CARCE agreements on state aids and involvement in European Commission advisory committees; and future autonomous community participation in the Council. Discussions also focused on the 1996 intergovernmental conference, EU challenges to the Basque taxation regime and Basque preferences on structural fund reforms. Castro and Ugalde have characterised the 'life' of the Bilateral Commission as 'excessively languid' and 'unpromising', and criticised it for apparently failing to discuss more 'assiduously' EU issues like taxation, Europol and Schengen, which affect distinctive Basque competencies (2004: 158). It is difficult to evaluate the significance and conduct of these discussions because, like its multilateral counterparts, detailed material such as agendas or minutes of meetings have not been made public. Nevertheless, it is fully apparent that this body, not having met since June 1999, cannot currently serve as a platform allowing Basque and central governments to share powers in EU decisionmaking.

One more promising outcome following establishment of the Bilateral Commission was that it ended the Basque government's formal boycott of the CARCE. Once the Bilateral Commission was set up, the Basque government signed up to CARCE agreements such as the 1990 agreement on state aids, the 1992 institutionalisation agreement and the 1994 agreement extending the CARCE's thematic ambit (see Table 3.3 above). But despite a more intensive engagement in multilateral fora since the constitution of the Bilateral Commission, the Basque government has not yet engaged fully with the CARCE and Sectoral Conference system. It has the lowest attendance rate of all autonomous communities at Sectoral Conference meetings.[23] The Basque government has not signed up to CARCE agreements on autonomous community involvement in European Commission and ECJ legal proceedings. But, more fundamentally, the Basque government has not signed up to the CARCE's pivotal 1994 Agreement, even though it continues to participate in Sectoral Conference activities derived from, or related to, this Agreement (Roig 1999b: 202).

Like its earlier positions on the CARCE, the Basque government's position on the Sectoral Conferences is sustained by a critique of the Sectoral Conferences themselves and suspicions about the motives behind central government preferences on the design of the Spanish EU participation system in general. Basque government critiques of the design and functioning of the Sectoral Conferences subscribe to most of the negative evaluations described earlier and need not be recounted here (see Diego 1994; Ortuzar 1998: 15;

Castro and Ugalde 2004: 153; Gobierno Vasco 2003: 17). The Basque government has repeatedly espoused replacing the decentralised Sectoral Conference system with a single interautonomous community body which would negotiate common positions to be concerted later in a second body also involving the central government (Diego 1994; Gobierno Vasco 1996). These bodies would include representatives of state and autonomous communities with responsibility in EU matters and, where appropriate, representatives with responsibility for different policy sectors.

Another explanation for the Basque government's stand against the Sectoral Conference system can be found in more general differences between Basque and central authorities over the appropriate balance between internal and external mechanisms for autonomous community participation in EU affairs (Roig 1999b: 202), which will be discussed in more detail in the next chapter. Furthermore, Basque rejection of the Sectoral Conference system has reflected suspicions that these coordination mechanisms were a central government strategy to undercut Basque autonomy. This was especially evident in reactions to the controversial 1992 *acuerdos autonómicos* (Autonomy Agreements), which the two main statewide parties negotiated in order to bolster the Sectoral Conference system, among other things. As López points out, the 1992 Autonomy Agreements:

> aroused enormous distrust due to their tendency to establish homogenising, standardising and multilateralised relations between the state and all the autonomous communities, omitting the singularity of the 'nationalities' compared to the 'regions', and neglecting the fact that the first – Catalonia, the Basque Country and Galicia – constituted sociological and political realities different from the other [autonomous communities]. (2002: 52, my translation)

Political parties and intergovernmental relations

In Spain, relations among and between political parties can constitute an additional form of intergovernmental relations. More specifically, collaboration among nationalist, regionalist and statewide parties, and the internal dynamics of politics within parties governing at multiple territorial levels, can provide important channels for governments to influence each other's policies. In part this is due to aspects of Spanish political culture, such as a tendency for party elite to conflate interinstitutional relations with *intra*party relations (Aja 2003: 237) and for party elite to conduct *inter*party negotiations with an eye to party fortunes in multiple territorial arenas (Reniu 2002: 180). But, first and foremost, the role that political parties play in intergovernmental relations is a consequence of the structure of the party system in Spain.

At the state level, parties fielding candidates in all parts of the country (statewide parties) compete with a range of minority nationalist and regionalist parties who between them have captured around 10 per cent of seats in all general elections since the early 1980s (Gunther *et al.*, 2005: 205–12; www.elmundo.es, accessed 10 June 2006). The consolidation of the party system by the end of that decade confirmed the permanence of three principal statewide parties: the centre-left PSOE, the conservative PP and the smaller leftist coalition centred on the communist party, IU. The largest share of non-statewide party votes in general elections has always gone to Catalan nationalists, particularly the moderate Christian-democratic Convergence and Union (CiU, *Converència i Unió*) which has won between ten and eighteen seats since 1977, although the Basque nationalists in PNV, who have won between five and eight seats, have almost always come second to CiU (Gunther *et al.*, 2005: 205–12; www.elmundo.es, accessed 10 June 2006). In both places and in Galicia, other minority nationalist parties have won seats, as have regionalist parties from Andalucía, Aragón, Canary Islands, Navarre and Valencia.

More significantly, only four of nine general elections since the transition to democracy have allowed a single party to command an absolute majority of seats in the Spanish parliament. However, Spanish central governments have always been run by a single party because, when the largest party lacked an absolute majority, party elites preferred minority government to coalition government (Reniu 2001 and 2002). As Josep Maria Reniu's work shows (summarised in Table 3.5), the minority governments of the centrist Union of the Democratic Centre (UCD, *Unión de Centro Democrático*), led by the former Francoist reformers Adolfo Suárez and Leopoldo Calvo Sotelo, were based on more *ad hoc* relations with different political parties. More recent minority governments of the PSOE, led by Felipe González, and of the PP, led by José María Aznar, have been based on more formal agreements, mostly with Catalan and Basque nationalist parties and regionalists from the Canary Islands Coalition (CC, *Coalición Canaria*). The current PSOE administration, led by José Luis Zapatero, has less stable arrangements for parliamentary support than its immediate predecessor, but has often relied on a variety of minority nationalist and regionalist parties from Catalonia, Canary Islands and Galicia.[24]

Changing patterns of government formation at the state level can have a significant impact on the development of the state of autonomies more generally, but have also had some relevance for autonomous community participation in EU decisionmaking. Catalan nationalists – particularly CiU – have been the principal winners of pacts with statewide parties for government formation, largely because the arithmetic of parliamentary majorities has made their votes indispensable.[25] They were able to prise important concessions from both PSOE and PP governments, including new powers (such as policing, ports, land use and traffic management) and reforms giving autonomous communities more control over their finances. For its part, the PNV, with a much smaller share of seats in the Spanish parliament, has been much less influential (Heller 2002). PNV demands have focused on calls for

Table 3.5 State-level minority governments and principal supporters

Government	Period of government	Type of government	Principal supporters
Suárez I (UCD)	1977–79	Minority	Informal and *ad hoc*
Suárez II (UCD)	1979–81	Minority	Informal and *ad hoc*
Calvo Sotelo (UCD)	1981–82	Minority	Informal and *ad hoc*
González I (PSOE)	1982–86	Majority	
González II (PSOE)	1986–89	Majority	
González III (PSOE)	1989–93	Majority[a]	
González IV (PSOE)	1993–96	Minority	Formal CiU, PNV
Aznar I (PP)	1996–2000	Minority	Formal CiU, PNV, CC
Aznar II (PP)	2000–4	Majority	–
Zapatero I (PSOE)	2004 to present	Minority	Informal and *ad hoc*

Source: My compilation from data, concepts and analysis in Reniu 2001 and 2002 and correspondence with the author.
Notes: [a] After the 1989 elections, the PSOE won 175 seats, one short of an absolute majority. However, because radical Basque nationalists from *Herri Batasuna* refused to take up their four seats in the Spanish parliament, the PSOE had a *de facto* majority (Heller 2002: 669–70). CC = Canary Coalition (regionalists); CiU = Convergence and Unity (Catalan nationalists); PNV = Basque Nationalist Party; PP = Popular Party; PSOE = Spanish Socialist Workers Party; UCD = Union of the Democratic Centre.

the completion of resource transfers from central to Basque authorities, transfers necessary for the practical application of competencies assigned in the Basque autonomy statute. Basque financial relationships with the state, regulated by the 1981 Economic Agreement (*Concierto Económico*), were another important issue for the PNV, especially during the PP's first term of government, when the two parties successfully negotiated a renewal of the Basque quota (*cupo*) paying for state services (see chapter six). The CC's terms for supporting PP and PSOE minority governments have largely focused on obtaining recognition of the special economic and geographical difficulties facing the islands (Heller 2002: 673 and 678).

Both the CiU and the PNV placed demands for increased participation in EU policymaking on the political agenda during periods of minority government at state level (Heller 2002; López 2002: 55; Sinova 1993: 196). In a general sense, this helped elevate the importance of autonomous community participation in EU decisionmaking on the Spanish political agenda (see, for example, Roig 2002: 141), but in some cases there was a clear link between minority nationalist demands and concrete events: The PP's 1996 'Governability Pact' with CiU, for instance, led to the creation of an autonomous community representative in the Spanish permanent representation to the EU and measures allowing autonomous communities to participate in state delegations in European Commission advisory committees (see chapter four). It is probably more than a coincidence that the constitution of the Basque-State Bilateral Commission for European affairs coincided, after five difficult years of negotiations, with the PSOE's first period of minority government, and that the only five meetings held since its constitution took place between 1996 and 1999, during the PP's period of minority government. Subsequent chapters in this book will return to examine the impact of these party relationships, especially their impact on Basque government EU campaigns.

Statewide, minority nationalist and regionalist parties also compete at autonomous community level and here, patterns of government formation may also provide opportunities for political parties to assume responsibility for institutional relations between governments. In almost all cases, both the PP and PSOE field candidates in autonomous community elections. Between them, they have had a hand in the government of every single autonomous community at some point, and in most cases the statewide parties have dominated autonomous community politics, either governing alone or as senior partners in coalitions with minority nationalist or regionalist parties. Moreover, the fortunes of statewide parties at autonomous community level have tended to reflect their fortunes at the state level, so that when the PSOE or the PP have been strong in Madrid, they have tended to be strong in autonomous communities too.

This has had a variety of implications for intergovernmental relations. As Reniu observes, the formation of government coalitions may often take into account the dynamics of government formation and party competition at different territorial levels: parties with established relations at autonomous community level may extend such alliances to state level and vice versa; or the regional branch of a statewide party may be required to adjust its conduct to suit the needs of governing arrangements at the state level (2001 and 2002). It also gives autonomous community leaders an opportunity to call on their party colleagues in Madrid to advance the interests of their autonomous community and gives them good reason to expect a more sympathetic ear from the central government than they might get if it were governed by another political party (Aja 2003: 236–7; Fernández Manjón 2001: 253–93). Moreover, the frequent occurrence of a statewide party's simultaneous involvement in state and autonomous community government has allowed party managers to use party structures and discipline to try to keep autonomous communities in line with central government policy, although this has not been possible in every case (Aja 2003: 236–7; Fernández Manjón 2001: 253–93). A case were it does appear to have been decisive has been the PP's ability to undermine autonomous community agreements on arrangements for autonomous community participation in the EU's Council, which is discussed more fully in chapter four.

Roig (2002 and 1999b) has also observed some of these dynamics in the conduct of the CARCE and the Sectoral Conferences more generally, which has clear implications for autonomous community involvement in EU decisionmaking. Roig argues that the balance of power between parties running state and autonomous community governments can be a decisive factor affecting both the behaviour of autonomous communities and the effectiveness of sectoral conferences. He observes that autonomous community representatives tend to focus much less actively on the interests of their autonomous communities and more on the dynamics of state level politics in the presence of state-level ministers from their party (Roig 2002: 251). Furthermore, he argues that autonomous community representatives from the same party as the minister are less likely to oppose central government positions or even consent to multilateral agreements that will condition ministers' actions (Roig 1999b: 212).[26]

There have been opportunities for political parties to channel institutional relations between the Basque autonomous community and the central government on many occasions since democratisation. Even though the PNV has dominated Basque government formation since 1980, it has often had to share power with other political parties. From 1987 to 1998 the most important of these coalition partners was the PSE-PSOE, the Basque branch of the statewide PSOE (see Table 2.2).[27] This period coincides with a significant portion of the PSOE's sixteen years running the central government from 1982 to 1996. Due to its informality and the lack of detailed research on interterritorial relations within the PSOE, it is difficult to assess with much precision what the impact of simultaneous PSOE party involvement in state and Basque governments was. However, there is testimony from the PSE-PSOE suggesting that it did at least on occasion have some leverage with their PSOE colleagues in Madrid (Antolín 2001). In the Basque parliament, PSE-PSOE members often defended actions and policies of the PSOE central government, suggesting at the very least a synchronicity of interests between the Basque branch and central party apparatus. Some academic commentary has put the relationship in starker terms: as a proclivity for PSE-PSOE leaders to 'make the centralist logic of their mother party their own' (Letamendia 1997b: 37). There is also evidence that the PNV considered its PSE-PSOE coalition partner's links with Madrid of significance: The PNV was not shy to demand concessions from the PSOE central government – on banking and industry competencies and infrastructure allocations, for instance – in the course of negotiations with the PSE-PSOE on Basque government formation (de Esteban 1992: 337; Ayala, El Correo, 14 November 1990, p. 10). Chapter five examines the impact of this relationship on European policymaking in greater detail.

In conclusion, it is possible to argue that, from a historical perspective, Spain's EU membership has shaped the territorial distribution of power in Spain, largely because it has taken many years to construct the cooperation system in place today. The slow development of this system not only became a source of tensions between Basque and central authorities, it imposed substantial limits on autonomous communities' ability to influence EU decisions affecting their policy competencies. The central government still has many opportunities to dominate the state's EU decision-system and some institutions have important shortcomings. Nevertheless, the central government has gradually reconciled itself to the idea that autonomous communities should share power in EU decisions affecting their competencies, as the list of agreements in Table 3.3 and further discussion in chapter four testify. There is now much clearer evidence of collaboration among autonomous communities, and among autonomous communities and central government authorities, in the formation, and representation in the EU's Council, of state EU decisions. Some important shortcomings in the Spanish system for autonomous community participation in EU decision-making are gradually being overcome. Analysis of the evolution of Basque and other autonomous communities' participation in EU-level institutions presented in chapter four further substantiate these points.

Notes

1 Senate powers in 'territorial matters' include approval of autonomous community cooperation agreements; distribution and regulation of the state's regional development fund and disciplining autonomous communities who may act against state 'general interests'. In addition, the Senate may present legislative proposals drafted by autonomous communities to the Congress of Deputies, issue opinions on government economic plans and is involved in constitutional reform, ratification of international treaties and certain key state appointments.

2 The Senate has limited time to veto a legislative proposal or suggest amendments and the Congress of Deputies can overturn these fairly easily. Furthermore, the Senate has no formal role in appointing (through presidential investiture) or dismissing (through constructive no confidence motion) the Spanish government.

3 Reglamento del Senado, *Boletín Oficial de las Cortes Generales (BOCG)*, Series I, 119, 9 May 1994, p. 1.

4 Ley 8/1994, de 19 de mayo, *BOE*, 120, de 20 Mayo, p. 15513.

5 Such activities may take place outside of the Mixed Commission as well, including compliance with the requirement that the government inform parliament about the conduct of European Council summits in the plenary of the Congress of Deputies.

6 Technically this was a *proposición no de ley* (non-legislative proposal), *Boletín Oficial del Parlamento Vasco (BOPV)*, 156, 6 March 1998, p. 13658.

7 Technically this was a *proposición no de ley* (non-legislative proposal), *BOCG, Cortes Generales*, Series A, 145, 11 November 1997, p. 2

8 *Diario de Sesiones de las Cortes Generales (DSCG)*, *Comisiones*, 89, 4 March 1998, p. 1823.

9 *BOCG, Congreso*, Series D, 258, 23 March 1998, p. 30.

10 *BOE*, 257, de 27 de octubre, p. 33815.

11 *BOE*, 269, de 10 de noviembre, p. 34741. Replaced in 1997, *BOE* 189, de 8 de agosto, p. 24191.

12 Ley 2/1997, de 13 de marzo, *BOE*, 64, de 15 de marzo, p. 8518.

13 Law 2/1997 also made provision for participation of representatives of the

autonomous cities, Ceuta and Melilla, who are represented by members of their respective governing councils.

14   Published summaries of matters discussed are sparse, do not clearly distinguish EU and domestic issues or describe points debated. According to MAP officials, verbatim records of discussion are rare and unpublished minutes do not provide great detail (interview 13 December 2006).

15   As a number of authors point out, the Spanish central government embraced German proposals for the creation of the CoR at its own initiative, but autonomous communities were invited to participate in formation of the state negotiating position and were generally supportive of central government proposals (Calonge and Sanz 2000: 39; Parejo and Betancour 1996: 187–9; Ortúzcar *et al.* 1995: 36–40).

16   By contrast, Eduard Roig, a close observer of the CARCE, argues that much of the substance of the autonomous community position on the 1996 intergovernmental conference reinforced positions already expressed by the central government and distanced itself from some of the more radical demands of EU regions. Even then, he argues, the common position found little distinctive echo in central government thinking and some autonomous communities were disappointed that the central government did not support the Amsterdam Treaty's Declaration by Germany, Austria and Belgium on Subsidiarity (Roig 1998: 525–9; 2001: 514).

17   I would like to thank the ministry for public administration for confirming this point in an interview with senior functionaries on 13 December 2006.

18   This view was also articulated at length in interviews with MAP officials on 13 December 2006.

19   See investiture speech of Sr. Rodríguez Zapatero, *DSCG, Congreso, Pleno y Diputación Permanente*, 2, 15 April 2004, p. 19.

20   See investiture speech of Sr. Rodríguez Zapatero, *DSCG, Congreso, Pleno y Diputación Permanente*, 2, 15 April 2004, p. 19.

21   *Acta constitutiva de la Comisión Bilateral de Cooperación Administración del Estado – Administración de la Comunidad Autónoma del País Vasco para Asuntos relacionados con las Comunidades Europeas,* Madrid, 30 November 1995. Bilateral commissions specifically for European affairs have also been established between the state and the Catalan, and the Canary Islands autonomous communities.

22   Information confirmed in correspondence with Basque government in October 2005.

23   I would like to thank the ministry for public administration for confirming this point (interview December 2006).

24   I would like to thank Josep Maria Reniu for his interpretation of this arrangement. Zapatero was 'invested' as president of the government with the support of his party and from *Esquerra Republicana de Catalunya* (ERC, Republican Left of Catalonia), *Izquierda Unida, Iniciativa per Catalunya- Els Verds* (IU-ICV United Left, Initiative for Catalonia – Greens), *Coalición Canaria* (CC, Canary Islands Coalition) and *Bloque Nacionalista Galego* (BNG, Galician Nationalist Block). According to the Spanish constitution, candidates for the post of 'president of government' (equivalent to prime minister) must find the support of a majority of parliamentarians in the Congress of Deputies before taking up government office. This procedure is called investiture.

25   In the 1993 elections, PSOE won 159 seats (37.63 per cent of vote), PP won 141 seats (34.76 per cent of vote); CiU won 17 seats (4.94 per cent of vote) and the PNV won 5 seats (1.24 per cent of vote). In 1996, PP won 156 seats (38.79 per cent of vote), PSOE won 141 seats (37.63 per cent of vote), CiU won 16 seats (4.6 per cent of vote); PNV won 5 seats (1.27 per cent of vote) and CC won 4 seats (0.88 per cent of vote). The lower house of the Spanish parliament has 350 seats.

26   Roig also observed that the dynamics of state-level politics could easily spill over to

intergovernmental relations: In 1995, he argues, the work of the Sectoral Conferences and the CARCE were paralysed by the atmosphere of extreme tension between the two statewide parties as the balance of power in autonomous community governments fell to the PP, while the PSOE lived out the dying days of their administration in Madrid (Roig 2002: 151).

27 This party merged with the nationalist *Euskadiko Ezquerra* (EE, Basque Left), in the mid-1990s to form PSE-EE-PSOE.

4

The Basque presence in Brussels

From the mid-1980s, regions across Europe mobilised to call for EU treaty reforms that would, as Charlie Jeffery (2004) put it, 'let regions in' to EU decision fora. Various contributions to Constitutional Treaty debates show that many EU regions still want a bigger role in EU decisionmaking (Jeffery 2004; Keating 2004; Bourne 2006).[1] In this chapter, I examine EU and state-level responses to these demands, particularly creation of the CoR and a widening of regional participation in state delegations to EU bodies. Analysis of domestic debates and arrangements permitting Basque and other autonomous communities' involvement in EU bodies provides further material for evaluating both powersharing practices within Spain and patterns of conflict and cooperation in Basque and Spanish central government relations. Furthermore, examination of Basque government involvement in EU decision fora helps identify the scope of 'external', European dimensions of Basque selfgovernment.

I begin analysing the CoR, disputes over the Basque government delegation in Brussels and autonomous community access to Community Courts. Later sections explore the sometimes polemical process by which Basque and other autonomous communities gained a role in European Commission advisory committees, the Spanish Permanent Representation to the EU and state delegations to the EU's Council.

The Committee of the Regions

The decision, made during Maastricht Treaty negotiations, to create a specialised Committee of the Regions responded to both technical and political rationales (Millan 1997; Jeffery 1995 and 2002: 328–31; Calonge and Sanz 2000: 30–42). On the one hand, the European Commission wanted to extend consultation with, and access to expertise of, regions and local authorities, who had become increasingly involved in EU policy implementation. At the same time, 'bottom up' demands came from EU regions, who wanted greater participation in EU decisionmaking as 'compensation' for EU incursions into their decision powers. Such demands were forcefully articulated by the German *Länder* domestically and corralled into a something of an EU regions' agenda through a series of *ad hoc* conferences and the work of bodies like the Assembly of European Regions. The Spanish government was initially in favour of channelling regional participation in EU decisionmaking via the existing Economic and Social Committee (ESC), but later signed up to a joint German-Spanish proposal setting out the basic features of what later became the CoR (Calonge and Sanz 2000: 39). This was, as a number of authors point out, a central government initiative, which was not the subject of an explicit agreement with autonomous communities (Calonge and Sanz 2000: 39; Parejo and Betancour 1996: 187–9 and 194). Nevertheless, autonomous communities generally supported the initiative and their joint position on the future CoR was, according to these authors, 'taken into account' by the central government during Maastricht Treaty negotiations (Calonge and Sanz 2000: 39; Parejo and Betancour 1996: 187–9 and 194).

The body created at Maastricht, and (lightly) amended by both Amsterdam and Nice Treaties, is composed of 344 representatives of local and regional authorities from all member states and an equal number of alternates. According to treaty provisions – currently grouped in articles 263–5 of the Treaty Establishing the European Community (henceforth European Community (EC) Treaty) – CoR members must hold a regional or local authority electoral mandate, or be politically accountable to an elected assembly. Membership lasts four years but is renewable. Treaty provisions prohibit CoR members being bound by mandatory instructions and require them to be completely independent and perform their duties 'in the general interest of the Community'. In practice, it is unrealistic to expect members to ignore the individual interests of their regions, especially if the member is an elected official in a powerful EU region (Jeffery 2002: 330; Ortega 2003: 32). Indeed, many argue that participation by senior politicians from powerful regions gives the CoR its political clout (Loughlin 1997: 160; Ortega 2003: 25), even if it is probably 'unthinkable' that powerful regional presidents participate in the CoR's more mundane activities (Diego 1995: 1019).

The treaties give Spain twenty-one seats in the CoR. In accordance with a CARCE agreement later taking the form of a 1993 Senate motion, all seventeen autonomous communities may propose a representative and an alternate each, with the remaining four CoR members proposed by the Spanish Federation of Provinces and Municipalities.[2] The Basque autonomous community is represented by its president, although the president's alternate (José María Muñoa) frequently assumes this task. The formula for distributing CoR seats was not without controversy. Some wanted to increase the share of local authority representation in the CoR, while others, including the Basque government and the PNV, looked forward to the day when the CoR might be a regions-only chamber (Calonge and Sanz 2000: 167; Gobierno Vasco 1993: 65).[3] Applying the logic inherent in the concept of *hecho diferencial*, the PNV at one point proposed giving two seats each to the historic nationalities (that is, the Basque Country, Catalonia and Galicia) (Calonge and Sanz 2000: 166).

The CoR was set up to be an advisory body to the European Commission, Council and (after the Amsterdam Treaty) the EP. The range of matters on which it may issue opinions potentially covers all areas of EU policy. When considering new legislative proposals the Council and European Commission must seek CoR opinions in ten policy areas: initially, economic and social cohesion (including structural funds), transEuropean infrastructure networks, health, education and culture; and, after the Amsterdam Treaty, employment policy, social policy, the environment, vocational training and transport. Together with the EP, these institutions are free to solicit CoR views on any other matters and the CoR may issue opinions on matters with regional relevance considered by the ESC. Using its own initiative powers, the CoR may issue opinions on any other matter it considers appropriate. Between 1994 and 2003, the CoR issued an average of sixty opinions (or equivalent positions) per year (CoR 2004).

Despite the scope of its consultative powers, the CoR has significant weaknesses. Its opinions are not binding and may be ignored by other EU institutions. It cannot use a power of delay, such as that pioneered by the early EP, because the Council and European Commission can impose a one-month time limit for the issue of CoR opinions. The CoR's relationship with various EU institutions – and thus political influence – varies. The European Commission, which lent its support to the CoR from the outset, appears to take the CoR seriously (Jeffery 2002: 341; Warleigh 1999: 29–31).[4] EP support for creation of the CoR and frequent cooperation between them at committee level is underpinned by something of a rivalry over competing claims to represent European citizens (Millan 1997: 6; Warleigh 1999: 25–6; Jeffery 2002: 342). The Council has some powers to control the CoR; it formally appoints CoR members based on member state proposals and, until the Amsterdam Treaty, endorsed the CoR's rules of procedure. But CoR and Council relations have been, at best, distant.[5]

The CoR struggles to overcome the handicap of diverse membership and a variety of political cleavages. Four political groups – representing conservative, social democratic, liberal and nationalist/regionalist persuasions – acknowledge ideological cleavages. Representatives of regions, on the one hand, and local authorities, on the other, may have wildly different competencies, resources, political standing at home and different expectations about the CoR's role (Jeffery 1995 and 2002; Millan 1997; Christiansen 1996; Keating 2004). Commentators have also observed a north-south divide, especially in matters relating to the structural funds. Cleavages are managed through a careful distribution of CoR leadership positions and consensual decision styles that see many opinions issued unanimously or with large majorities (Warleigh 1999, 40–1; Jeffery 2002: 335). An inevitable consequence of these bridging efforts, however, has often been resort to the lowest common denominator and a tendency to deliver bland opinions (McCarthy 1997: 440; Jeffery 1995: 254 and 2002: 343). More generally, the CoR has struggled, as Charlie Jeffery argues, to resolve fundamental disputes over whether its role is to provide technocratic expertise or democratic representation, with consequent confusion over what its 'added value' for the EU should actually be (2002: 327).

The Basque government saw creation of the CoR as a significant but insufficient step (see Gobierno Vasco 1993: 63–5; 1996: 15; 1998 and 2003: 18–19; 2004). It was praised for embodying the first formal recognition of the regional level in the EU's institutional architecture and for promoting collaboration among Europe's regions, and among regions and EU institutions. Despite certain misgivings, discussed below, the Basque government has been actively involved in the CoR, largely because it is 'the only body in the decisionmaking process that allows the participation of regions as such' (Gobierno Vasco 2004: 5). It has also provided, according to the Basque government, an opportunity to project a positive image of the Basque Country in general, its government, identity and 'know-how' (Gobierno Vasco 1998: 9 and 2004: 59).

Despite entreaties that CoR members be independent, serve general EU interests and eschew mandatory instructions, Basque CoR representatives are clearly Basque government representatives. Basque CoR participation is organised from the seat of the Basque government in Vitoria with support from its Brussels office, and internal administrative procedures allow all government departments to respond to, and propose amendments for, CoR opinions (Gobierno Vasco 1998: 6 and 2004: 33). An indication of Basque commitment to CoR activity is that such procedures have produced, between 1994 and 2004, a total of 335 proposals for amendments, with around two-thirds (232) being adopted by the CoR (Gobierno Vasco 2004: 41). Basque government activity in the CoR tends to focus on EU regional policy, education, culture and institutional issues.[6] The CoR has taken a specific interest in Basque politics on a number of occasions, often at the initiative of the Basque representative.[7]

The Basque government has always hoped for a CoR different from the one created at Maastricht and, like many other EU regions, has become increasingly critical. In November 2002, for instance, the Basque government signed the 'Florence Declaration' of the Conference of Presidents of Regions with Legislative Powers, stating that the CoR did not meet the expectations of regions (see www.regleg.org, accessed 8 July 2005). With other EU regions (Keating 2004; Jeffery 2004) and indeed the CoR itself,[8] the Basque government has supported calls to: enhance the status and powers of the CoR by elevating the CoR to the rank of an EU institution (rather than a 'mere' advisory body); give it a meaningful role in enforcement of subsidiarity and access to the ECJ to protect its prerogatives; extend CoR powers of consultation; and require other EU bodies to explain why they depart from CoR opinions. The Basque government has also supported proposals to create a bicameral CoR, with a separate chamber for regions with legislative powers.

The Convention on the Future of Europe, which included the input of six CoR representatives, and the follow-up intergovernmental conference, which approved the Constitutional Treaty, supported some of these proposals. If the Constitutional Treaty comes into force, the CoR will be given, among other things, a role in subsidiarity enforcement and access to the ECJ. Within Spain, proposals for CoR reform have not been particularly controversial. During debates on the Constitutional Treaty many autonomous communities, minority nationalist parties and the two main statewide parties supported most of the above-mentioned proposals for strengthening the CoR (Bourne 2006: 5–8).

Overall, the CoR can be seen as a 'breakthrough' (Millan 1997: 3) or a something of a 'revolution' (Calonge and Sanz 2000: 28) for the EU; it provided the first formal recognition of the regional and local level in the EU's institutional architecture. It has since delivered hundreds of opinions on a wide range of issues of importance to EU regions. However, on its own, the CoR provides poor 'compensation' for regional powers transferred to the EU (Diego 1995: 1021). Individual regions' views must potentially be reconciled with those of over three hundred regions and local authorities and there is no guarantee that collective views will be taken into account in EU decision processes. Not surprisingly, many EU regions, including Basque authorities, have sought other means to manage the overlap of regional and EU powers.

The Brussels Office and Judgement 165/1994

For the Basque government, effective participation in EU decisionmaking could not rely solely on domestic mechanisms coordinating state and autonomous community views, or on Basque involvement in the CoR (see, for instance, Gobierno Vasco 1993 and 1996). These had to be complemented by other forms of autonomous Basque presence in the EU and autonomous community involvement in state EU delegations. However, for many years, the central government argued that the Spanish constitution justified limitations on autonomous community activity in the EU (Mangas and Liñán 2004: 515–6; Aja 2003: 165; Börzel 2002: 104–6). Article 149.1 of the Spanish constitution gives central authorities exclusive competence over 'international relations' and a range of other international matters such as external commerce, customs and tariffs, defence and the armed forces, immigration and asylum. Furthermore, article 93, which authorised cession of competencies to international organisations (like the EU), makes central authorities (government and parliament) responsible for compliance with EU treaties and laws. Differences over the permissible scope of Basque autonomy abroad were bought to a head in the Constitutional Court when the central government challenged the Basque government's right to an official EU delegation.

In 1986, the Basque government joined the growing ranks of EU regions and local authorities with an information office in Brussels. Formally, the Basque Brussels office was that of the *Sociedad para la Promoción y Reconversión Industrial* (SPRI, Association for Promotion and Industrial Reconversion), a development agency ascribed to the Basque government's department of industry. In addition to the promotion of industrial development and the creation of employment, SPRI's office in Brussels sought to gather information and represent, defend and coordinate Basque interests before the EC (Santamaría, *El Correo*, 29 September 1988; Barón, *El Correo*, 10 February 1987). The (PSOE) Spanish central government tolerated this, and similar arrangements for other autonomous communities, until the Basque Brussels office was moved from the PSE-PSOE-controlled department of industry to the PNV-controlled department for the presidency (Torres, *El Correo*, 29 September 1988). A 1988 decree situated the Brussels office in the Cabinet for Affairs related to the EC, which was responsible for 'supporting and advising departments and other bodies of the autonomous community on matters related to the European institutions'.[9] More controversially, the Cabinet and its Brussels office were 'to coordinate relations between Basque public institutions and European Community bodies'.

The problem with these new arrangements was not so much a change of responsibilities. The central government considered it acceptable for SPRI, like many other companies, foundations, business representations, lobbies and autonomous communities in Brussels, to provide information about EU decision processes and make contacts with policymakers (Torres, *El Correo*, 29 September 1988). However, with the change of ascription to the department of the presidency, the Basque government purportedly changed the legal status of their representation in Brussels; they had converted it from a 'lobby', given it 'representativeness', and 'institutionalised it as an "embassy"' for formally coordinating relations between Basque and EU authorities (Torres, *El Correo*, 29 September 1988 and 10 September 1988). The central government considered this an 'invasion' of its competencies and an attempt to establish an 'independent representation' before an international organisation (Torres, *El Correo*, 29 September 1998).

The Basque government downplayed the political significance of the new arrangements (Torres, *El Correo*, 10 September 1988; Santamaría, *El Correo*, 29 September 1988). Representatives argued that the Brussels office was merely a 'body for assisting and advising' a variety of interests on EU activities, programmes and laws. At the same time, it argued that some form of

Brussels office was 'absolutely indispensable' for the defence of Basque interests in the EU and for the 'responsible' and 'efficient' exercise of Basque competencies. The Basque government minister then responsible for the Brussels office, Juan Ramón Guevara, described the central government's response as an anachronistic, 'nineteenth-century conception of the state'.

There were various attempts to resolve the issue before it reached the courts, including a high-level meeting between central and Basque government ministers, which considered alternative legal formulas for a Basque Brussels office (Torres, *El Correo*, 29 September 1988). But these came to nothing and, some six years later, the Constitutional Court made a ruling in the much cited judgement 165/1994 of 26 May 1994.[10] The judgement vindicated the Basque government and concluded that to do otherwise risked an 'emptying out' of autonomous community competencies and a reorganisation of the constitutional distribution of power (Carrera 1994: 41).

The central government had argued that the Basque government's attempts to establish direct relations with EU bodies breached article 149.1.3 of the Spanish constitution reserving international relation activities for central state authorities. It also argued that the Basque autonomy statute confined Basque government activity to the territorial limits of the autonomous community. In its ruling against these arguments, the Constitutional Court recognised that, if every form of external activity were corralled into the central government's exclusive competence in international relations, many autonomous community competencies would cease to exist in practice (Carrera 1994: 41).

The Court also made important distinctions between 'international relations' and relations with the EU. The transfer of autonomous community competencies to the EU level created a very different legal order from that traditionally established in international relations. The EU-level legal system was, in certain respects, 'internal' to the legal systems of member states. This partly 'internal' nature of the EU legal order, and the relevance of EU activities for the exercise of autonomous community competencies, gave autonomous communities a legitimate interest in EU developments. It further ruled that 'international relations' ought to be narrowly conceived to cover matters pertaining to 'international order', such as the negotiation of treaties, entering into international obligations and external representation of the state. If the Basque Brussels office limited itself to gathering information about EU activities and did not stray into this 'hard core' of international relation activities, direct relations between Basque and EU institutions would not violate the constitution.

The victory was important in a number of ways. It gave the Basque government the 'satisfaction' of being able to open an official delegation in Brussels and gave judicial backing to its interpretation of the permissible scope of autonomous community 'foreign policy' activities (Ayala, *El Correo*, 31 May 1994; Pescador, *El Correo*, 5 February 1996). More generally, the ruling deflated central government arguments limiting autonomous community participation in EU bodies and helped pave the way for many of the reforms outlined in the rest of the chapter.

Autonomous communities and state EU delegations

Within two years of the Constitutional Court's judgement 165/1994, important steps were made to extend the presence of autonomous communities 'beyond the state' by increasing their profile in state EU delegations. A key trigger was a change of government in Madrid and installation of a PP minority government reliant on parliamentary support from minority nationalist and regionalist parties (see Table 3.5). In its 'governability pact' with the Catalan nationalists of CiU, the PP had, among other things, conceded on two longstanding autonomous community demands – participation in the European Commission's advisory committees relating to autonomous community competencies and the creation of a Spanish version of the German *Länderbeobachter* (*Länder* Observer).

For autonomous communities, participation in a portion of the European Commission's hundreds of advisory committees – something already open to regions in other member states – was attractive for a number of reasons (Matia 2003: 166; Lucas 2000: 116–18; Roig Molés 2002: 359–65). Committee membership provides opportunities to gather insider information about and to influence future EU laws at very early stages of the decision process. The committees could also influence European Commission decisions about the execution of EU laws, a process which routinely involves autonomous communities. Following the PP's pact with CiU, the CARCE agreed rules allowing autonomous communities to participate in fifty-five European Commission committees for the period 1998–2002. After positive evaluation of this experience, the number of committees available for autonomous community participation was extended to ninety-five for the period 2003–6.[11]

Practices and rules governing participation in European Commission committees make autonomous communities protagonists in domestic decisionmaking processes, but leave ample provision for central government control in 'external' stages.[12] Each four years, autonomous communities decide among themselves which of their number will represent them collectively on the various committees. Two autonomous communities – each responsible for successive two-year periods – are usually selected for each committee. The autonomous community representative for each committee is responsible for forwarding relevant information to all other autonomous communities, facilitating the formation of collective autonomous community views on committee business and representing those views in the committee itself. The autonomous community forms part of the state's delegation to the committee, which central government representatives lead. Central government representatives vote and speak on the delegation's behalf, unless both state and autonomous community representatives agree otherwise. In the formation of its views on committee business and when voting, the central government is obliged to take collective autonomous community positions properly into account.

These provisions gave the Spanish EU participation system more generally an important boost (Börzel 2002: 131–2; Roig 2002: 373). Roig argued, for instance, that the incentive of participation in European Commission committees produced authentic experiences of interautonomous community cooperation, and more intense and satisfactory experiences of collaboration, than that habitually taking place in the Sectoral Conferences (Roig 2002: 252, 278–9). There were noted deficits, however. Some European Commission committees discussed matters of particular interest to autonomous communities, such as those on structural funds and regional development. Others were of less interest, either because committees did not deal with important EU business or because they did not deal with matters affecting autonomous community competencies or interests (Matia 2003: 166; Castro and Ugalde 2004: 170). Indeed, there were some committees no autonomous community wanted to attend. More generally, effectiveness was highly dependent on the political will – and administrative capacity – of individual autonomous communities, who were responsible for passing on and undertaking the difficult task of searching for common positions among interested autonomous communities (Roig 2002: 374; Castro and Ugalde 2004: 171).

The Basque government had called for participation in European Commission committees for many years (Gobierno Vasco 1993) and it made full use of new rules once given the opportunity. Between 1998 and 2002, the Basque government represented autonomous communities in thirteen of the fifty-five available committees and subsequently, in fourteen of the ninety-five available committees between 2003 and 2006 (Castro and Ugalde 2004: 168–73). During the period 1999–2002, the Basque government attended more European Commission committee meetings than any other autonomous community. As Castro and Ugalde explain, this was due to the Basque government's elevated commitment to participation in EU bodies and the relative importance and high activity levels of its assigned committees (especially agriculture and rural development) (2004: 171).

The Basque government characterised the new arrangements as an important step towards consolidation of a more effective EU participation system, but otherwise its praise was lukewarm (Ortuzar 1998).[13] The new arrangements were seen as 'excessively timid', were criticised for taking in only a limited number of European Commission committees, and for excluding some committees of particular interest to autonomous communities. Above all else, Basque leaders insisted that autonomous community participation in European Commission committees was not a substitute for their involvement in the more powerful Council, or its committees and working groups.

Soon after the PP took office in Madrid in 1996, the CARCE agreed to establish a *consejería* (department), and the figure of a *consejero* (department head, representative) *para asuntos autonómicos* (for autonomy affairs) in the Spanish Permanent Representation to the EU.[14] The Permanent Representation (REPER) is the state's formally accredited body in Brussels, responsible for representing the Spanish state in the EU and for managing its EU affairs. The post of *consejero* was inspired by the *Länder* Observer (*Länderbeobachter*), established in Germany as early as 1957. The Observer is responsible for passing EU information to *Länder* and the *Bundesrat,* can participate in federal government meetings on EU issues and in state delegations to various EU bodies, including the Council (Börzel 2002: 61; Roig 2002: 187–92).

The CARCE's 1996 agreement made the *consejero* exclusively responsible for the REPER's relations with autonomous communities' Brussels offices and for channelling information to autonomous communities. It permitted the *consejero* to attend CARCE meetings and, tantalisingly, opened up the possibility that the *consejero* 'form part of the Spanish delegation in all meetings [of EU bodies] directly affecting autonomous community competencies'. Unlike the *Länder* Observer, who is appointed by *Länder* ministers (Börzel 2002: 61), the Spanish *consejero* was less clearly an autonomous community representative. The postholder would be a central government functionary, appointed by the state ministry for foreign affairs and dependent administratively upon the state ministry for public administration. In the appointment procedure, the views of the autonomous communities would merely be 'heard' in a meeting of the CARCE plenary. Moreover, when the central government came to implement the 1996 CARCE agreement, there were no provisions operationalising a role for the *consejero* as an autonomous community 'observer' in EU bodies. In short, arrangements in Spain were more a useful 'administrative reorganisation' than a new instrument for autonomous community participation in EU decisions (Roig 2002: 203; Matia 2003: 160).

Nevertheless, the PP central government characterised the new *consejero* and REPER's department for administrative affairs as an 'important achievement' in the evolution of the Spanish EU participation system and considered the more robust information distribution system envisaged a 'valuable resource in the complex world of EU politics' (Fernández 1998: 23). Others also recognised that the *consejero* and the REPER's new autonomy affairs department could provide a variety of useful services for autonomous communities, including: provision of tailored and expert 'insider' knowledge; improved coordination among levels of government; an illustration for EU actors of the domestic significance of autonomous communities; and enhanced opportunities for autonomous communities to scrutinise central government actions in the EU (Roig 2002: 199–203; Matia 2003: 163). Early assessments of the work of the *consejero* were generally positive. Cienfuegos concluded that, after the first year, the first *consejero* (Guillermo Ardizone García) had 'correctly completed the basic functions for which his post had been created' (1997b: 199).[15]

The Basque government had long proposed the creation of an autonomous community observer in the REPER as a measure to help 'normalise' and improve the efficiency of information flows and relations between state and autonomous community bodies in Brussels (Diego 1995: 1025–6, see also Gobierno Vasco 1993: 31). However, evaluations of the 1996 REPER reforms were far from glowing. The Basque government's then secretary general for external action, Andoni Ortuzar, argued that arrangements had not 'met expectations of autonomous communities' and saw problems with the way the post had been defined and structured (1998: 15). The fluid exchange of information between REPER and the Basque Brussels office was a noted problem for the Basque government (Diego 1995: 1025),[16] but Ortuzar did not think the new *consejero* would be able to resolve it (1998: 15).[17]

Nearly ten years later, following another change of government at state level and the installation of a PSOE minority government (see Table 3.5), the role of the *consejero* and the REPER's department for autonomy affairs were revisited. In conjunction with the PSOE government's commitment to extend autonomous community participation to the EU's Council (see below) a new CARCE agreement in 2004 enhanced the representative function of the *consejeros* (now plural) and their access to EU decision fora.[18] The 2004 CARCE agreement allowed autonomous communities to propose (by way of consensus reached in the CARCE) candidates for civil service and *consejero* positions in the REPER's department for autonomy affairs. These employees would form an integral part of the REPER and be responsible to REPER's leaders. They would also be accountable to the CARCE, which would be regularly informed about their activities and could dismiss the *consejeros* they had proposed.

The *consejeros* and the REPER's department for autonomy affairs gained new powers, which, in addition to the transmission of EU documentation to autonomous communities and relations with their Brussels offices, would include: arranging contacts with other sectoral departments of the REPER; monitoring autonomous community participation in Sectoral Conferences and contributing to that participation by providing timely information on EU negotiations; identifying and keeping autonomous communities informed about critical points in EU negotiations; monitoring European Commission and ECJ proceedings that could affect autonomous communities; and facilitating contacts between autonomous community and EU representatives. More fundamentally, the *consejero* could now participate in Council working groups on behalf of autonomous communities. The political importance of this new role can be more fully understood through examination of broader disputes about participation in the Council, a matter to which I now turn.

The long road to Council participation

Participation in the EU's Council – only authorised since December 2004 – has been one of the most sought-after and most controversial, Basque EU demand. The Council is composed of representatives of the member state governments and works at three main levels. In the Council proper, decisions are made by ministerial representatives from each member state. The Committee of Permanent Representatives (COREPER), made up of member states' ambassadors to the EU, and around two hundred specialised committees and working groups made up of member state delegates, resolve many issues before they reach the Council. Autonomous communities wanted to participate in the Council and its preparatory bodies because the Council is pivotal in the EU's decisionmaking system and because it regularly deals with matters relating to autonomous community competencies. Even though the Council shares many legislative powers with the European Commission and, increasingly, with the EP, all EU laws must find support in the Council. Participation in Council preparatory bodies is important not only because they make many decisions later rubber-stamped by ministers but because participation provides indepth and timely information about the conduct of negotiations, views of different member states and prospects for different policy outcomes.

Before Maastricht, the EC Treaty did not permit anyone other than central government ministers to be Council members or to vote (Sobrino 1998: 50–1). Central government representatives could be accompanied by others, and some creative interpretations of internal regulations allowed Belgian regions and, mostly through the offices of their Observer, the German *Länder* to participate in some Council business (Sobrino 1998: 63–7; Fernández de Casadevante 2001: 87). The Maastricht Treaty redrafted article 146 of the EC Treaty (now article 203) to permit regional ministers authorised by their state to be Council members, although this was not explicit.[19] Representatives must act on behalf of their state – rather than their own region – and each member state must authorise one representative to vote in its name (Sobrino 1998: 64; Mangas and Liñán 2004: 533–4).

The Treaty does not specify which regions, from which states, should participate in Council meetings. These were questions which, in accordance with the principle of internal autonomy (discussed in chapter one), are left to member states. Most federal and regionalised states in the EU – including Belgium, Germany, Austria, the United Kingdom, and now Spain – allow regional participation in the Council. As the following discussion shows, the path to authorisation of Spanish autonomous community Council participation has been long and acrimonious. In certain respects, it recalls events elsewhere in Europe, particularly the preMaastricht struggles of German *Länder* for influence in EU decisionmaking. In both Spain and Germany, regional governments have promoted the goal of Council participation through the application of domestic pressure and collaboration with regions from other states (Jeffery 1997: 55–7). Similarly, it took central government elite in both countries many years to embrace the idea that, insofar as it affected regional competencies, EU policy was no longer foreign policy in the traditional sense (Jeffery 1997; Börzel 2003: 58–79). In contrast to their Spanish counterparts, however, *Länder* have been able to use powers to authorise German constitutional reforms to insist on both EU treaty and domestic reforms enabling extensive participation in the Council (Jeffery 1997 and 2004; Börzel 2002: 71).

The Basque government, and especially Basque nationalist parties, called for Council participation even before the Maastricht Treaty formally opened up the possibility (Ortuzar 1998: 13). Their demands became increasingly insistent after Maastricht, when the EP and CoR declared their support and, more importantly, as regions from other federal and regionalised states came to routinely attend Council meetings (Gobierno Vasco 1993, 1996 and 2003; Diego Casals 1994; Ortuzar 1998). For the Basque government – and eventually most Basque political parties[20] – Council participation ensured European integration did not unduly affect the internal distribution of political power in Spain and prevented, as one Basque government report starkly put it, the 'emptying out' of selfgovernment (Gobierno Vasco 1993: 25). Like Basque government attempts to open a delegation in Brussels, disputes over Council participation exposed many of the tensions permeating relations between Basque and central governments more generally.

Basque nationalists, the Basque government and many other autonomous communities took various steps to push Council participation onto the political agenda. In 1998, Basque nationalists introduced a resolution in the Spanish parliament,[21] based on an earlier Basque parliament resolution,[22] calling on the PP Spanish government to permit Council participation and, more controversially, to allow autonomous communities to lead certain state Council delegations. In what represents a high point in an otherwise difficult relationship on this issue, the PNV and the PP agreed a formula allowing the Mixed Commission for the EU to unanimously call on the (PP) central government to facilitate autonomous community participation in the Council.[23] Not long afterwards a Basque nationalist (EA) deputy initiated a very similar motion approved in the Congress of Deputies.[24]

In December 1998, the Basque government gave notice that direct relations with the EU would be part of obligatory negotiations with the central government to renew the 1981 Economic Agreement (*Concierto Económico*) (Álvarez, *El Correo*, 18 December 1999). As chapter six spells out more fully, the Economic Agreement establishes a distinctive form of taxation devolution in the Basque Country which has raised some concerns at the EU level. In this context, Council participation was relevant to Economic Agreement negotiations because EU debates affected Basque taxation powers and because, according to the Basque government, it could help EU authorities 'better understand' that the Economic Agreement was not a 'camouflage for subsidies' or a special 'privilege that undermined competition laws' (Aizpeolea, *El País*, 17 May 2001; Ibarretxe 1998: 190).

The PP initially appeared willing to discuss this point (Aizpeolea, *El País*, 17 May 2001), but it soon became a serious sticking point in negotiations and a major source of tension between Basque and central authorities (López 2002: 82–6). Indeed, despite pressure from the Basque provinces and the business community (Aizpeolea, *El País*, 30 November 2001), Basque and central authorities could not reach agreement in time to ensure a new Economic Agreement was in place before the old one ran out. The central government extended the validity of the old Agreement by decree but refused to proceed with negotiations until the Basque government gave up its demands for Council participation (Aizpeolea, *El País*, 31 December 2001). The central government treasury minister responsible for negotiating the new Economic Agreement, Cristóbal Montoro, argued it was 'absurd' to discuss autonomous community participation, which was a multilateral issue, in bilateral negotiations with Basque authorities. Moreover, echoing the increasingly categorical line of President Aznar, Montoro declared: 'We are not facing a question [to be dealt with] between equals. The Spanish government possesses [competence for] external representation and is not going to negotiate it bilaterally with the Basques' (Aizpeolea, *El País*, 31 December 2001).[25]

The episode aroused mutual suspicions (Aizpeolea, *El País*, 31 December 2001). As López argues in his study of Basque and central government relations, the central government veto on Basque Council participation prompted some Basque leaders' most biting critiques of the PP government, including the charge that the central government sought to 'roll back' prior autonomy gains (*regresión autónomica*) (2003: 86). Settlement was reached nearly two months after the Economic Agreement renovation deadline had passed and only after Basque negotiators completely renounced linking Economic Agreement negotiations to Council participation (Aizpeolea and Damborenea, *El País*, 21 February 2002).

Similarly, the above-mentioned Basque nationalist parliamentary initiatives turned out a disappointment. Throughout the 1990s, many other autonomous communities signalled stonger interest in Council participation.[26] Once the parliament's Mixed Commission had agreed the principle of autonomous community participation in the Council, autonomous communities pursued a variety of initiatives to promote it. A series of meetings in 1999 produced an autonomous community agreement expressly supported by fourteen autonomous communities and supported with reservations by the three PP autonomous communities, Valencia, Murcia and Cantabria (Gorriaran, *El Correo*, 4 January 2000). This agreement was scuppered, according to journalists and opposition parties, due to a central government-directed manoeuvre which saw the PP-controlled autonomous communities initially entering reservations later withdraw their support on the grounds that the proposal 'lacked maturity' (*El Correo*, 4 January 2000).[27]

Within the CARCE a working group, composed of representatives from Extramadura, Catalonia, Galicia and La Rioja, studied possible formulas for Council participation (Castro and Ugalde 2004: 180; Aizpeolea, *El País*, 14 December 2001). Its proposal favouring autonomous community participation in Council meetings under central government tutelage was rejected by the central government ostensibly because the working group exceeded its mandate by considering political rather than merely technical questions (Castro and Ugalde 2004: 180; Aizpeolea, *El País*, 14 December 2001).[28] The PP also initiated a divisive debate, regarded by many as a delaying tactic, on the nature of exclusive autonomous community competencies affected by the EU (Castro and Ugalde 2004: 178–9; Roig 2002: 367–8 and Matia 2003). This complex debate allowed the PP to adopt restrictive views on the possible scope of autonomous community Council participation, in contrast to the permissive interpretation adopted by many autonomous communities (Roig 2002: 367–8; Matia 2003).

PP reliance on minority nationalist parties' support during its first term of government made it expedient for the party to give way – or at least appear willing to debate – the issue of Council participation. After 2000, when the party won an absolute majority in the general elections, the PP no longer needed to do so (see Table 3.5).[29] When Basque, Catalan and Galician nationalists reintroduced the text of the 1998 Basque resolution that had previously led to unanimous agreement favouring Council participation, the PP rejected the resolution.[30] Similarly, an April 2001 legislative proposal on Council participation introduced in the Spanish parliament by the Balearic Islands was rejected with PP votes.[31] The party even had to diffuse a counteroffensive within its own ranks, led by Manuel Fraga Iribarne, founder and former leader of the PP, but from 1990 to 2005 president of the Galician autonomous community (Aizpeolea, *El País*, 26 January 2002).

The PP's manoeuvres provoked deep criticisms from opposition parties and reinforced negative assessments of the CARCE and the Sectoral Conferences.[32] Some saw failure to progress on the issue of Council participation as a threat to the very foundations of the state of autonomies.[33] By its second term, the PP government clearly rejected Council participation outright. PP minister of foreign affairs, Abel Matutes, emerged as a profound critic of autonomous community Council participation. He thought it 'would generate dysfunction, be ungovernable and simply be grounds for confrontation between the contrasting interests of different autonomous communities'; or, to use his more colourful metaphor, it would plunge the state's Council delegation into the anarchy of a 'cage of crickets' (*una jaula de grillos*) (Gurruchaga, *El Mundo*, 5 March 1998; Segovia, *El Mundo*, 5 March 1998). In 2001, President Aznar articulated similar views and effectively reverted to arguments employed by the preceding PSOE administration in its case against the Basque Brussels office. Aznar argued that autonomous community

Council participation would not be permitted because the constitution gave central state authorities exclusive competence in international affairs (Aizpeolea, *El País*, 14 December 2001 and 31 December 2001; Matia 2003: 192–4).

It was not until the return of a PSOE administration – again a minority administration dependent on support from smaller parties, including minority nationalists (see Table 3.5) – that stalemate was broken. Prior to the March 2004 general election, PSOE autonomy policy explicitly endorsed Council participation (PSOE 2003) and President Zapatero promised to carry through on the commitment.[34] In 2004, the CARCE finally agreed rules for one autonomous community minister to represent all other autonomous communities in Spanish delegations to four out of nine Council formations.[35] Selected Council formations – employment, social policy, health and consumer affairs; agriculture and fisheries; environment; education, youth and culture – were chosen for being most likely to deal with issues affecting autonomous community competencies. The CARCE's 1994 Agreement on the Sectoral Conferences (see chapter three) would apply when other Council formations dealt with matters affecting autonomous community competencies.

These arrangements hinged on the viability of the Sectoral Conferences and the ability of autonomous communities to reach common positions on EU matters, hitherto a weak point of the Spanish EU participation system. Ten Sectoral Conferences were paired up with the four EU Councils selected for autonomous community participation. These Sectoral Conferences would develop their own procedures for designating an autonomous community Council representative, determine which matters on Council agendas were of interest to autonomous communities, and update autonomous communities on Council negotiations. In a procedure similar to that employed for European Commission committees, designated autonomous community representatives would: coordinate negotiation of a common position among autonomous communities declaring an interest in a Council agenda item; conduct negotiations with the central government; appoint its own specialists to attend relevant meetings of the Council's preparatory bodies; and advise the state's Council delegation on autonomous communities' common positions. If the head of the delegation agreed, and if there was a common position, the designated autonomous community would be authorised to speak in Council debates.

The head of the state's Council delegation – a central government representative in all cases – would be responsible for the conduct and conclusion of negotiations, and autonomous community participation would be conditioned by the need for unity and flexibility in EU negotiations. However, the 2004 Agreement urged both state and autonomous community authorities to respect principles of 'loyalty' and 'mutual confidence' and required the state delegation to take autonomous community common positions decisively into account throughout negotiations.

MAP studies (2005 and 2006b) examining implementation of the 2004 CARCE agreement provides evidence of a new vitality in the Spanish EU participation system. According to the reports, all relevant Sectoral Conferences adopted rules to implement the 2004 Agreement and designated autonomous community representatives for participation in each selected Council formation. By December 2006, representatives from fifteen autonomous communities had participated in Council meetings; and representatives from autonomous community administrations, or the REPER's department for autonomous affairs, had attended Council committee and working groups on over 450 occasions (MAP 2005: 21–41; MAP 2006b: 23–58). Autonomous community ministers were authorised to speak in the Council on eleven occasions; on four occasions in either Catalan or Galician languages (MAP 2005: 16; MAP 2006b: 19–20). In an important turn-around for the Spanish EU participation system in general, MAP provides evidence of more intensive horizontal cooperation among autonomous communities. In 2005–6, their representatives met on at least twenty-seven occasions to prepare for Council meetings and adopted twenty agreements that were then discussed in further meetings with representatives of central government ministers (MAP 2005: 11–15; MAP 2006b: 13–19). Autonomous community participation in the Council appears to have provided a strong incentive for autonomous communities to overcome extremely languid practices of horizontal cooperation.

The Basque government was actively involved in all aspects of the new arrangements in its first year, but was not selected as autonomous community representative for the second. In 2005, Basque government ministers represented autonomous communities at two meetings of the employment, social policy, health and consumer affairs Council and representatives of the Basque government's Brussels office attended fifteen meetings of its working groups (MAP 2005: 21–42). In both years, the Basque government was involved in preparatory work for Council meetings; sometimes organising and often attending meetings with other autonomous communities, signing up to autonomous community agreements, and attending at least one meeting with central government ministers on behalf of other autonomous communities (MAP 2005: 11–13; MAP 2006b: 58–116).

Regions and Community Courts

In a limited number of circumstances, the EC Treaty gives regions and local authorities standing before the Community Courts. The Treaty gives Community Courts – the ECJ, the Court of First Instance (CFI) and since the Nice Treaty, judicial panels – powers to promote the observance and implementation of EC law, and the unity of the supranational legal order. If a member state fails to fulfil an obligation under the Treaty or secondary legislation, the European Commission or another member states may initiate 'infringement proceedings' (articles 226–7). Member states or separate EU institutions may challenge the legality of the acts of EU institutions (and call for their full or partial annulment) (articles 230–1). They may also challenge an EU institutions' failure to act if this infringes the Treaty (article 232). When a national court considers a dispute raising issues of EC law – such as interpretation of the Treaty, or questions about the validity of the acts of EU bodies – the ECJ may (and in some cases must) be asked to deliver a binding opinion in a 'preliminary' ruling procedure (article 234). In addition, Community Courts rule on the award of damages to individuals for the actions or inaction of EU institutions or officials, and on whether international agreements entered into by the European Community are compatible with the Treaty (St Clair Bradley 2002).

Regional, local or other territorial entities within member states have limited standing before Community Courts. Infringement proceedings under articles 226–7 can only be initiated by member states, rather than individual regions, and a member state as a whole is responsible for infringements, even if committed by substate entities (Ordóñez 2003: 144–8; Evans 2003: 484–5). In proceedings for annulment under articles 230–1, however, there is more scope for an autonomous role for regions. As Andrew Evans explains, article 230 distinguishes between the standing of 'privileged', 'semi-privileged' and 'non-privileged' applicants (2003: 485). Member states, the Council, the European Commission and, since the Nice Treaty, the EP have 'privileged' standing, or full rights, to challenge the legality of the acts of EU institutions before the ECJ. In contrast, the Court of Auditors, the European Central Bank and, if the Constitutional Treaty enters into force, the CoR, are 'semi-privileged' applicants with standing for the purpose of protecting their prerogatives. And finally, regions, local authorities and other territorial entities – as 'natural or legal persons' – constitute 'non-privileged' applicants, who may challenge EU acts addressed to them or of direct and individual concern to them (Evans 2003: 485; see also Ordóñez 2003: 148–53). While preliminary ruling cases under article 234 are essentially procedures facilitating cooperation among national and Community Courts, when regional or local authorities are implicated in national disputes from which questions about Community law are drawn, the region will be able to intervene in ECJ deliberations (Ordóñez 2003: 154; Sobrido Prieto 2003: 367).

The CARCE has negotiated a number of agreements regulating the participation of autonomous communities in EU legal proceedings, the most recent of which was agreed in 1997 (see Table 3.3).[36] If an infringement proceeding were launched against the Spanish state and affected autonomous community competencies, the latter would be informed of this fact by central authorities; would remain in permanent contact with relevant state officials throughout the procedure; and have opportunities to provide relevant information and meet with both central government and European Commission representatives involved in the matter. The Secretary of State for Foreign Affairs and the European Union would, however, remain the principal interlocutor with EU bodies, mediating requests such as deadline extensions and transmitting state responses.

In accordance with the 1997 Agreement, autonomous communities are able to request that the state bring actions against EU institutions and that it intervene in a preliminary ruling case affecting autonomous communities. A central government body involving representatives from various ministries is responsible for determining whether the state would pursue autonomous community requests and central government representatives take final decisions (Ordóñez 2003: 155–6).[37] MAP representatives attend the committee when matters affect autonomous community competencies and autonomous communities expressing an interest in the initiation of ECJ proceedings will be invited to express their views (Ordóñez 2003: 155–6). If the committee agrees to go ahead with an autonomous community request, or if an infringement proceeding ends up in the ECJ, autonomous communities can designate lawyers or advisors to assist the state lawyer (responsible to the central government ministry of justice) in actions before the ECJ.

The Basque government did not sign up to the 1997 CARCE agreement laying down these rules, or its more limited predecessor, negotiated in 1990 (see Table 3.3). The earlier agreement was unsatisfactory for the Basque government because it only dealt with cooperation in infringement and preliminary ruling procedures (Gobierno Vasco 1993: 40), a concern later addressed in the 1997 Agreement. A second critique, not addressed in the 1997 Agreement, was that autonomous communities were conceived as subordinate to the state, even when exclusive autonomous community competencies were affected (Gobierno Vasco 1993: 40). The Basque government's preferred alternatives included state representatives taking instructions from autonomous communities and defending their interests in the ECJ; or permitting autonomous community representatives to defend their own interests in the ECJ as 'state representatives' (Gobierno Vasco 1993: 40).

With other autonomous communities and EU regions, Basque authorities have repeatedly called for treaty reforms that would enhance the standing of regions in ECJ proceedings (Jeffery 1997 and 2004; Roig 1998: 524; Bourne 2006; Evans 2003; 489–90). Current arrangements are regarded as 'insufficient' for the defence of Basque competencies (Gobierno Vasco 2003: 18). Basque authorities have called for regions with legislative powers to have the same standing as member states in the Community Courts; for a regional right to protect their competencies through the courts; and for a right to challenge violations of the subsidiarity principle (Gobierno Vasco 1993: 40; 1996: 17; 2003: 23 and 2005b: 10).

An autonomous community common position prepared for the EU's 1996 intergovernmental conference called for treaty reforms allowing regions with legislative competencies to bring annulment cases (under article 230) on the same terms as member states (Roig 1998: 524). The proposal did not prosper. The issue was aired again during the Convention on the Future of Europe, found support from minority nationalist parties and the PSOE, but was rejected by the PP. Spokespersons for the PP were concerned that unmediated regional access to the ECJ would politicise and overload Community Courts (Bourne 2006).

The foregoing discussion should make it clear that 'Europe' is now an integral element of Basque selfgovernment. The Basque government has means for an autonomous role in EU politics through the CoR, its Brussels office and, in some circumstances, in the Community Courts. It may form part of state delegations in EU bodies such as European Commission advisory committees and the Council, which has provided many opportunities for collaboration with other autonomous communities and with the central government.

However, Spain's EU membership opened a new front in broader disputes about Basque selfgovernment. Disagreements over Basque participation in EU bodies were played out in the Constitutional Court, state parliament and even in taxation devolution negotiations. These differences were, in essence, about the permissible scope of Basque selfgovernment and whether it ought to extend to activity outside the state. It took many years for the central government to agree that an EU presence was a legitimate expression of Basque selfgovernment.

Alongside weaknesses in the Spanish system of intergovernmental relations discussed in chapter three, historic and contemporary limitations on Basque and other autonomous communities' involvement in EU decision fora reduced their ability to influence EU decisions affecting their competencies. Even the Constitutional Court recognised that central government dominance of EU decisionmaking threatened to undermine regional power. However, this chapter provided additional evidence that the central government has gradually overcome its reluctance to share power in EU decisionmaking. Autonomous community information offices in Brussels have been incorporated into state EU decisionmaking networks, the Spanish REPER has been reformed to better serve autonomous community interests, and state delegations to EU bodies – especially the Council – give autonomous communities a much larger role in the representation of state interests in EU politics.

Notes

1   For CoR views see CoR, 8 July 2002, CdR 127/2002 fin. Many EU regions also called for measures to reduce EU incursions into regional spheres of governance.
2   *BOCG, Senado*, Series I, 30, 18 October 1993, p. 2.
3   *DSCG Senado, Pleno*, 18, 20 October 1993, p. 251.

4   The European Commission has established internal procedures to ensure the CoR is informed about its activities; its representatives attend many CoR meetings and it generally goes beyond Treaty requirements, for instance, by providing feedback on the impact of CoR opinions (Warleigh 1999: 29–31).

5   Representatives of the state holding the rotating Council presidency frequently attend CoR plenary sessions, but more general indications are that the Council treats the CoR with indifference. It tends to consult the CoR only when it has to and refuses to give feedback on CoR opinions (Warleigh 1999: 28–9; Jeffery 2002: 341; Ortega 2003: 29).

6   A Basque representative was assigned to CoR committees dedicated to these topics and, between 1998 and 2001, the Basque alternate (Muñoa) served as rapporteur for five opinions relating to these general themes (Gobierno Vasco 2004: 33, 35–7).

7   In 1998, for instance, the CoR adopted a declaration in favour of peace in the Basque Country; in 2000, after ETA assassinated Basque parliamentarian Fernando Buesa and councillor Jesús María Pedrosa, the institutional affairs committee held a minute of silence; and in April 2003 the CoR held a hearing on 'attacks and threats against local and regional politicians in the Basque Country', involving Basque politicians from different political parties (Gobierno Vasco 2004: 44; CoR 2004: 59–60).

8   July 2002, CdR 127/2002 fin.

9   Decreto 89/1988, *BOPV*, 86, 5 May 1988, p. 2528, see articles 4 and 23.

10   *BOE*, 151, suplemento, 25 June 1994, p. 68.

11   *Informe sobre el proceso de participación de funcionarios de las Comunidades Autónomas en los comités de ejecución o de comitología durante el periodo 2003–2006*, CARCE, www.map.es (accessed 8 August 2006).

12   *Reglas sobre la participación autonómica en los comités de ejecución de la Comisión Europea*, 10 March 2003, www.map.es (accessed 8 August 2006).

13   See also preamble to Basque nationalist group's 1998 resolution on autonomous community participation in the Council, *BOCG, Congreso*, Series A, 145, 11 November 1997, p. 3 and *BOCG, Congreso*, Series D, 47, 19 July 2000, p. 29.

14   *BOE*, 302, 16 December 1996, p. 37314; *Real Decreto* 2105/96, de 20 de septiembre, *BOE*, 229, 20 September 1996, p. 28394.

15   According to Cienfuegos, the *consejero* had held many meetings with, and transmitted abundant, but appropriately filtered information to, autonomous communities and had worked 'naturally elbow to elbow with autonomous communities in matters of interest to them' (1997: 199).

16   According to then Basque government director of European affairs, Juan Luis Diego Casals, in 1995, 'Central [government] ministers are officially sent any information that arrives [from EU institutions] on matters relating to their competence. Autonomous communities must, first, find out if information exists, secondly, ask for it and later hope that it is not denied to us on the understanding that it is confidential information' (Diego 1995: 1025). More generally, relations between the Basque delegation in Brussels and the Spanish permanent representation were characterised as 'sporadic', if subject to improvement depending on the inclinations of the permanent representation (Diego 1995: 1024).

17   Ortuzar argued that 'the truth is that it gives us very little ... one person to attend to the demands of seventeen autonomous communities cannot cope with the thousands of pages of information of interest to autonomous communities and send them to their destinations' (1998: 15).

18   *BOE*, 64, 16 March 2005, p. 9372.

19   Article 203 of the EC Treaty now reads: 'The Council shall consist of a representative of each Member State at ministerial level, authorised to commit the government of that Member State.' Various Basque government position papers on EU treaty reforms call for regions with legislative powers to be given explicit treaty authorisa-

tion to participate in Council meetings affecting their competencies and interests (see Gobierno Vasco 1996: 18 and 2003: 17).

20 See interventions of different political parties in Basque parliamentary debate on autonomous community participation in the Council, *Diario de Sesiones del Parlamento Vasco (DSPV)*, 86, 20 February 1998, pp. 65–103. Reactions to central government rejections of Basque hopes for Council participation could be bleak. According to a 1993 report: 'There is no greater marginalisation or failure to recognise the political power that the state confers to the [Basque] autonomous community than denying it permission to attend and participate in [the Council of ministers] and its committees' (Gobierno Vasco 1993: 28).

21 Technically this was a *proposición no de ley* (non-legislative proposal), *BOCG, Cortes Generales*, Series A, 145, 11 November 1997, p. 2.

22 Technically this was a *proposición no de ley* (non-legislative proposition) *BOPV*, 156, 6 March 1998, p. 13658.

23 *DSCG, Comisiones Mixtas*, 89, 4 March 1998, p. 1823.

24 *BOCG, Congreso*, Series D, 258, 23 March 1998, p. 30.

25 As a substitute for full involvement in the Council, the central government apparently offered to 'invite Basque representatives to form part of the Spanish delegation in the economic and finance Council when taxation matters directly affecting Basque taxation measures were debated' (*El País*, 6 January 2002, in López 2003: 85). But this was not sufficient for Basque negotiators.

26 Although autonomous communities run by minority nationalists have tended to push hardest on this issue, autonomous communities run by the PSOE later joined the cause, especially after the PSOE joined the ranks of opposition at the state level after 1996.

27 See also views of Sr. Guardans i Cambó in *DSCG, Congreso, Pleno y Diputación Permanente*, 109, 2 October 2001, pp. 5292–3.

28 A second, even more modest report, was also rejected, when certain PP-governed autonomous communities again appeared to 'modify', throughout the course of a CARCE meeting, their previous position of support for the report (Castro and Ugalde 2004: 180; Aizpeolea, *El País*, 14 December 2001).

29 In the early years of the PP's first term of government, PP spokespersons were conciliatory, if more committed to enhancing internal participation of autonomous communities than expanding channels for external participation (see, for instance, intervention of Secretary of State for Territorial Administration, Jorge Fernández, and PP spokesperson in the Congress of Deputies, Sr. Martínez Casañ, *DSCG, Comisiones Mixtas*, 89, 4 March 1998, pp. 1824–26.

30 *BOCG, Congreso*, Series D, 47, 19 July 2000, p. 29; *BOCG, Congreso*, Series D, 68, p. 5; *DSCG, Congreso, Pleno y Diputación Permanente*, 27, 26 September 2000, p. 1198. See also debates with Secretary of State for European Affairs, Sr. de Miguel y Egea, *DSCG, Comisiones Mixtas*, 24, 19 December 2000, p. 469.

31 *BOCG, Congreso*, Series B, 130–1, 6 April 2001, p. 1; *BOCG, Congreso*, Series B, 130–2, 9 October 2001, p. 1; *DSCG, Congreso, Pleno y Diputación Permanente*, 109, 2 October 2001, p. 5286.

32 For example, PNV critiques that 'the Sectoral Conferences don't serve any purpose' (Aizpeolea, *El País*, 14 December 2001).

33 See comments by Basque nationalist (EA) Begoña Lasagabaster, by Galician nationalist, Sr. Aymerich Cano, Catalan nationalist Sr. Guardans i Cambó, and critique of PSOE's Sr. Moragues Gomila, DSCG, *Congreso, Pleno y Diputación Permanente*, 109, 2 October 2001, pp. 5286–95.

34 See investiture speech of Sr. Zapatero, *DSCG, Congreso, Pleno y Diputación Permanente*, 2, 15 April 2004, p. 19.

35   *BOE*, 64, 16 March 2005, p. 9372.
36   *BOE*, 79, 2 April 1998, p. 11352.
37   This body is called the Commission for Monitoring and Coordinating Actions Related to the Defence of the Spanish State before the ECJ (*Comisión de Seguimiento y Coordinanción de las Actuaciones Relacionadas con la Defensa del Estado Español ante el Tribunal de las Comunidades Europeas*).

5

More allies, more influence? The Atlantic Arc and transEuropean networks

In this chapter I examine a Basque government campaign to promote an ambitious high-speed train (HST) project linking Basque towns into Spanish and European transport networks. The Basque HST project, known locally as the 'Basque Y', aims to link Bilbao, San Sebastián and Vitoria in the Basque Country south to Madrid and north, across the Pyrenees, to France and the rest of Europe. The project has been a major Basque government priority since the 1980s, and is considered key for future economic prosperity, although it has raised concerns about environmental and social costs. The transregional and transnational nature of HST networks, and the territorial distribution of competencies, gives other regions, states and the EU a stake in decisions on the Basque Y. Basque authorities have thus been dependent on the decisions of other political actors to see the project through, which has provided incentives for Basque authorities to develop complex lobbying strategies. In short, the Basque Y is a policy decision subject to the dynamics of a multilevel polity.

Examination of the Basque government's strategy to promote the Basque Y provides an opportunity to consider whether EU decisionmaking resembles multilevel interest aggregation, where regions, alongside state and EU actors, are influential. The relative importance of domestic interest aggregation processes, and the practical utility of various channels for Basque participation in EU decisionmaking, can be assessed. Analysis of alliance strategies should determine whether cooperation among regional and supranational authorities enhanced Basque influence. And finally, the case study should provide insights into the conduct of Basque and central government relations in more routine aspects of EU decisionmaking. The chapter begins with a review of autonomous community, state and EU competencies in rail transportation and Basque government collaboration with other Atlantic Arc regions. Following sections examine domestic interest aggregation and the efforts of Basque and Atlantic Arc regions to influence EU bodies.

The mosaic of European transport policy

Transport policy demonstrates the veracity of the observation that EU, state and regional authorities 'share control over many activities that take place in their respective territories' (Marks *et al.* 1996: 346). The first rail link, between Barcelona and Mataró, was initiated in the 1840s and was soon followed by rail construction in the Basque Country (Mayor Menéndez 1999: 222–4; Magdalena 2003). A line between Madrid and the Basque town Irún, near the French border, was built from 1856, followed, not long afterwards, by a line between Bilbao and Madrid (Gobierno Vasco 2001: 66). General Franco's regime nationalised the railways in 1941 and created two publicly owned companies still in operation today: *Red Nacional de los Ferrocarriles Españoles* (RENFE, Spanish National Rail Network) and *Ferrocarriles Españoles de Vía Estrecha* (FEVE, Spanish Narrow-Gauge Railways). The transition to democracy and 1978 constitution introduced radical changes in the regulatory regime for railways by giving both central authorities and autonomous communities important powers.

Article 149.1.21 of the Spanish constitution gives central authorities responsibility for railways and land transport passing through the territory of more than one autonomous community, including establishment, organisation, operation and inspection of railways and tramways (Benzo 1993: 32). Largescale railway infrastructure projects are a central government competence by virtue of article 149.1.24 (Spanish constitution), which gives it responsibility for public works of 'general interest' or those whose construction affects more than one autonomous community.

Article 148.1.5 (Spanish constitution) – and subsequently, all seventeen autonomy statutes – allows autonomous communities to acquire competence over railways (and land transport) within their territorial limits (Benzo 1993: 20). Basque authorities acquired both legislative and executive powers over Basque railways (and land transport), which were among the first services transferred from central authorities in the early transition period (Magdalena 2003: 45). There are now four rail networks operating in the Basque autonomous community, run by four companies, dependent on three different administrations: RENFE and FEVE, owned by the central government; *Euskotren*, owned by the Basque autonomous community; and, at the local level, the Bilbao metro, owned by the Biscay Transport Consortium (*Consorcio de Transportes de Bizkaia*).

Soon after acquiring these powers, the Basque government developed ambitious plans. Railways had not kept pace with rapid economic growth in the 1960s and 1970s and, despite increased investment in recent decades, including the high-profile Bilbao metro, significant problems remain. Major problems include an old and ageing railway infrastructure, much longer travel times than those offered by other forms of transport and a serious downturn in demand (Gobierno Vasco 2001: 53–4). There are grave deficiencies in railway links between the three major Basque cities – Bilbao, Vitoria and San Sebastián – and between Basque towns, Spanish and European railway networks (Gobierno Vasco 2001: 54, 58). Government reports have repeatedly identified economic costs of poor infrastructure endowment, including negative effects on the competitiveness of Basque businesses and isolation from dynamic areas of economic activity (see for example Gobierno Vasco 1988 and 2001).

In the late 1980s, the Basque government conceived the 'Basque Y' as one important means of addressing such problems. The Basque Y is a proposal for the construction of a HST network that would link the three Basque capitals into state and European HST networks. It takes its name from the shape created by the project's route plan, which links Bilbao to San Sebastián (and France) with a further link south from each of these cities to Vitoria (and other parts of Spain) (Gobierno Vasco 1989 and 2001) (See Map 5.1). Difficult terrain, particularly in mountainous parts of the Basque Country, makes the project ambitious, requiring an estimated cost of some 4 billion euros to place tracks suitable for travel of up to 230 kilometres per hour and cut travel times between Bilbao, Vitoria and San Sebastián to an average of thirty minutes (www.yvasca.com, accessed 19 December 2006).[1]

Despite its keen interest in the project, the Basque government depends on the central government for its execution. The project is only viable if linked into long distance routes extending outside Basque territory, making its construction a central government competence (Gobierno Vasco 2001: section 2.2). In the late 1980s, the PSOE central government – enjoying its second term in office, an absolute majority in the Spanish parliament (see Table 3.5), and a period of economic prosperity – committed to a programme of largescale investment in railways modernisation. In April 1987, it approved the Railways Transport Plan 1987–2000 (*Plan de Transporte Ferroviario 1987–2000*). This Plan, which envisaged an investment package of 2.1 billion pesetas (in 1986 prices), sought both to increase the capacity of the rail network and make provision for HSTs reaching speeds of up to 200 kilometres an hour (*Ministerio de Transportes, Turismo y Comunicaciones* (MTTC, Ministry of Transport, Tourism and Communications) 1987: 31 and 45). A few years later, the government approved the more ambitious Master Plan on Infrastructures 1993–2007 (*Plan Director de Infraestructuras 1993–2007*). With an overall projected budget of between 10 and 13 billion pesetas (in 1992 prices) for the 1993–2007 period, and focusing on more than just transport infrastructure, the Plan envisaged a budget of 1.7 billion pesetas just for HST projects (*Ministerio de Obras Públicas, Transportes y Medio Ambiente* (MOPTMA, Ministry for Public Works, Transport and the Environment)

1994: 399). These plans were updated in 2005, when the Spanish central government approved the Strategic Transport and Infrastructure Plan 2005–2020 (*Plan Estratégico de Infraestructuras y Transporte* 2005–20). Some 48 per cent of the envisaged 250 billion euro investment package for the fifteen-year period would be dedicated to strengthening the railways (*Ministerio de Fomento* 2005: 3–4).

EU transport policy developments in the late 1980s and 1990s soon made the EU part of this policy mosaic. The EC Treaty envisaged a common transport policy from the outset and reforms have been agreed in most major EU treaties. Member states' transport rules, procedures, systems and investment priorities can affect the functioning of the common market (Artis and Lee 1997: 221; Stevens 2004): State transport decisions may discriminate against foreign service providers or constitute barriers to trade; the configuration of transport systems, particularly the presence or absence of international links at state borders, can affect the free movement of people and goods; and transport links can affect economic and social cohesion, depending, for example, on the extent to which they link less economically developed, or peripheral regions, and more dynamic centres of economic activity.

Treaty rules affecting transport are concentrated in separate titles of the (amended) EC Treaty, one on transport (Title V, articles 70–80) and one on transEuropean networks (Title XV, articles 154–6). Title XV, of most relevance to Basque government HST ambitions, was the product of Maastricht negotiations, and provides for an EU role in the establishment and development of transEuropean networks in transport, telecommunications and energy infrastructures. This role includes establishing guidelines for transEuropean networks (covering objectives, priorities and broad lines of measures); implementing measures to ensure interoperability of national networks (particularly technical standardisation); the coordination of national policies affecting transEuropean networks; and identifying and supporting projects of common interest (which must also be supported by the member state concerned) through feasibility studies, loan guarantees, interest rate subsidies or Cohesion Fund grants. The Cohesion Fund was another Maastricht Treaty creation designed to help poorer EU states cope with the requirements of economic and monetary union. It provided financial contributions to environment and transport infrastructure projects for states whose per capita gross national product was less than 90 per cent of the EU average. Until the 2004 enlargement, Spain was the major Cohesion Fund beneficiary, a portion of which has been used for HST development.[2]

Significant progress towards liberalisation of transport markets and development of a common transport policy only really took off in the wake of the single market programme (Stevens 2004: 47–55; Nichol and Salmon 2001: 217). Indeed, railways has been one of the most difficult transport modes to subject to EU measures, due to traditions of state control, railways' political sensitivity and the cost of correcting technical incompatibilities in state railway systems (Stevens 2004: 89–92; Knill and Lehmkuhl 2000: 69). One aspect of renewed interest in transport policy during the late 1980s and 1990s were attempts to harness the integrative potential of advances in railway technologies through development of an EU-wide HST network. Major events in the development of the EU's policy on HSTs are listed in Table 5.1.

Table 5.1 Blueprints for the development of EU high-speed train networks

Date	Agreement
1. December 1990	Council Resolution drawing up an outline plan and specifying priority measures for an EU HST network, including identification of key network links
2. December 1994	Essen European Council endorsment of fourteen priority transport projects, including HSTs
3. July 1996	European Parliament and Council Decision setting out community guidelines for development of transEuropean transport networks, including identification of projects of common interest
4. April 2004	European Parliament and Council Decision amending July 1996 Decision on community guidelines for development of transEuropean transport networks and identifying projects of common interest

Notes: 1. Council Resolution of 17 December 1990, *Official Journal of the European Communities (OJ)*, C33, 8 February 1991, pp. 1–3; 2. Bulletin of the European Communities, 12–1994, point I.6 and I.37; 3. Decision no. 1692/96/EC of 23 July 1996, OJ, L228, 9 September 1996, pp. 1–104; 4. Decision no. 884/2004/EC of 19 April 2004, OJ, L167, 7 April 2004, pp. 1–39.

In order to bring the Basque Y into being, the Basque government needed to develop a strategy to find support from the central government and to include the Basque Y in these EU transport network blueprints.

The Atlantic Arc regions' lobby and collaboration with Aquitaine

A key element of its Basque Y strategy has been promotion of, and participation in, an EU regions' lobby. Part of the strategy focused on the idea of an 'Atlantic Arc', which is a spatial concept demarcating territories with similar socioeconomic features and a unifying idea for transnational regions' organisations. Basque collaboration with Atlantic Arc regions has also pursued other compatible objectives, including an autonomous role in EU policymaking and closer ties with Aquitaine, the neighbouring region in France encompassing the French Basque Country.

The 'Atlantic Arc' is one of a number of European macroregions identified by policymakers and academics. Its boundaries are rather fluid, sometimes defined differently by different authors and institutions (compare del Castillo *et al.* 1992: 84; The Atlantic Arc Commission 2005; European Commission in Wise 2000: 867 and 873). Broader definitions usually include all regions and small states (Republic of Ireland and Portugal) along the Atlantic seaboard from as far north as Scotland and as far south as Andalusia. Conceptualisation of the Atlantic Arc as a space within Spain includes regions in northwestern Spain: The Basque Country, Cantabria, Asturias, Galicia, Castilla y León, Navarre and La Rioja (del Castillo *et al.* 1992) (See Map 2.1).

The principal characteristic of the Atlantic Arc is its relative isolation from principal axes of growth and economic dynamism in Europe (del Castillo *et al.* 1992: 81; Luaces 2004). European growth and prosperity are concentrated spatially along the so-called 'dorsal', which extends from the centre of England (including London), through the north of France (including Paris), the Benelux states, the south of Germany and connects with Switzerland and industrial northern Italy (del Castillo *et al.* 1992: 78; Luaces 2004: 10–12). In recent decades, this zone of economic growth and dynamism has extended towards the Mediterranean, creating a 'Mediterranean Arc' centring on Rome, Marseilles, Barcelona and Valencia (Luaces 2004: 10–12; del Castillo *et al.* 1992: 79; Calvo and López 1998: 171). The Spanish part of the Mediterranean Arc – especially the northeastern regions of Catalonia, Valencia and Murcia – has emerged as a relatively coherent and dynamic economic space experiencing relatively long periods of economic growth compared to many other parts of Spain (Calvo and López 1998: 173; MOPTMA, 1994: 54).

Component regions of the Atlantic Arc suffer from a range of economic problems and constitute a less cohesive economic space. In Spain, Cantabria, Asturias and the Basque Country faced serious industrial crises; others faced problems like population decline or low productivity in primary areas of economic activity (del Castillo *et al.* 1992: 82–7). The regions lack sufficiently integrated economic structures, and networks linking regions internally or connecting them with more dynamic areas of economic activity. These problems have been exacerbated by transport infrastructure deficiencies (in railway, airport and certain road provisions) (del Castillo *et al.* 1992: 88).

This conception of the Atlantic Arc as a socioeconomic space with economic problems and something of a shared fate became a useful weapon for Atlantic regions. The idea of a needy area facing further marginalisation as European market integration progressed allowed Atlantic regions to formulate their objectives as a call for social solidarity. More specifically, Atlantic regions argued that failure to establish suitable transport links accentuated their peripheral character and deepened economic problems.[3]

The idea of the Atlantic Arc helped provide political glue for creation of a series of regional organisations used by the Basque government as part of its strategy to promote its transport priorities in Spain and the EU. The Basque government was actively involved in the Conference of the regions of the Southern European Atlantic (CSEA), founded in April 1990. This organisation was later absorbed into the Atlantic Arc Commission, another interregional association formed in 1989 (see below). While it was active, the CSEA incorporated around a dozen regions from France, Spain and Portugal (Castro and Ugalde 2004: 186–7; Iriondo 1997: 132).[4] Its main priority was to respond to members' difficulties competing in what was then the early days of the EU's single market programme (Castro and Ugalde 2004: 186). Defending and promoting modern means of transport along the Atlantic Arc, including highways, international airports, ports – and HSTs – was another priority objective (Iriondo 1997: 132–3).[5]

The Basque government was actively involved in this organisation, constituting along with the French regions Aquitaine and Poitou-Charentes, one of its founding members (Iriondo 1997: 132; Castro and Ugalde 2004: 186–7). The Basque president attended meetings annually in the early 1990s and hosted some of its meetings (Castro and Ugalde 2004: 413–26; Iriondo 1997: 132–3). Basque representatives occupied leading positions, notably Conference president and chair of a committee on railway infrastructure (Iriondo 1997: 132–3; Galende, *El Correo*, 28 April 1990). One of the achievements of this organization was negotiation, in April 1990, of a 'Common Declaration on the Development of Infrastructure in the Southern European Atlantic', calling on central governments and EU institutions to amend proposed EU HST routes to account for southern Atlantic regions' preferences (Galende, *El Correo*, 28 April 1990). These included calls for construction of the Basque Y and a HST route crossing the Spanish French border through the Basque Country. Proposals were first elaborated by the CSEA's railways infrastructure committee, chaired by the Basque transport minister, Pedro Ruiz de Alegría (Galende, *El Correo*, 28 April 1990).

A second EU regions' body – the Atlantic Arc Commission – was formed within the Conference of Peripheral Maritime Regions (CPMR) in 1989. The CPMR was established as a Breton initiative in 1973 with two principal aims: to unite peripheral regions in Europe to counterbalance prosperous regions at Europe's geographical centre; and to promote common initiatives jointly exploiting advantages offered by their maritime and coastal resources (Iriondo 1997: 138).[6] The Atlantic Arc Commission, one of six geographical commissions, includes thirty Atlantic regions and specifically aims 'to overcome the handicap of their peripheral geographical situation' (Iriondo 1997: 139).[7] Like the CSEA, transportation is a priority area, particularly improvement of internal and external accessibility, intermodality and the development of maritime links.

A major thrust of Atlantic Arc Commission activity has been EU-orientated. Indeed, the organisation defined creation of a 'political instrument for defence of common Atlantic interests in the EU' as one of its fundamental objectives (Wise 2000: 866). It has sought to influence EU debates on a variety of issues, including spatial planning, maritime safety, regional policy reform, the Constitutional Treaty and transEuropean networks (www.crpm.org, accessed 20 July 2006). According to Mark Wise, 'persistent petitioning [involving] frequent meetings with EU officials and MEPs as well as European Commissioners and relevant ministers' have enabled the Atlantic Arc representatives to influence the content of EU structural fund legislation in their favour and to increase allocations of EU structural funds in the Atlantic zone (2000: 872–80).[8]

The Basque government has played an active role in this association (Gobierno Vasco 1999). A comparative measure developed by Mark Wise to gauge different regions' degree of involvement in Atlantic Arc Commission activities ranks the Basque Country above average (2000: 885–6). The Basque government has held a number of leadership roles, including longterm coordinator of the Atlantic Arc's transport working group.[9] The transport working group aims to make transport and infrastructure proposals and to have a greater say in 'state and European Commission decision making processes' and its priorities include influencing revision of transEuropean transport network guidelines. Led by the transport working group, the Atlantic Arc Commission recently elaborated a joint proposal on EU plans to revise transEuropean transport networks and held meetings with EU officials (www.crpm.org, accessed 20 July 2006).

Multilateral cooperation with Atlantic Arc regions has been complemented by intensive bilateral collaboration with the neighbouring French region, Aquitaine. Aquitaine is contiguous with the northern tip of the Basque autonomous community, Navarre and part of Aragón. The three Basque provinces – *Lapurdi, Behe-nafarroa* and *Zuberoa,* collectively known as the *Iparralde* (Northern Basque Country) – lie within the Aquitanian department, *Pyrénées-Atlantiques.* Informal political relationships have long spanned the border between France and Spain. During the dictatorship, the republican Basque government-in-exile found refuge in the French Basque Country and it became a refuge for ETA activists from the 1960s (Ahedo 2004: 22). Although much stronger in Spain, Basque nationalism has a foothold in France, which supports transnational political relationships, particularly among the Basque nationalist left (Ahedo 2004).

Formal political links developed slowly. After what one author called 'various decades of mutual ignorance', presidents of the Basque autonomous community and the Aquitanian Regional Council met in April 1989 (Garamendia 2002: 75; Marugán, *El Correo,* 3 October 1989). In October of the same year, the two governments signed the Protocol of Collaboration between the Basque Autonomous Community and the Region of Aquitaine (*Protocolo de Colaboración entre la Comunidad Autónoma Vasca y la Región de Aquitania*). Navarre was soon bought into the fold with signature of a new Protocol of Cooperation between the three regions in February 1992. However, by 2000, increasingly difficult relations between governing parties in the Basque autonomous community and the Foral Community of Navarre prompted Navarre to withdrew its cooperation and negotiate a separate Protocol with Aquitaine (Garamendia 2002: 81; Delgado, *El Correo*, 25 January 2000).

Despite this sour note, cooperation between Aquitaine and the Basque Country proceeded. The partnership is sustained by a permanent institutional framework, agreements, joint actions, frequent meetings and a Cooperation Fund financing a range of crossborder projects (Garamendia 2002; Letamendia 1997a; Castro and Ugalde 2004: 186–7 and 262–72). Both 1989 (Basque-Aquitaine) and 1992 (Basque-Navarre-Aquitaine) versions of the Protocols signalled that EU developments – particularly the single market, economic and monetary union, regional policy reforms – were important prompts for collaboration and identified Atlantic Arc cooperation as a priority (see also Letamendia 1997a).[10]

As mentioned above, one of the early achievements of this partnership was cooperation, with the French region of Poitou-Charentes, to found the CSEA. Cooperation to influence EU HST plans has continued as an enduring aspect – and according to some authors an increasingly central element (Castro and Ugalde: 2004: 273–4; Luaces 2004: 71) – of the Basque-Aquitanian partnership. This has taken the form of both technical and political cooperation.[11] Political cooperation has included efforts to promote common HST transport priorities in EU policymaking through further multilateral and bilateral initiatives. In 2003, following agreement reached at a joint Basque-Aquitanian summit, the two regions created a new body, *L'association Priorité T.G.V. Sud Europe Atlantique* (Priority Southern European Atlantic HST Association) (Castro and Ugalde 2004: 272). This body, whose membership is almost identical to the abandoned CSEA, aims to lobby for realisation of an Atlantic HST link (Castro and Ugalde 2004: 272). It was agreed that the first president of this new association would be Alain Rousset, president of Aquitaine, while the Basque Country would continue to coordinate their activities on transport matters in the Atlantic Arc Commission (Castro and Ugalde 2004: 272–3; *Plataforma Logística Aquitania-Euskadi*, 2001). Furthermore, in 2003 the two regions signed a joint declaration calling for the construction of the Basque Y and a HST between Dax (France) and Vitoria (Basque Country) and Madrid (Spain) by 2010 and for their inclusion in a list of the EU's priority 'quick start' projects (Castro and Ugalde 2004: 247–8).[12] They sent this to both the European Commission and central governments in Spain and France (Castro and Ugalde 2004: 247–8).

Conflict, cooperation and relations with central government

Projects to modernise Basque railways have been identified as priorities in Spanish transport infrastructure blueprints since the 1980s.[13] However, the

Basque Y has been of secondary importance compared to HST projects in the south of Spain and projects in the northeast along the Mediterranean Arc (MTTC 1987: 31; MOPTMA 1994: 133). As early as December 1988, the central government decided it would begin construction of Madrid-Seville HST and Madrid-Barcelona routes ahead of others (MOPTMA 1994: 148). Construction of a HST route to Valencia would come at a later date (MOPTMA 1994: 133). Large parts of the Seville-Madrid-Barcelona-France line have now been completed (Ministerio de Fomento 2005: 94; Arroyo, El País, 5 May 2006). By contrast, the Basque Y has been in the planning stage for over a decade, with financial commitments in place by 2006,[14] and construction only now at an early stage (Ormazabal, El País, 5 May 2006; www.yvasca.com, accessed 20 December 2006).

Central government decisions to prioritise transport infrastructure investment in the Mediterranean Arc rather than the Atlantic Arc were controversial. In 1989, Basque government minister for the presidency, the PNV's Juan Ramón Guevara, described the decision as 'an act of hostility to the Basque Country', and accused the central government of using 'political' rather than 'technical' or 'economic' criteria for decisions (El Correo, 12 January 1989). The PNV party secretary, Josu Bergara, called the decision 'prejudicial', 'against history' and 'electoralist' and argued that it 'impeded the [Basque autonomous community] from being as best prepared and equipped as possible to face the challenges' of the single market programme (Bergara, El Correo, 20 February 1989). The EE's leader, Juan María Bandrés, described decisions to prioritise the Mediterranean Arc as a 'gift' by the ruling Andalusians to their own people (Marugán, El Correo, 12 February 1989).[15] The Basque government transport minister, PSE-PSOE's Enrique Antolín, called central government preferences 'extremely confusing' and promised to 'ask for explanations' (Fontova, El Correo, 12 January 1989).

Other Atlantic Arc autonomous communities were also critical, including some governed by the PSOE (Santos, El Correo, 18 September 1989). Some responded by participating, alongside the Basque autonomous community, in interregional associations like the CSEA and Atlantic Arc Commission, and in joint initiatives to promote transport infrastructure modernisation in their territories (Santos, El Correo, 18 September 1989; Marugán, El Correo, 21 July 1990).

It was against this background that the central government chose to promote inclusion of two Spanish HST links to France in EU networks – an Atlantic link, including the Basque Y, and the Seville-Madrid-Barcelona lines. Before the Council agreed the first EU HST network map in December 1990 (see Table 5.1), central government transport minister José Barrionuevo insisted that Spanish EU negotiators would push for both a Basque route through Irún and a Catalan route through Port Bou or La Junquera (Torres, El Correo, 3 October 1989a and 3 October 1989b; Pescador, El Correo, 17 October 1989; see also El Correo, 16 July 1990). From this point onwards, the

Map 5.1 EU transEuropean transport network plans for Spain

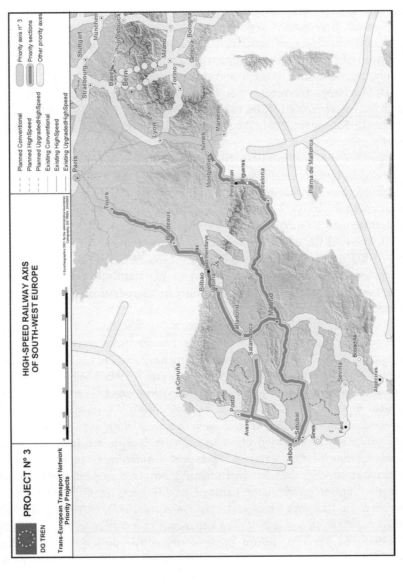

Source: High-Speed Railway Axis of South-West Europe, © European Communities, 2006, http://ec.europa.eu/ten/transport/maps/doc/axes/pp03.pdf.

Basque government had reason to be satisfied its priorities would form part of transEuropean transport network plans. In 1990, the Council established the principle, carried over into the Essen European Council's fourteen priority projects and both 1996 and 2004 transEuropean transport networks guidelines (see Table 5.1), that the Basque Y would be part of the EU's transport network (see Map 5.1).

Central government reports identify many factors considered in the formation of railway infrastructure preferences such as these, including the condition of existing railway infrastructure provision, spatial distribution of population, economic growth and environmental issues (MTTC 1987 and MOPTMA 1994). Electoral cycles, clientelism and other political factors may also have been involved (Ross 1994: 203; Díaz and Tijeras: 1991; Marugán, El Correo, 12 February 1989). What role did autonomous community preferences play?

Spanish transport infrastructure blueprints and EU transport policy were discussed in two Sectoral Conferences – the National Transport Conference (Conferencia Nacional de Transportes) and the Sectoral Conference for Infrastructure and Territorial Planning (Conferencial Sectorial de Infraestructuras y Ordenación del Territorio) (Ortúzar et al. 1995 and MAP 1996). The CARCE's 1994 Agreement on autonomous community participation in EU decisions through the Sectoral Conferences (see chapter three) designated the former for cooperation in EU transport policy in general, while the latter was allocated responsibility for cooperation in transEuropean transport network decisions.

Both are among the least active Sectoral Conferences (See Table 3.4). The National Transport Conference only met thirteen times between 1987, when it was created, and 2005. It did meet during key stages in the development of Spanish and EU policies on HST networks and a 1995 MAP report characterised autonomous community participation in EU transport policy discussions as 'intense' (Ortúzar et al., 1995: 180).[16] Summaries of matters discussed show that the central government's Railways Transport Plan 1987–2000, which included plans to improve Basque railways, was on the agenda of one of the National Transport Conference's plenary meetings (Ortúzar et al. 1995: 262–5). This meeting, however, was held in June 1988, after the central government Council of Ministers (consejo de ministros) approved the Railways Transport Plan (in April 1987). EU transport policy was discussed at all but one of the Conference's plenary meetings (Ortúzar et al. 1995: 262–5). The 'future horizon of railway policy' was specifically mentioned as a topic for an October 1994 meeting held after publication of the European Commission's proposal for what became the 1996 transEuropean transport networks guidelines (see Table 5.1). However, it is not clear whether the proposal was discussed. There is no record that central government and autonomous communities reached agreement on state or EU HST network plans at any meetings of this Conference.

The Sectoral Conference for Infrastructure and Territorial Planning, has met even less frequently (see Table 3.4). Until 2005, when it met once, the Sectoral Conference only met on three occasions, all in 1993.[17] The central government's Master Plan on Infrastructures 1993–2007, which included the Basque Y and supported HST links to France via the Basque town of Irún, dominated the agenda of this Sectoral Conference during its short period of activity.[18] Meetings were held before the Master Plan was approved by the central government Council of Ministers, but there is no record that autonomous communities and the central government reached agreements on the Master Plan in this Sectoral Conference. Indeed, the central government argued it was only obliged to inform – rather than consult – autonomous communities in the formulation of the Master Plan on Infrastructure, given its exclusive competencies in this policy area (MAP 1996: 94 and 103). The Conference was not convened during negotiation of EU transEuropean network legislation between 1994 and 1996 (MAP 2001: 67) or 2001 and 2004 (www.map.es, accessed 20 November 2006).

Formal procedures for bilateral EU collaboration among Basque and central government were not in force until late 1995 (see chapter three). This was too late to be relevant for many state and EU decisions affecting EU HST networks plans, including the 1990 Council decision and the 1994 Essen lists of priority projects. The first meeting of the Basque-State Bilateral Commission for EU matters was held on 1 July 1996 (Castro and Ugalde 2004: 157), within only a few weeks of – and too late to influence – the final outcome of the EU transEuropean transport network Decision adopted on 23 July 1996. It has not met since 1999. Bilateral agreements relating to the Basque Y have been negotiated outside the framework of this Bilateral Commission, including a 2006 agreement setting out financial commitments for construction of the Basque Y.[19]

There is ample evidence that Basque and central government representatives met less formally for bilateral discussions on HST plans, evidence which includes testimony by various Basque transport ministers (Antolín 2001: 764–6; Ruiz de Alegría 2001: 1070; Bergara 2001, 1156) and press reports (Rojo, *El Correo*, 23 February 1989; Torres, *El Correo*, 27 September 1988). In the late 1980s, such meetings culminated in negotiation of an Infrastructures Pact, agreed between Basque and central governments in February 1989. In addition to improving Basque ports (Bilbao and Pasajes) and airports (especially Bilbao), the pact included commitments to continue technical studies for Basque Y construction and for the central government to defend inclusion of a Basque HST link to France in EU network plans (Antolín 2001: 764; Torres, *El Correo*, 3 October 1989b). One problem with this pact was its informality. The central government resisted signing a formal text, which caused uncertainty in the Basque government about central government intentions (Torres, *El Correo*, 3 October 1989b; Ruiz de Alegría 1998: 1070).

Furthermore, there is evidence that party political links may have been an additional source of influence for the Basque government, particularly links between the PSOE-led central government and the PSE-PSOE, the Basque branch of the aforementioned statewide party. The PNV and the PSE-PSOE were the principal parties in coalitions running the Basque government for most of the period between March 1987 and July 1998 (see Table 2.2) and both were committed to construction of the Basque Y (Torres, *El Correo,* 27 September 1988).[20] During the first years of the PNV and PSE-PSOE alliance, a crucial period in negotiation of Spanish HST priorities, the PSE-PSOE was well placed to influence its central government colleagues. Two successive PSE-PSOE ministers held the transport portfolio in the Basque government: Enrique Antolín (1987–89) and Pedro Luis Ruiz de Alegría (1989–91).

The PNV sought to take advantage of the PSE-PSOE's relationship with the PSOE central government to advance Basque infrastructure priorities. After the October 1990 Basque autonomous community elections, for instance, the PNV sought to make central government concessions in Basque infrastructure provision one of its conditions for renewal of the PNV-PSE-PSOE governing coalition (Ayala, *El Correo,* 14 November 1990). Similarly, when the central government announced in early 1990 that it would prioritise construction of HSTs crossing the French border in Catalonia, the PNV called the decision 'an act of hostility towards the Basque Country *and* its coalition government' (my italics) (*El Correo,* 12 January 1989).

Antolín and Ruiz de Alegría, along with the PSE-PSOE Basque government vicepresident, Ramón Jáuregui, were involved in initiatives to pressure the central government over the Basque Y. Ruiz de Alegría was involved in the CSEA, chairing the transport infrastructure committee that put together a joint proposal on EU HST routes which included the Basque Y (Galende, *El Correo,* 28 April 1990). Member regions agreed to use the proposal to solicit support from their central governments and the EU (Galende, *El Correo,* 28 April 1990). Vicepresident Jáuregui led an initiative, with Aquitanian socialists, to promote the needs of the Atlantic Arc and HSTs were a high-profile agenda item (Zubirte, *El Correo,* 15 April 1989; Tellitu, *El Correo,* 14 October 1989).

Senior PSE-PSOE members such as Jáuregui, Antolín and Ruiz de Alegría were involved in many of the above-mentioned bilateral meetings between the Basque and central governments on Basque infrastructure provision. This included negotiation of the 1989 Infrastructures Pact, which was clearly conceived as negotiations between the political parties running these institutions (that is PSOE, PSE-PSOE and PNV) (Antolín 2001: 764–6). Representatives of Basque political parties (as opposed to just members of government) were involved in other meetings as well (Torres, *El Correo,* 27 September 1988). Significantly, in recent testimony on his time as Basque government transport minister, Antolín observed that, while negotiation of the 1989 Infrastructure Pact was sometimes difficult, the PSOE presence in both central and Basque governments eased negotiations (Antolín 2001: 764–6).

The Atlantic Arc and the search for EU allies

As we have seen, establishing contacts and lobbying EU policymakers has been part of the rationale for cooperation among Atlantic Arc regions. There is evidence of numerous contacts between European Commission officials and Atlantic Arc regions, and these have sometimes provided opportunities to promote Basque HST objectives (Wise 2000; Fontova, *El Correo*, 3 October 1990; Ubarretxena, *Deia*, 15 May 1993). Contacts have taken place in a variety of different contexts, including attendance at conferences or meetings discussing Atlantic Arc issues. They have also taken the form of formal meetings. For instance, prior to the 2004 Decision on transEuropean transport network guidelines (see Table 5.1), the Atlantic Arc Commission held a meeting with representatives of the European Commission's Transport and Energy Directorate-General, the EP and the French Transport ministry (www.crpm.org, accessed 20 July 2006). The Basque government actively sought to ensure its priorities would form part of the Atlantic Arc Commission's proposals, which were incorporated into a joint position agreed in Inverness on 20 June 2003.[21]

One contact of particular importance for the Basque government was Eneko Landaburu, who was European Commission director-general for regional policy between 1986 and 2000.[22] Although Landaburu was born in France and educated at the University of Paris, his surname betrays Basque roots. Landaburu played a role in Basque politics in the early democratic period, when he served as a PSE-PSOE deputy in the Basque parliament (between 1980 and 1981). As head of EU regional policy, Landaburu acquired an international reputation and was regarded as an influential figure in regional policy decisions (Gardner, *Financial Times*, 12 May 1993; Gardner, *Financial Times*, 21 June 1994; *Financial Times*, 3 February 1995; Groom, *Financial Times*, 1 December 1997). Basque officials frequently sought his insider's view on EU politics, which were often reported in the press or presented at conferences in the Basque Country (Pescador, *El Correo*, 12 February 1989; Vallejo, *El Correo*, 25 January 1989; Lezana, *El Correo*, 8 November 1998; Ubarretxena, *Deia*, 15 May 1993).[23] In one newspaper interview, Landaburu reportedly argued that without some form of 'ultramodern' transportation links (either road or railways) from the northeastern (or Atlantic) area of Spain through the Basque Country to France, there was a risk that this area would 'stay marginalised' (Vallejo, *El Correo*, 25 January 1989; see also Marugán, *El Correo*, 12 February 1989). He also commented, in relation to improving Atlantic transport links, that although the European Community 'could not impose decisions ... we could try to convince others it is necessary to do so' (Vallejo, *El Correo*, 25 January 1989).

The European Commission has often supported the interests of the Atlantic Arc and the Basque Y in EU HST decisions, but its policy positions have varied over time. At one point the European Commission proposed prioritising EU HST networks in the Atlantic Arc rather than the Mediterranean Arc.[24] Later, its position vacillated between prioritising HST links only along the Mediterranean Arc and then prioritising them along both Mediterranean and Atlantic Arcs.[25] From early 1990, however, European Commission proposals on longterm transport infrastructure networks stood by the position that the Franco-Spanish border should be crossed through both the Basque Country and Catalonia.[26] Before the finalisation in 2004 of the transEuropean transport network guidelines, the European Commission identified the need for an additional high capacity railway crossing across the central Pyrenees, but continued to support an Atlantic HST network including the Basque Y (European Commission 2001: 53).[27] It has frequently emphasised the importance of transportation policy for the integration of peripheral regions and its role in economic and social cohesion.

European Commission reports, proposals and contributions to parliamentary debates do not question the preferences of member states expressed collectively in the European Council (such as the 1994 Essen summit) and demonstrate a reluctance to question those of individual member states.[28] For the 2004 transEuropean transport network guidelines, the European Commission went out of its way to ensure member state preferences were taken into account in its proposals by creating the Van Miert high-level working groups of member state representatives.

Atlantic Arc regions, and the Basque autonomous community, have used links with the EP to promote their preferences on EU HST networks.[29] Spanish MEPs are elected by proportional representation from closed lists presented in a single electoral constituency covering the whole state (Newton 1997: 307–8). This presents an obstacle to regions forming direct links with MEPs because MEPs technically represent the whole state rather than an area within it. The electoral system also benefits statewide parties at the expense of those competing in only part of state territory (like minority nationalist or regionalist parties).[30] Nevertheless, it is possible to identify certain MEPs with clear links to the Basque Country, especially those from Basque nationalist parties who have won EP seats (that is, PNV, EA and EH). MEPs from other political parties may be linked to Basque politics by their simultaneous association with Basque branches of statewide parties.

The EP's powers have grown considerably and made it a potentially powerful ally. Initially, the EP was merely 'consulted' on proposals for EU HST networks. Nevertheless, MEPs with links to the Atlantic Arc tried to get the EP to back transport infrastructure projects of interest to individual and multiple Atlantic Arc regions. MEPs with links to regions in France, Portugal and Spain signed up to a number of motions for resolution, including one expressing concern that EU choices on HST priorities could 'accentuate the peripheral character of the regions bordering on the Atlantic' and calling for prioritisation of Atlantic HST routes like the Irún Spain-France link.[31] Three others concerned individual Atlantic Arc priority projects, including a proposal for EP support for the Basque Y HST link at Irún, which was proposed by Basque MEP (and former president of the Basque autonomous community) Carlos Garaikoetxea.[32] The EP responded positively to Atlantic Arc calls for support. The EP accepted key points of the above-mentioned motions from Atlantic MEPs, and called for proposed EU HST routes to link up all regions of the Iberian Peninsula within a reasonable period.[33] Additionally, Jean-Pierre Raffarin, when president of the Atlantic Arc Commission during much of the 1990s, used his EP seat to publicise Atlantic Arc concerns and to pressure other EU institutions to take Atlantic Arc needs into account.[34]

The EP acquired new powers with introduction of the codecision procedure in the Maastricht Treaty. Codecision, which was used for both July 1996 and April 2004 transEuropean network Decisions, gives the EP up to three chances to propose amendments and ultimately the right to veto proposals it does not support. However, as some MEPs lamented, EP influence in these cases was hobbled by prior European Council agreements and priority lists drawn up by member state representatives in the Christophersen and Van Miert working groups.[35] This meant that the EP could not amend specific projects (in 1996) or could only do so within very limited parameters (in 2004), although some of the proposals made in 1996 were eventually incorporated into proposals for 2004 guideline revisions.

Despite these obstacles, the EP proposed a large number of amendments to specific projects, including a number relating to Atlantic Arc road and rail links.[36] It also tried to incorporate an 'Atlantic Arc' clause into the 1996 guidelines, which sought to create obligations for future EU-wide rail projects to link peripheral regions of the Atlantic seaboard.[37] Using its powers under the codecision procedure, the EP defended this clause at both the first and second reading stages and tried to reinstate it after the clause was rejected by the European Commission and the Council.[38] However, there was not enough support to carry the Atlantic Arc clause to the final text, and EP debates at different stages of the process revealed that the Atlantic Arc was never an EP priority.[39]

By 2004, the inclusion of projects in transEuropean transport network guidelines was not a priority for Atlantic regions and the Basque government; they had already been confirmed in European Commission proposals and in the work of the Van Miert working group.[40] There were no EP proposals to amend maps relating to Atlantic HST routes.[41] The issue for Atlantic Arc, reflected in comments by the PNV's MEP, Josu Ortuondo, and the French socialist MEP Gilles Savary, was to encourage speedier implementation of projects already agreed.[42]

Given the degree of cooperation among Atlantic Arc regions, and activities in the EP, lack of activity in the CoR is striking. The CoR, which must be consulted on transEuropean transport network proposals, delivered opinions on both 1996 and 2004 transEuropean transport networks guidelines.[43] These opinions were first dealt with in the CoR's committees for transport and communications networks (1996 Decision); for transEuropean networks, transport and information society (2004 Decision) and for territorial cohesion policy (2004 Decision). The Basque CoR representative was not a member of any of these committees (Gobierno Vasco 1998 and 2004) and there is no evidence that the Basque government sought to propose any amendments to the relevant CoR opinions.

The CoR's draft and final opinions on the 1996 Decision emphasises the importance of consulting with regions, environmental considerations and 'welcome[s] the Commission's aim of integrating inaccessible regions, the island and peripheral regions ... more closely into the existing network'.[44] But there is no specific emphasis on transport needs of Atlantic regions. There were no proposals from other CoR members that it do so, although Yvon Bourges, a French member of the CoR linked to the Atlantic area, proposed, but failed to find support for, a very general statement on the need for priority projects to ensure a better spread of people and activities throughout the EU and for 'vitalizing the less developed regions particularly those on the periphery of the Communities'.[49]

The CoR's response to what would become the 2004 Decision was longer and in some respects more robust in its defence of linking peripheral regions into transEuropean transport networks. Its opinion stressed that the EU should 'improv[e] the access of the Communities' peripheral regions into the single market area' in light of the objectives of economic and social cohesion.[46] And, like its predecessor, this more recent CoR opinion emphasised the need for regional participation in decision processes, omitted specific mention of Atlantic regions' transport needs and generally refrained from mentioning specific projects.[47] The rapporteur for the CoR's opinion on this Decision was Ramón Luis Valcárcel Siso, president of the Spanish region of Murcia and, at the committee stage, Adela Barrero Flórez, representing Asturias in northeast Spain, managed to introduce two amendments emphasising balanced economic development, economic and social cohesion, and accessibility for peripheral regions.[48] At the plenary stage, other Spanish autonomous communities, mostly from the Mediterranean seaboard of Spain, but also including a representative from Galicia in Spain's northeast, jointly proposed a number of amendments, mostly related to the transportation needs of islands.[49]

The transport policy mosaic in contemporary Europe has clearly provided incentives for the Basque government to develop complex, transnational lobbying strategies. With their Atlantic Arc allies, the Basque government found some support from supranational authorities. However, this mostly took the form of very general statements recognising the needs of peripheral regions and passive acceptance of compatible preferences expressed by member state governments. Indeed, once central governments agreed the basic contours of transEuropean transport networks, other EU bodies did not really question them in fundamental ways. In this context, domestic interest aggregation processes were more salient. A variety of factors appear to have underpinned central government support for the Basque Y, including technical and broader public policy objectives and a shared interest in developing a modern, well-connected HST network in Spain. The appeals and shared interests of party colleagues involved in the Basque government (and other Atlantic Arc autonomous communities) may also have been relevant. There is little evidence that formal institutions and procedures were employed to channel autonomous community interests into transEuropean transport network decisions. Despite domestic disputes about prioritisation of Mediterranean over Atlantic Arc transport infrastructure, this case provides further evidence of collaboration among Basque and central governments in the pursuit of common EU objectives.

Notes

1   *BOE*, 157, 3 July 2006, p. 24942.
2   *OJ*, L130, 25 May 1994, p. 8; *OJ* L161, 26 June 1999, p. 61.
3   This argument, for instance, was frequently made in Basque parliament debates on Atlantic Arc cooperation and HSTs, see *DSPV*, 36, 11 November 1988, p. 35 and *DSPV*, 40, 17 February 1989, p. 22.
4   From France: Aquitaine, Centre and Poitou-Charentes; from Spain: Basque Country, Asturias, Galicia, Castilla y León, Andalucía, Extremadura, Cantabria, Navarre; and from Portugal: North and Centre regions.
5   Other goals were promoting cooperation among member regions' scientific communities and developing human resources in their area to attract and service firms (Iriondo 1997: 132–3).
6   Its membership of mostly maritime regions outside the European 'dorsal' has grown from twenty-three regions when it was first established to around a hundred and fifty regions today (www.crpm.org, accessed 20 July 2006).
7   Other priority areas are sustainable development, fisheries, research and innovation, and maritime safety (www.crpm.org, accessed 20 July 2006).
8   EU structural funds have contributed significantly to the funding of action plans – Atlantis I (1993) and Atlantis II (1996–99), for example – which supported a variety of joint projects, including establishment of FINATLANTIC SA, a public-private partnership providing funds and business expertise for transnational enterprises, or tourism projects like a transnational 'Atlantic cycle route' or an 'Atlantic walking trail' (Wise 2000: 875). A number of transport projects have also been funded, such as the ARCANTEL scheme, through which six Atlantic cities sought to rejuvenate ports through use of information technology and the 'Atlantic skyways' concept, which looked at ways to improve airlinks along the Atlantic Arc (Wise 2000: 874).
9   I would like to thank the Basque government for confirming this point (interview 20 December 2006).
10 In both the 1989 (Basque-Aquitaine) and 1992 (Basque-Navarre-Aquitaine) Protocols the partner regions also agreed to 'establish and develop ... permanent institutional relations' to exchange useful information on, and where appropriate, harmonise, their respective policies in economic and social spheres, training and research, and cultural and linguistic heritage. The 1992 Protocol added transport

infrastructure to this list of policy areas. Furthermore, both the 1989 and 1992 Protocols endorsed cooperation to develop and study resources needed for projects of common interest; support collaboration among public, professional and private entities based in their regions; cooperate to deal with the social and economic consequences of the removal of border controls.

11   The two regions have sought to harmonise their transport priorities through technical studies and joint planning. In an annexe to their 1989 Protocol, the two regions agreed to fund joint studies on the demand for and potential traffic flows that could be generated by a HST link between Paris and Madrid via Irún. In 1992, they established a budget, specifications and timetable for conducting a technical study to 'fuse and harmonise' their separate railway plans and for economic analysis examining costs, investment needs and likely sources of finance for the EU's proposed Dax-Vitoria HST link. More recently, the two regions established the Logistical Platform Basque Country-Aquitaine (*Plataforma Logística Aquitania-Euskadi*), which aims to integrate the transport infrastructure networks of Aquitania and the Basque Country (Luaces 2004: 67; *Plataforma Logística Aquitania-Euskadi* 2001: 8).

12   See also *Noticias de Euskadi: Boletín de información sobre la Comunidad Autónoma del País Vasco*, 'Euskadi y Aquitania exigen el desarrollo del Tren de Alta Velocidad', 67, 2003, p. 3.

13   The 1987 Railways Transport Plan proposed adapting rails between the Basque towns of Bilbao and Vitoria for train speeds of between 160 and 200 kilometres an hour and improvements in the track linking the Basque Country to Madrid via Zaragoza (MTTC 1987: 31–2). By publication of the 1994 Master Plan on Infrastructures, planned HST access to the Basque Country had improved markedly, with inclusion of the Basque Y in the state HST network (MOPTMA, 1994: 133 and 148). The Strategic Transport and Infrastructure Plan (2005) included the Basque Y among its plans for a basic network and for high usage lines (Ministerio de Fomento 2005: 94).

14   *BOE*, 157, 3 July 2006, p. 24942.

15   Both Felipe González, the president of the Spanish government, and other leading figures in the PSOE, such as Alfonso Guerra, were from the Andalusian capital Seville, one of the first cities to benefit from HST links.

16   The Conference plenary met once or twice a year between 1988 and 1995, except for 1993 when it did not meet. Meetings were held intermittently from then on, once in 2000, twice in 2001 and once in 2005 (Ortúzar *et al.* 1995: 262 and www.map.es, accessed 20 November 2006). The Conference's technical and administrative support body, *Comisión de Directores Generales de Transportes* (Transport Directors-General Committee), composed of senior officials from both levels of administration, met more frequently at between four and seven times a year (between 1986 and 1993) (Ortúzar 1995: 265).

17   Up to 1995, it only met once at a technical and administrative level (in 1991) (Ortúzar *et al.* 1995: 286–7).

18   It was the only matter discussed at the first two meetings and one of only three matters discussed at the final 1993 plenary meeting (Ortúzar et al 1995: 286–7).

19   *BOE*, 157, 3 July 2006, p. 24942.

20   See contributions by PNV and PSE-PSOE parliamentarians in *DSPV*, 36, 11 September 1988, p. 35 and *DSPV*, 40, 17 February 1989, p. 22.

21   The Basque government made proposals for inclusion of the Vitoria-Dax HST link in the new list of 'quick start' priority projects and a joint proposal with the French Region of Aquitaine. Minutes of Atlantic Arc Commission transport working group, Bilbao, 17 November 2003; Minutes of Transport Intergroup Committee of the CPMR, Brussels, 4–5 December 2003 (www.cprm.org, accessed 20 July 2006).

22   *International Who's Who*, 65th edition (London: Europa Publications, Taylor and

Francis, 2002), p. 879. I would like to thank the Basque government for confirming this point (interview 20 December 2006).

23 Landaburu was also mentioned in the majority of interviews I conducted with Basque politicians and officials as a particularly useful EU contact. One European Commission official also observed that Landaburu made efforts to receive Basque delegations.

24 COM (86) 341 final, 30 June 1986, annexe II and III.

25 COM (86) 341 final, 30 June 1986; COM (89) 238 final, 5 June 1989; COM (89) 643 final, 18 December 1989; OJ, C34, 14 February 1990, p. 13.

26 COM (82) 231 final, 11 June 1992; COM (94) 106 final, 7 April 1994; COM (96) 16 final, 24 January 1996.

27 COM (2001) 544 final, 2 October 2001.

28 European Commission 2001: 53; COM (2001) 544 final, 2 October 2001; Debates of the European Parliament, 2 October 2001; 30 May 2002; 10 March 2004 (www.europarl.europa.eu, consulted 15 November 2006).

29 Atlantic Arc regions have used contacts with the EP for other objectives too. According to Wise, a multinational 'Atlantic Group' of thirty-five MEPs proved influential in getting EP support for EU-financed regional development projects in the Atlantic area (2000: 872).

30 Not surprisingly, this has frequently led Basque nationalists (and others) to call for the creation of regional electoral constituencies for the EP (see for example, Gobierno Vasco 1993, 1996a and 2003)

31 Motion B3–1083/90 in *Report of the European Parliament Committee on Transport and Tourism on a Community Railway policy*, A3–0339/90, 30 November 1990.

32 Motion B2–789/88 and Motion B2–1229/88 in *Report of the European Parliament Committee on Transport and Tourism on the problems of the Railways*, A2–119/89, 25 April 1989; Motion B3–1857/90 in *Report of the European Parliament Committee on Transport and Tourism on a Community Railway policy*, A3–0339/90, 30 November 1990.

33 European Parliament Resolution, *OJ*, C281, 19 October 1987, p. 72.

34 Written Question E-35/1995, *OJ*, C103, 23 January 1995, p. 53; Written Question E-169/1995, *OJ*, C326, 6 December 1995, p. 1; Written Question E-826/1995, *OJ*, C196, 31 July 1995, p. 50.

35 Committee on Regional Policy, Transport and Tourism Report, A5–0135/2002, 23 April 2002, pp. 27–9. See also Debates of the European Parliament, 2 October 2001; 30 May 2002; 10 March 2004 (www.europarl.europa.eu, consulted 15 November 2006). The Christophersen group proposals informed the list of priority projects agreed at the Essen European Summit and later 1996 transEuropean transport network guidelines. The Van Miert group's proposals informed the 2004 transEuropean transport network guidelines.

36 See, for instance, European Parliament resolution, *OJ* C151, 19 June 1995, especially amendments 50, 52 and 90.

37 See European Parliament resolution, *OJ* C151, 19 June 1995, Amendment 91 'In the Annexes maps and links for the trans-European rail network must take into consideration links with the peripheral regions of the Atlantic seaboard so as not to exclude these regions from future projects'; European Parliament decision on Council common positions, *OJ*, C 17, 22 January 1996, Amendment 86 'Links with the peripheral regions of the Atlantic seaboard must be taken into consideration so as not to exclude these regions from future projects'.

38 For European Commission's rejection of the clause see COM (96) 16 final, 24 January 1996. Council's rejection of the Atlantic Arc noted in *OJ*, C17, 22 January 1996, page 58.

39 Debates of the European Parliament, 18 May 1995; 12 December 1995

(www.europarl.europa.eu, consulted September 1999).

40 High-Level Group on the TransEuropean Transport Network, 27 June 2003 (www.europa.eu, consulted 19 November 2006).

41 Committee on Regional Policy, Transport and Tourism Report, A5–0135/2002, 23 April 2002; Committee on Regional Policy, Transport and Tourism Report, A5–0110/2004, 25 February 2004; EP legislative resolution, 20 May 2002, P5_TA(2002)0264; EP legislative resolution 11 March 2004, P5_TA(2004)0173; EP legislative resolution 21 April 2004, P5_TA(2004)0332.

42 Debates of the European Parliament, 2 October 2001; 30 May 2002; 10 March 2004 (www.europarl.europa.eu, consulted 15 November 2006).

43 *OJ*, C210, 14 August 1995, p. 34; *OJ*, C278, 14 November 2002, p. 7. The CoR also delivered an opinion on a 2001 White Paper on Transport Policy (European Commission 2001), see *OJ*, C192, 12 August 2002, p. 8.

44 Draft opinion of CoR transport and communications networks committee, CdR 91/94, 15 July 1994; Revised draft opinion of CoR transport and communications committee, CdR 91/94 rev. 26 July 1994; Opinion of the CoR, *OJ* C210, 14 August 1995, p. 34

45 Record of proceedings of 4th plenary 27/28 September 1994, CdR 190/94, 27 October 1994.

46 Opinion of the CoR, *OJ*, C278, 14 November 2002, p. 7. Similar views on the general importance of the interests of peripheral regions were expressed in draft opinions, see Draft Opinion of the Commission for Territorial Cohesion Policy, CdR 284/2001, 18 February 2002; Draft Opinion of the CoR, CdR, 284/2001 rev. 1, 4 April 2002. It was also expressed in a working document produced by the CoR's Commission for TransEuropean Networks, Transport and Information Society, CdR 95/2001, 12 November 2001.

47 The CoR did, however, include mention of one specific project to improve the navigability of the Danube.

48 Amendments, Draft Opinion of the Commission for Territorial Cohesion Policy, 5 March 2002, CdR 284/2001 Am. 1–10.

49 Record of Proceedings, 44th plenary 15/16 May 2002, CdR 146/2002, 29 May 2002; Amendments, 44th plenary of the CoR, 15 and 16 May 2002, CdR 284/2001 rev.1 Am. 1–11.

6

Basque taxation devolution and the EU's competition imperative

This chapter examines a key episode in a long-running dispute between Basque, central government and certain EU bodies about the scope of politically sensitive Basque taxation powers. The devolution of extensive taxation prerogatives was a central element of the selfgovernment formula negotiated by Basque and central state elite after the dictatorship. The daily application of these powers, however, became controversial. Basque and central authorities confronted each other in the courts and the issue often provoked biting recriminations, especially from Basque nationalists, for whom these taxation prerogatives represent a modernisation of historic practices of selfgovernment. Once Spain joined, various EU bodies took an interest in Basque taxation measures, particularly their compatibility with competition imperatives of the EU's common market. By the late 1990s, the EU began to ask questions which threatened to put new limits on the exercise of Basque selfgovernment in taxation matters. All of this was at stake when the ECJ began to examine Basque taxation measures in a 'preliminary ruling' case close to completion in 1999, which is the principal focus of this chapter.

This case provides a pertinent setting for examining the role that EU actors might play in the legitimisation – or indeed delegitimisation – of regions as authoritative decisionmakers. Officials within the European Commission and the ECJ adopted positions about whether or not it was appropriate, given the objectives of the common market, for substate authorities to adopt certain kinds of taxation initiatives within their territories. The dispute provides another instance in which to examine the dynamics of relations between Basque and state central authorities. Their response to EU-level challenges would have to accommodate a complex set of circumstances. The case involved sensitive issues about Basque selfgovernment and was linked to domestic disputes about Basque taxation, while political incentives made some form of cooperation between Basque and central authorities desirable.

I begin with an examination of the distinctive features of the Basque taxation regime and its political salience in contemporary Basque politics. The second section describes the evolution of EU challenges to Basque taxation measures and examines arguments developed by the European Commission and the ECJ's advocate general, Antonio Saggio, about their compatibility with common market rules. The final section examines Basque government strategies to 'defend' taxation powers against EU challenges and how Basque and central authorities managed to navigate their way through the complexities of this case.

The political significance of the Concierto Económico

It would be difficult to overstate the contemporary political and symbolic importance of Basque taxation devolution. These taxation prerogatives represent a modern form of what the Spanish constitution calls the 'historic rights' of Basque provinces. During the middle ages, Basque provinces developed their own foral laws (*fueros*) regulating governing institutions and customary practices. When the provinces were separately absorbed into the Kingdom of Castille from the thirteenth century, the foral laws set out the mutual rights and obligations of the Crown and each province (de la Cierva 1997: 71–6; Pérez Arraiz 1994: 24–9). Among the rights granted to the latter, was the possibility of rejecting royal edits contrary to local foral laws and exemptions from taxation and military service outside Basque territories. Furthermore, the foral laws established a system in which authority was shared between the monarch, whose representatives managed the affairs of interest to the Crown locally, and provincial institutions, which governed their own private affairs in accordance with distinctive local customs and traditions (de la Cierva 1997: 71–6).

While foral laws in other parts of the Spanish state had been abolished in the eighteenth century, they survived in the Basque Country and Navarre until the nineteenth century. By that time, however, the foral laws were increasingly questioned by those who sought to liberalise and modernise the Spanish state. The defeat of Basque provinces, who sided with the 'old regime' against the liberals in the Carlist civil wars of 1833–39 and 1872–76, provided opportunities to dismantle remaining foral laws. Following defeats in the first Carlist war, an 1839 law subordinated the foral laws to the imperatives of 'constitutional unity' and set in motion a process culminating, after the last Carlist war, in their abolition by 1876. The emasculation of what are now called 'historic rights' became a seed for the development of Basque nationalism and one of its principal grievances against the Spanish state (de la Granja 1995; Letamendia 1994). Claims about the ancient 'original sovereignty' of the Basque territories under the foral laws continue to feature among legitimising rationales employed by Basque nationalists to bolster demands for selfdetermination.

In 1878, the foral laws were replaced with the system of the Economic Agreement (*Concierto Económico*), which gave governing institutions in Álava, Guipúzcoa and Vizcaya significant autonomy over taxation matters (Pérez Arraiz 1994: 45–83). Political elite in Navarre negotiated the modernisation of its foral regime in 1841 and from that point onwards, Navarese institutions exercised taxation prerogatives similar to those of Álava, Guipúzcoa and Vizcaya. Economic Agreements were periodically renewed until 1937, when they were abolished for Guipúzcoa and Vizcaya, which the regime of the dictator General Franco branded 'traitor provinces' for having sided with the democratic second republic during the Spanish civil war. Economic Agreements remained in force for Álava and Navarre, however, which had supported the Francoist insurgents.

Restoration of the Basque taxation regime was a central element of the new democratic constitutional and legal order established after Franco's death in 1975. Alongside general provisions for selfgovernment, and the recognition of certain cultural and political differences, the restoration and modernisation of Basque taxation powers was both an act of reconciliation and a measure to encourage the integration of Basque citizens into the new democratic system (Carr and Fusi 1981; Corcuera 1991; Tamayo 1991). Basque taxation prerogatives, among other things, are guaranteed in the 1978 constitution's first additional disposition, which promises to 'protect and respect the historic rights of the foral territories'. The 1979 Statute of Gernika, which regulates the powers of the Basque autonomous community, confirmed the contemporary legitimacy of the Economic Agreement system. In 1981, Basque and central authorities negotiated a new Economic Agreement for Álava, Guipúzcoa and Vizcaya, which was updated in 2002.[1] Similar arrangements were made for the Foral Community of Navarre, currently enacted in the 1991 Economic Agreement (*Convenio Económico*), reformed in 1997 and 2003. (Due to my focus on politics in the Basque autonomous community, this chapter will not examine taxation arrangements in Navarre.) The new Economic Agreements maintained their traditional character as 'pacts' to be elaborated and modified through negotiations among central and Basque authorities. When formally enacting the Economic Agreements in the Spanish parliament, a single reading procedure is employed where parliamentarians issue a vote (to accept, reject or abstain) on the text negotiated by Basque and central authorities, without introducing amendments altering its content.

In both its 1981 and current version, the Economic Agreement for Álava, Guipúzcoa and Vizcaya gave these 'historic territories' competence to 'maintain, establish and regulate, within their territories, their taxation system' and responsibility for 'levying, administration, settlement, inspection, revision and collection of the taxes and duties comprising the(ir) taxation system'.

Basque authorities are competent to regulate and collect the majority of taxes levied in their territories, including personal income tax, corporation tax, inheritance and gift taxes, among others (Aja 2003: 87). Furthermore, the Basque historic territories transfer a preagreed amount of their tax revenue to the state, called the quota (*cupo*). The quota is a fixed amount negotiated every five years to pay a share of state services not assumed by the historic territories and Basque autonomous community. In contrast, the system applied to finance other autonomous communities (except Navarre) sees income generated by their more limited taxation powers bolstered by a share of central government taxation receipts, with some light variations for the Canary Islands (Aja 2003: 134–47).

The Economic Agreements impose some limitations on Basque taxation powers. While most important taxes are regulated by the historic territories, some remain exclusive state competence. Since 2002, these have been reduced to import duties and import levies included under Excise Duties and Value Added Tax. The Basque taxation regime must have 'regard' to the general tax structure in Spain and the constitutional principle of interterritorial solidarity. All parties to the Economic Agreement are to be guided by the principle of 'fiscal harmonisation' which includes the requirement that historic territories maintain an overall tax burden 'equivalent' to that of the rest of Spain. 'Harmonisation' also requires historic territories to:

> respect and guarantee freedom of circulation and establishment of persons and the free movement of goods, capital and services throughout the territory of Spain, without giving rise to discrimination or a lessening of the possibilities of commercial competition or to distortion in the allocation of resources.

They must also comply with international agreements and treaties entered into by the state.

It is important to note that while taxation competencies belong to the historic territories, institutions of the Basque autonomous community do play a role in this field. The Basque government takes part in ongoing Economic Agreement negotiations; the Basque parliament approves laws related to coordination, harmonisation and collaboration among the historic territories; and, crucially, the Basque government has taken a lead defending the Basque taxation system before the EU.

All main Basque nationalist parties and statewide parties, including those habitually governing at the state level, accept the contemporary legitimacy of the Economic Agreement system. The 2002 Economic Agreement, for instance, was approved in the Spanish parliament with near unanimity and support from all main parties represented in the parliament.[2] However, misgivings have been raised about the implications of certain Economic Agreement reforms and about certain measures operationalising the Economic Agreement. Concerns have been raised about purported 'privileges' granted to Basque citizens through the Economic Agreement system, its effects on the fiscal unity of the state, the equality of tax burdens and financial 'solidarity' with the rest of the state (Pérez Arraiz 1994: 241–51). Such issues have been raised since negotiation of the Statute of Gernika (Tamayo 1991: 110) and, more recently, they motivated PSOE's abstention in a parliamentary vote approving Economic Agreement reforms in 1997.[3]

Initially, taxation measures operationalising the Economic Agreement produced few significant tensions (Zubiri 2000: 113–28). In the late 1980s, however, when the historic territories began introducing measures creating profounder differences between Basque and common taxation systems, conflict increased. From 1988, the Spanish government initiated a series of legal challenges, sometimes with support from the governments and business confederations of neighbouring autonomous communities. Basque corporation tax rules, including tax credits for certain kinds of productive investments and so-called 'fiscal vacations', which provide tax exemptions or reductions for new companies, were a particular focus of legal challenges (*El País*, 2 March 1999; Ortiz de Arri, *El País*, 9 June 1999; *Expansión*, 7 October 1999). Such laws have been challenged on the grounds that measures were 'dispropotionate' and distorted the free movement of goods, persons, capital and services within the state.

Tension between Basque and central authorities over application of the Economic Agreement increased considerably during the 1990s. Indeed, by January 2000, there were around a hundred central-government-initiated challenges to Basque taxation measures awaiting judgement in the courts (Zubiri 2000: 114). This judicialisation of the Economic Agreement set in train lengthy processes of challenge, counter-challenge and appeal, which could take years to resolve (Zubiri 2000: 114). The press routinely came to refer to the disagreement with metaphors of 'war' and moves to resolve them with those of 'peace' (Damborenea and Ortiz de Arri, *El País*, 18 January 2000 and 19 January 2000; Oregui, *El País*, 23 January 2000). Senior figures in the Basque government and historic territories accused the central government of wanting to undermine the Economic Agreement. The PNV's Félix Ormazabal (when deputy general of Álava) considered key court judgements a 'campaign, orchestrated in Madrid by the statist parties to harass and demolish everything Basque' (Angulo, *El País*, 3 March 1999). The PNV's Josu Bergara (when PNV deputy general of Vizcaya), made similar charges against the central government, commenting that 'we live in perpetual fear and harassment by those who challenge our historic rights' (Fuentes, *Expansión*, 15 January 1999). Senior figures from the central government, including Rodrigo Rato (when Economics Minister), Juan Costa (when Secretary of State for Finance) and Josep Piqué (when Industry Minister) repeatedly denied these charges, arguing that the central government did not question the Economic Agreement itself, only the way it had been applied (Angulo, *El País*, 3 March 1999; Álvarez, *El Correo*, 3 March 1999 and 4 May 1999; Lezana, *El Correo*, 7 March 1999).

EU challenges to Basque taxation prerogatives

The EC Treaty gives the European Commission powers to supervise member state activity which might affect free trade between member states and competition between European firms – both basic ingredients of the EU's common market. EU institutions' concerns about Basque taxation measures have been similar to those arising in Spain, focusing on the potentially distorting effects of tax credits, reductions or other concessions, on competition and free movement. While in its earlier investigations the European Commission showed some sensitivity towards the historical and political significance of Basque tax prerogatives, in more recent episodes European Commission and ECJ officials came to defend positions which would ultimately reduce the scope of Basque taxation prerogatives.

In 1988, the European Commission launched the first of a series of procedures questioning the legality of Basque taxation measures under EU rules. In its 1993 Decision,[4] the European Commission ruled that certain Basque tax measures were illegal because they contravened treaty provisions relating to the free movement of persons. However, in an unusual move, it granted a short transition period to allow the negotiation of amendments to the Economic Agreement (Pariente de la Prada 1994: 205). The European Commission justified this decision with reference to 'the special features of this case and the historical nature of the tax relationship between the central government and the Basque Country'.

The conclusion of this episode, however, did not put an end to acrimony over Basque taxation measures. Indeed challenges from the EU level increased significantly (Zubiri 2000: 191–3; Muguruza 1999; Sobrido 2003). In the late 1990s, the European Commission initiated further proceedings questioning the legality of specific tax concessions granted to individual firms in the Basque Country, including those promised as part of a deal to attract the much sought-after South Korean firm Daewoo. As Table 6.1 shows, Community Courts were soon drawn into the affair as Basque authorities began appealing European Commission Decisions and when, in 1997, a Spanish court asked the ECJ to make a preliminary ruling on the legality of Basque measures offering tax deductions and exemptions to encourage productive investments. In cases involving EU law, national courts must refer questions about the interpretation of EU law to the ECJ in what is known as a 'preliminary ruling' procedure. This request for a preliminary ruling arose in a case which had been initiated by the Spanish central government in the national courts, a fact which would later complicate collaboration among Basque and central authorities when it came to defending the Basque taxation regime before the ECJ.

Table 6.1 Basque taxation measures before European Community courts 1997–2006

Action	Issues	Outcome
1. Preliminary ruling referred by Spanish Court to ECJ	In a case bought to national courts by the Spanish government against urgent Basque tax measures aiding investment and promoting economic activity, the national court asked the ECJ to interpret treaty provisions on free movement and state aid.	An ECJ advocate general characterised tax measures as state aid and provisions contravening freedom of establishment, but the case was archived before ECJ reached judgement (see below).
2. Annulment proceedings against Commission Decision 1999/718/EC	Basque authorities and the firm Daewoo challenge characterisation of certain economic advantages, grants, tax credits and reductions in tax base given to Daewoo as illegal state aid.	The CFI accept a partial annulment, but Álava's 45 per cent tax credits for certain investments were characterised as illegal state aids. An ECJ appeal failed.
3. Annulment proceedings against Commission Decision 2000/795/EC	Alavan authorities challenge initiation of proceedings and suspension of measures granting tax credits and reducing the tax base for the firm Ramondin, measures characterised as illegal state aid.	The CFI upheld characterisation of measures as illegal state aid. An ECJ appeal failed.
4. Annulment proceedings against initiation of European Commission investigation	Basque authorities challenge initiation of investigation into schemes offering 45 per cent tax credits for investments in new fixed assets. They argue tax measures at issue are not illegal state aid.	CFI reject all Basque authorities' arguments.
5. Annulment proceedings against initiation of European Commission investigation	Basque authorities challenge initiation of investigation into schemes offering reduction of tax base by 99, 75, 50 and 25 per cent over four years for new businesses. They argue tax measures at issue are not illegal state aid.	CFI reject all Basque authorities' arguments

Table 6.1 Continued

Action	Issues	Outcome
6. Annulment proceedings against Commission Decision 2001/168/ECSC	Basque authorities challenge characterisation of tax deductions for steel undertakings' export activities as illegal state aid.	CFI ruled case was inadmissible because Basque authorities were not entitled to initiate proceedings. An ECJ appeal failed.
7. Annulment proceedings against various Commission Decisions.	Basque authorities challenge characterisation of measures providing tax exemptions for new companies as illegal state aid.	Judgements pending (as of 20 October 2006)
8. Annulment proceedings against various Commission Decisions	Basque authorities challenge characterisation of Basque taxation measures providing 45 per cent tax credits for investments in new fixed assets and reductions of 99, 75, 50 and 25 per cent in the tax base for new firms.	Judgements pending (as 20 October 2006)
9. Infringement proceedings against Spain	Initiated by the European Commission for Basque authorities' failure to comply with various Commission Decisions relating to taxation measures offering 45 per cent tax credits and concessions for new firms.	Judgement pending (as of October 2006)

Notes: **1.** *OJ* C41, 7 February 1998, p. 9; Opinion of Mr. Advocate General Antonio Saggio of 1 July 1999, European Court Reports, 2000, I-01037; *OJ* C135, 13 May 2000, p. 10. **2.** *OJ* L292, 13 November 1999, p. 1; *OJ* C156, 29 June 2002, p. 16; *OJ* C180, 27 July 2002, p. 9; *OJ* C180, 27 July 2002, p. 11; *OJ* C6, 8 January 2005, p. 2. **3.** *OJ* L318, 16 December 2000, p. 61; *OJ* C156, 29 June 2002, p. 16; *OJ* C191, 10 August 2002, p. 15; *OJ* C191, 10 August 2002, p. 16; *OJ* C6, 8 January 2005, p. 3. **4.** *OJ* C71, 11 March 2000, p. 8; *OJ* C351, 4 December 1999, p. 29; *OJ* C19, 25 January 2003, p. 28. **5.** *OJ* C55, 26 February 2000, p. 2; *OJ* C19, 25 January 2003, p. 28. **6.** *OJ* L60, 1 March 2001, p. 57; Order of the CFI, 11 January 2002; *OJ* C213 6 September 2003, p. 4. **7.** Relevant Commission Decisions are: 2003/28/EC, *OJ* L17, 22 January 2003, p. 20; 2003/86/EC, *OJ* L40, 14 February 2003, p. 11; 2003/192/EC, *OJ* L77, 24 March 2003, p. 1; *OJ* C144, 15 June 2002, p. 52. **8.** Relevant Commission Decisions are: 2002/820/EC of 11 July 2001, *OJ* L296 of 30 October 2002, p. 1; 2002/894/EC of 11 July 2001, *OJ* L314, 18 November 2002, p. 26; 2003/27/EC of 11 July 2001, *OJ* L017, 22 January 2003, p. 1; 2002/892/EC of 11 July 2001, *OJ* L314, 18 November 2002, p. 1; 2002/540/EC of 11 July 2001, *OJ* L174, 4 July 2002, p. 31; 2002/806/EC of 11 July 2001; *OJ* L279, 17 October 2002, p. 35; see also *OJ* C331, 24 July 2001, pp. 29–32; *OJ* C348, 8 December 2001, p. 24. **9.** Relevant Commission decisions are listed in point 8. above. *OJ* C21, 24 January 2004, p. 21.

Additionally, Basque taxation measures came to be questioned in the context of the EU's fiscal harmonisation agenda, gathering steam in the wake of economic and monetary union (Zubiri 2000: 194; Muguruza 1998; Radaelli 1999). In December 1997, EU finance ministers unanimously approved a Code of Conduct on Business Taxation which aimed to tackle harmful tax competition.[5] In the Code, member states agreed not to introduce new tax measures which might harm competition and to reexamine existing measures, amending or eliminating harmful laws and practices as soon as possible. Basque tax measures featured on the agenda of the Fiscal Policy Group, a team of high-level member state representatives given the task of detecting potentially harmful taxation practices and to propose modification or abolition (Zubiri 2000: 194; Muguruza 1998: 7; *El País*, 31 May 1999).

By the late 1990s, the ECJ's preliminary ruling case had come to take centre stage and it is this episode which I examine in detail in the rest of the chapter. The Basque taxation measures at issue – one for each historic territory – offered tax deductions and exemptions for the creation of new companies and other productive investments. For instance, in Guipúzcoa, regulations offered deductions of between 5 and 100 per cent for business investment in activities such as acquisition of new fixed assets, research and development, export promotions, capital investment in small and medium-sized businesses, creation of permanent employment and workforce training.[6] Newly established businesses could, under certain conditions, be exempt from paying company tax for ten years. In its preliminary ruling petition, the Spanish court – Superior Court of Justice of the Basque Country (*Tribunal Superior de Justicia del País Vasco*) – asked the ECJ to consider whether these taxation incentives were incompatible with articles 43 (ex 52) and 87 (ex 92) of the EC Treaty on, respectively, freedom of establishment and the prohibition of state aids. The matter of compatibility with provisions on freedom of establishment was the lesser issue and, according to specialist commentators, was resolved by 1997 modifications of the Economic Agreement (Muguruza 1999: 8–9; Zubiri 2000: 192).

The central issue of the case was the essentially technical matter of defining the nature of the Basque taxation system for purposes of EU competition law. On the one hand, the taxation regimes of the historic territories could be considered part of the Spanish state's common system of taxation, a view held by the European Commission and the ECJ advocate general assigned to the case, Antonio Saggio.[7] On the other hand, the taxation regimes of the historic territories could be considered distinctive systems, equivalent to the general taxation systems of other, individual member states.[8] This is the position Basque authorities and the Spanish central government defended. The distinction was important because it determined which treaty provisions covered regulation of the disputed taxation measures.

If the Basque taxation regimes were characterised as part of the Spanish state's common system, Basque taxation measures attributing a competitive advantage to businesses operating in the Basque Country would be considered 'regional state aid'. In this case, EC Treaty articles 87 and 88 (ex 92 and 93) would apply. Article 87 establishes, with some exceptions, the principle that state aids which 'distort or threaten to distort competition' are illegal, while article 88 gives the European Commission extensive powers to supervise and approve plans to grant or alter state aids. On this interpretation of the nature of the Basque taxation systems, Basque authorities' powers to act in the field of taxation would be limited in two ways. In the first place, their taxation measures would have to be approved by the European Commission like other state aids. Secondly, as specialist commentators point out, the scope of the historic territories' autonomy to regulate tax contributions of companies operating in the Basque Country would be significantly reduced (Muguruza 1999: 9–10; Zubiri 2000: 197–8). More specifically, it would open the way for legal challenges to tax measures which lowered companies' taxation obligations relative to those in effect in the rest of the state. This would imply, as Zubiri spells out, an 'emptying out of a substantial part of the content of the Economic Agreement ... and the loss of an important instrument of economic regulation' (2000: 197).

In contrast, if the taxation regimes of the historic territories were considered distinctive systems equivalent to those of other individual member states, those very same taxation measures may not be considered regional state aids. Rather, as the ECJ's advocate general Antonio Saggio explained, they could be considered 'measures of a general character that form part ... of the political-economic decisions of the state, uncontrollable at the Community level within the terms of articles 87 and 88 and subject ... to other less rigorous Treaty provisions'. The less rigorous treaty provisions referred to were those in article 93 (ex 99) of the EC Treaty, which set out procedures for the Council to harmonise state taxation legislation where this helped operation of the common market. On this interpretation, Basque authorities would still be required to comply with provisions of the Treaty. However, they would not have to submit measures like those challenged in this case for European Commission approval and the scope of objectives their taxation measures could pursue would be wider than that allowed with the alternative interpretation.

The European Commission and the advocate general supported this second interpretation. Both considered it appropriate to prioritise the objectives of the common market rather than accept asymmetrical forms of taxation devolution like that in the Basque Country as a special case. The advocate general argued that if the internal organisation of a state were a satisfactory justification,

> the state could easily avoid the application, in a part of its own territory, of [European] Community provisions on state aids simply by introducing modifications in the internal distribution of competencies ... so as to be able to invoke the 'general' character of the measures applied in this particular territory.

For his part, the competition commissioner Karel van Miert acknowledged that he too considered disputed applications of the Basque taxation regime a 'dangerous precedent' (Segovia, *El Mundo*, 15 July 1999). In short, if the peculiarities of the Basque taxation system were considered acceptable, other EU states might then devolve taxation prerogatives like those exercised by Basque authorities, which would, in turn, amplify distortions to competition in the common market.

In theory, at least, the European Commission and the advocate general could have taken an opposite view. They could have recognised the uniqueness of historic traditions and practices upon which taxation devolution in Spain is based and made the Basque taxation regime a special case. This would have involved incorporating the practices of shared sovereignty in taxation matters prevalent at state level into the EU system, a move that would have added a new dimension to the already complex pattern of shared sovereignty in the EU. Earlier, the European Commission had considered the Basque taxation regime a 'special case' when it was necessary to rectify problems with the Economic Agreement, but when it came to the competition imperatives of the common market, the European Commission's view was less sanguine. Successive competition commissioners (Karel Van Miert and Mario Monti) emphatically denied questioning the legitimacy of the Basque taxation regime as such and declared that their concern was in the way it had been applied (Segovia, *El Mundo*, 15 July 1999; *El Correo*, 17 September 1999). But with the advocate general, the European Commission nevertheless considered the distribution of taxation competencies within a state 'merely a formal circumstance' which could not justify preferential treatment given to businesses regulated by Basque taxation laws.

Similar issues were raised in a more recent case involving income and corporation tax reductions in The Azores, Portugal.[9] It is not entirely clear how ECJ judgements affect the Basque Economic Agreement, but the case shows an important evolution in EU thinking on how regional taxation measures ought to be evaluated in state aid rulings (Pescador, *El Correo Digital*, 7 September 2006; *El Correo Digital*, 7 September 2006a and 2006b). While the European Commission continued to hold its restrictive view, the ECJ accepted that, under certain conditions, it would be appropriate to evaluate both regional and member state taxation matters according to similar criteria for state aid purposes. The conditions were that contested taxation decisions were made by regional or local authorities with a separate, constitutionally-specified, political and administrative status; that the central government could not directly determine the content of the taxation measure; and that financial consequences of the measure were met by the region itself, rather than being offset by aid or subsidies from another region or the central government. Although the ruling does not refer to Basque authorities, the Economic Agreement appears to meet these criteria. Basque leaders considered the ruling 'important' and 'positive', and argued that it must 'end political and legal attacks' on the Economic Agreement and Basque selfgovernment (*El Correo Digital*, 7 September 2006b). It remains to be seen how the judgement will affect national and EU-level disputes on Basque taxation measures.

Conflict, cooperation and the defence of devolution

In the months leading up to July 1999, when the advocate general published his influential opinion in the preliminary ruling case before the ECJ, fears and suspicions about the implication of EU challenges to the Basque taxation regime reached a peak.[10] Senior figures in the Basque government and the historic territories pointed to dramatic consequences if the ECJ ruled against them. EU-level challenges were interpreted as an attack on the Economic Agreement and the constitutional framework in which 'historic rights' were enshrined (Lezana, *El Correo*, 7 March 1999). The president of the Basque government, Juan José Ibarretxe, spoke of the impending 'death' of the Economic Agreement (Ormazabal, *Cinco Días*, 4 July 1999). The PNV's Josu Bergara (when deputy general of Vizcaya) saw the ECJ case as an event in which 'our [right to] be or not to be is at stake' and threatened 'revolt and non-cooperation' on the part of Basque institutions (Álvarez, *El Correo*, 4 May 1999; Fuentes, *Expansión*, 15 January 1999). The PNV's Román Sudupe (when deputy general of Guipúzcoa) considered a renegotiation of political formulas guaranteeing 'historic rights' in order if Basque authorities lost the ECJ case (Lezana, *El Correo*, 7 March 1999). The Basque government's spokesperson, Josu Jon Imaz, accused central and EU authorities of trying to impose 'uniformity' (Álvarez, *El Correo*, 4 May 1999).

At a deeper level, doubts were raised about whether 'prior mental schemes' were behind EU officials' perceived failure to appreciate the 'real' nature of the Economic Agreement as an 'independent taxation system in itself'.[11] This impression has been articulated in interviews with Basque politicians conducted by the author, but also in newspaper reports and parliamentary debates. Rafael Larreina, when secretary-general of EA, thought 'the Commissioners are at the service of the states and for that reason they don't understand, or do not want to understand, [Basque tax powers]'.[12] José Ramón Bengoetxea, when EA's viceminister for employment in the Basque government, expressed similar views about the ECJ advocate general's 'failure', or 'unwillingness', to understand the nature of the Basque taxation system.[13] This concern persisted for many years after the ECJ initiated its preliminary ruling case, however. It was cited as a key motive behind Basque government insistence that the renovation of the Economic Agreement in 2001–2 be firmly linked with a Basque presence in the EU's Council (see chapter four). Basque participation in Council discussions of taxation matters was considered pressing, not only because Basque authorities had very extensive taxation powers affected by EU decisions, but also in order to help EU authorities 'better understand' that the Economic Agreement was not a 'camouflage for subsidies' or a special 'privilege that undermined competition laws' (Aizpeolea, *El País*, 17 May 2001; Ibarretxe 1998: 190).

It is interesting to note, however, that interpretations of the implications of EU challenges could divide along partisan lines. Indeed, when the Basque president, Juan José Ibarretxe, tried along rally support for an institutional declaration emphasising the EU 'threat' to the Economic Agreement, he found the support of most Basque nationalists and key business associations. However, the most important trade unions, the PSE-PSOE, the PPV and other Basque opposition parties did not sign up to the Declaration (*El Correo*, 23 July 1999).

In addition to concerns about misunderstanding in Brussels and Luxembourg, some Basque leaders were suspicious about the sincerity of central government commitments to defend the Economic Agreement (Lezana, *El Correo*, 7 March 1999; Álvarez, *El Correo*, 4 May 1999). Concerns followed from the high number of central-government-initiated challenges to Basque taxation measures in the Spanish courts. But the fact that one such central government legal challenge was the basis for the ECJ preliminary ruling case raised particular doubts. The central government rejected arguments questioning its commitment to defend the Economic Agreement in the EU. Senior government ministers promised, as Secretary of State for Finance Juan Costa announced, to:

> defend the Economic Agreement in every moment and the legislative powers that are derived from it ... [even if] at the internal level, the central and the Basque autonomous administrations disagree at times about certain uses that the [historic territories] make of their legislative powers (Pescador, *El Correo*, 4 May 1999).[14]

It was in this context, that Basque president Ibarretxe claimed defence of the Economic Agreement for the Basque government, a defence whose primary objective would be to make EU officials 'understand' the 'real' nature of the Basque taxation system (*El Correo*, 23 July 1999; Lezana, *El Correo*, 17 December 1998).

As spelt out in chapter four, regional, local and other territorial entities within member states have only limited standing before Community Courts (Ordóñez 2003; Evans 2003). However, as authors of disputed tax provisions, able to establish that EU acts were of direct and individual concern to them, Basque authorities have often participated as litigants in cases before Community Courts (see Table 6.1). Furthermore, as authorities implicated in national disputes giving rise to the preliminary ruling case under examination here, Basque authorities were able to intervene and submit arguments in ECJ deliberations (Lezana, *El Correo*, 4 May 1999; Pescador, *El Correo*, 4 May 1999). Throughout the course of various European Commission investigations into Basque taxation measures, Basque authorities maintained direct contacts with the European Commission. These contacts took a variety of forms, ranging from submission of information and observations, to formal meetings in Brussels and the Basque Country (Sobrido 2003: 435, 500).

Given that disputes were largely played out in the courts, Basque involvement or links with other EU bodies would be of limited use. In the EP and CoR Basque authorities could, at most, hope to publicise their cause and find moral support from other members. There is no evidence in Basque government reports on CoR activity that it used the CoR to such ends (Gobierno Vasco 1998 and 2004). Parties governing Basque authorities did, however, exploit political links with the EP through the agency of the Basque nationalist MEP, Gorka Knörr (EA). Knörr tabled a question to competition commissioner, Mario Monti, requesting further meetings with Basque delegates and asking for clarification on Monti's views about the compatibility of the Economic Agreement with the EC Treaty (*El Correo*, 17 September 1999).

Paradoxically, the involvement of both central and Basque authorities in this case provided ample opportunities for cooperation, even though they were rival litigants in the initial state-level dispute. Disagreement over Basque taxation measures had been aired in both the Senate's General Commission for Autonomous Communities, at the initiative of a Basque nationalist senator (EA), and in the Mixed Commission for the EU, at the initiative of the PSOE (then in opposition).[15] But neither of these bodies served as fora for the resolution of disputes or for negotiation of common positions on Basque taxation matters. In contrast, the dispute was an ideal agenda item for the Basque-State Bilateral Commission for EU affairs, given the specificity of Basque taxation powers. During the brief period in which the Bilateral Commission was operational, there is evidence that EU challenges to taxation measures were discussed in this forum (Castro and Ugalde 2004).

Despite Basque suspicions about central government intentions, Basque and central government authorities presented compatible arguments in the early stages of the ECJ proceedings. Both Basque and central authorities had been against the national court's decision to submit a preliminary ruling request to the ECJ in the first place (Sobrido 2003: 438; Muguruza 1999: 7). Basque and central authorities argued that the ECJ should not admit the preliminary ruling request because aspects of the disputed tax provisions supposedly conflicting with EU law had already been rectified (Sobrido 2003: 438; Muguruza 1999: 9).[16] Furthermore, as mentioned above, Basque and central authorities held the same view about the nature of Basque taxation systems in the EU context. In defence of this position, both Basque and central governments appealed to the sanctity of state constitutional arrangements underpinning Basque taxation prerogatives. They did not hold back from using the argument that a negative ruling 'would be the same as emitting a value judgement on the constitutional structure of the Spanish state'. The central government was even prepared to put its name to the argument that Basque taxation prerogatives were akin to those of any 'sovereign' taxation authority, and that differences between taxation competencies of the Spanish state and the historic territories were equivalent to differences between EU member states. At this time, the use of such terminology was not without political risk, given the intensity of domestic debates about the nature of Basque rights to selfdetermination, the future of Basque selfgovernment and appropriate responses to ETA's ceasefire in the immediate aftermath of the Lizarra Declaration (see chapter two).

Moreover, when the advocate general published his opinion rejecting the arguments of Basque and state authorities in July 1999, the risk that the ECJ might concur produced decisive collaboration. This point was a critical juncture. A ruling by the ECJ carried the risk of establishing an unwanted and restrictive definition of the Basque taxation system as ECJ doctrine. The implications of such a decision would provide, as one commentator described it, 'oxygen' for European Commission challenges characterising other Basque taxation measures as illegal state aid and raise the prospect of further legal challenges against Basque measures establishing lower tax obligations than those at state level (Muguruza 1999: 10). However, there was one way of resolving the question, or at least postponing it: The central government could withdraw the legal challenge in the Spanish court which had referred the question to the ECJ in the first place.

Pursuing this option in the wake of the advocate general's opinion, the initiation of negotiations among Basque and central government authorities returned the conflict to the realm of Spanish politics. In January 2000, after six months of intense negotiations, and more than ten years of disputes over Basque taxation measures, Basque and central government authorities agreed the so-called 'fiscal pact' (Armentia and Barrasa 2001; Zubiri 2000: 236–41; Damborenea and Ortiz de Arri, *El País Digital,* 19 January 2000). Significantly, the pact was negotiated outside the formal framework for collaboration between Basque and central authorities on EU matters. It was agreed in the Mixed Commission for the Quota (*Comisión Mixta del Cupo*), a special body established in the 1981 Economic Agreement for negotiating the formula for, and amount of, Basque contributions to state services (Armentia and Barrasa 2001; Alonso Arce 2004).

The pact, which had a lifespan of two years, was designed to reduce the judicialisation of the Economic Agreement and to promote more cooperative relations between Basque and central authorities. The central government agreed to withdraw pending legal challenges, while Basque authorities agreed to withdraw appeals against court decisions and to abolish or modify some of the most contentious tax measures. Basque and central government authorities agreed to create a *Comisión de Evaluación* (monitoring committee) to examine the appropriateness of existing and future measures. Furthermore, both parties promised to 'defend' the Economic Agreement in both domestic and international spheres.

In the short term, the fiscal pact produced the desired effect. Once the central government withdrew its suit against disputed Basque taxation measures, the Spanish court subsequently withdrew its request for the ECJ preliminary ruling and the case was dropped. In the longer term, this did not produce a definitive end to conflict over the compatibility of Basque taxation measures and EU law. Challenges continued in the national courts (Alonso 2005; Rodríguez 2005) and, as Table 6.1 shows, the European Commission and Basque authorities continue to argue over the legality of Basque taxation measures in the Community Courts.

Negotiation of what came to be known as the 'fiscal peace' took place in a context of acute political differences between the PP central government and the Basque-nationalist-run autonomous community government. This was the time of serious confrontation between Basque nationalist and statewide parties over responses to ETA's 1998 ceasefire and the Lizarra process (see chapter two). The fact that Basque and central authorities managed to negotiate the fiscal pact at such a difficult time raises some important questions. What explains their collaboration in taxation matters? There are a number of possible responses to this question.

Basque nationalists and parties governing in Madrid shared the legacy of the century-long history of conflict over taxation devolution and experience of shared taxation sovereignty. Both had reaffirmed their commitment to protect historic Basque prerogatives in this field as an integral part of the postFranco devolution settlement and in the course of subsequent Economic Agreement reforms. In other words, they both had a stake in the political compromise that underpinned the Basque taxation systems.

Another explanation may be found in the configuration of party-political links. The Economic Agreement had been a central element of an agreement reached between the PP and the PNV at the outset of the PP's period of minority government (see Table 3.5). The PP and the PNV had committed themselves to propel 'institutional dialogue' on the Economic Agreement (*La Vanguardia*, 30 April 1996), and, in 1997, the PP had agreed to amend the Economic Agreement to strengthen Basque powers in taxation matters. The legislative pact between the two parties did not prevent the PP government from challenging Basque taxation measures in the Spanish courts. But it did establish a prior pattern of cooperation on Basque taxation matters and an explicit recognition of the central government's commitment to the Economic Agreement. These developments made it more difficult, politically, for the Spanish central government to avoid supporting Basque authorities in the ECJ dispute.

Another factor explaining the central government's support may have been the proximity of ECJ proceedings to the March 2000 Spanish general election. By supporting the Basque position in the EU and, more specifically, negotiating the 'fiscal peace' just months before the election, the PP was able to diffuse what was a highly contentious and potentially damaging issue for the PP in the Basque Country. As one commentator suggested, president Aznar 'was trying to show public opinion in the Basque Country that his grave strategic differences with the PNV on the peace process are not going to affect institutional relations between his government and that of [the Basque nationalists]' (Aizpeolea, *El País Digital*, 4 January 2000).

Basque authorities had their own compelling reasons to seek a settlement. They had most to lose from a negative ruling because it was their taxation powers which were at stake. Basque businesses were unhappy with the level of uncertainty brought with the conflict and, as some of the Basque nationalists' most important supporters on the question of the Economic Agreement, their calls for central and Basque government negotiations had to be taken seriously (*El Correo*, 10 December 1999). Furthermore, the PPV's election victory in the historic territory of Álava in June 1999 meant the loss of an important Basque nationalist powerbase; when the PPV's-led administration in Álava began abolishing some of the most contentious taxation measures, the strength of the Basque position took a serious blow (Ortiz de Arri, *El País Digital*, 31 December 1999).

From the foregoing it is possible to conclude that supranational actors are not necessarily the champions of regional interests in EU politics. In this case, supranational actors supported ideas that would effectively reduce the scope of Basque taxation competencies. Furthermore, it is evident that, while relations between Basque and central authorities have rarely been easy, there may be more 'political glue' binding territorial authorities within Spain than those beyond it. EU authorities do not have the same stake in the historically significant political compromise that Basque taxation devolution represents. Nor do EU authorities need to act with an eye on the next election or take into account the interests of coalition or other types of party partnerships. In the Basque taxation dispute all these factors were present and may have provided deeper foundations for constructing a strategic coalition between Basque and central government authorities.

Notes

1 Ley 12/1981, de 12 de mayo, *BOE*, 127, 28 May 1981, p. 11677; Ley 12/2002, de 23 de mayo, *BOE*, 124, section 1, 24 May 2002, p. 18617.
2 *DSCG, Congreso, Pleno y Diputación Permanente*, 155, 18 April 2002, p. 7897.
3 *DSCG, Congreso, Pleno y Diputación Permanente*, 94, 24 June 1997, p. 4714.
4 Decision 93/337/EEC of 10 May 1993, *OJ* L134, 3 June 1993, p. 25.
5 *OJ*, C2, 6 January 1998, p. 2.
6 *Normativa Foral* 11/1993 (Guipúzcoa), *BOPV*, 175, 14 September 1993, p. 8335.
7 Opinion of Mr. Advocate General Antonio Saggio of 1 July 1999, *European Court Reports*, 2000, I-010371 July, Luxembourg 1999.
8 See text of Opinion of Mr. Advocate General Antonio Saggio of 1 July 1999, *European Court Reports*, 2000, I-01037. See also statement by Secretary of State for Economy, Sr. Montoro Romero in *DSCG, Comisión Mixta para la Unión Europea*, Series A, no.

113, 29 July 1997, p. 1112.

9   Case C-88/03, *OJ*, C112, 10 May 2003, p. 11 and *OJ*, C261 of 28 October 2006, p. 1.

10 According to ECJ procedure, the advocate general's position is delivered before the ECJ makes its final judgement and is not binding. However, the advocate general's opinion is extremely influential given that the ECJ follows the advocate general's advice in most cases (Kennedy 2006: 128).

11 Comments by Rafael Larreina, when secretary-general of EA *DSPV*, no. 6, 12 February 1999.

12 These views were expressed in an interview with the author on 15 September 1999, Vitoria, the Basque Country.

13 Interview with author, 24 September 1999, Vitoria, the Basque Country.

14 For similar statements by Josep Piqué, central government Industry Minister see Álvarez, *El Correo*, 4 May 1999).

15 See *DSCG, Senado, Comisiones*, 160, 23 June 1997, p. 1; *DSCG, Senado, Comisiones*, 166, 30 June 1997, p. 1; *BOCG*, Series A, 114, 29 July 1997, p. 4; *DSCG, Comisiones*, 59, 16 June 1997, p. 1110.

16 Opinion of Mr. Advocate General Antonio Saggio of 1 July 1999, *European Court Reports*, 2000, I-01037.

CONCLUSION

Construction of the Spanish state of autonomies was a political juncture of historic importance for the Basque Country. Devolution provided tools to address many longstanding grievances and fears: It ended the historic exclusion of Basque nationalism from government; Basque government policies helped address the decline of the Basque language; Basque police services operate alongside state security services; Basque provincial institutions, traditions and powers have been given new life; and the Basque elite have an institutional foothold from which they can conduct relations with state authorities. Devolution, in some form or other, has been embraced by the majority of Basque citizens. It has not, however, resolved nationalist conflict. Deep divisions in Basque society persist; divisions defined by complex patterns of identification and entrenched political cleavages. A large number of Basque citizens want more autonomy than that which many others are happy to accept. Basque institutions have, at some points, served as a consociational framework regulating such differences. However, since the late 1990s, this institutional framework has been a source of tension in Basque society as major parties adopted contrasting positions about whether, and how, to reform it. Democratisation and devolution provided a setting in which ETA struggled to maintain credibility and operational capabilities, but it still remains to be seen whether democratisation and some form of devolution can close ETA down for good.

The EU has been much more than a trivial or incidental aspect of Basque experiences of selfgovernment. The observation that governance in the EU is now, in a general sense, multilevel governance, holds true for the Basque case. Basque, state and EU competencies overlap in many spheres and EU policies affect Basque powers and interests, including some with special symbolic and political salience. EU rules and institutional adaptations within Spain have gradually opened up channels for a Basque presence in Europe. This now involves a role for Basque political actors in the representation of autonomous community interests, and those of the Spanish state, in various EU bodies. Basque authorities have developed an elaborate European policy encompassing preferences on both longer-term issues, like the future path of European integration, and more routine EU policy and legislative processes. They have dedicated public resources and developed an institutional apparatus to execute this European policy.

These activities have been a logical adaptation to changes which have seen many Basque competencies also became EU competencies. They have given form to other political goals, such as aspirations for a semi-autonomous foreign policy role, for developing networks of contacts beyond the Spanish state, or for deepening ties between Basque territories on either side of the French-Spanish border. These political rationales help explain why Spain's EU membership has become an issue of some significance in relations between Basque and central state authorities.

The observation that European integration is relevant for Basque selfgovernment is only one of the conclusions that can be drawn from this research. I also address a series of research questions probing the impact of European integration on Basque political power and on patterns of conflict and cooperation between Basque and central authorities. I now turn to discuss findings and conclusions for each of these research questions.

The EU and Basque political power

In the opening pages of this book, I argued that in order to exercise political autonomy – that is to promote and protect features distinguishing the Basque political community from others and to formulate policies that differed from those of other political entities – Basque authorities had to have some capacity to achieve two things: a capacity to influence decisions about public policy in their favour, and an ability to escape the control of other political actors, at least some of the time. The postFranco devolution settlement endowed Basque authorities with powers and resources enabling them to meet these conditions. However, studies on European integration and regional governance suggest that being part of the EU may have an effect – sometimes positive, sometimes negative – on the capacity of regional authorities to influence decisions in their favour or to escape the control of other political actors. In short, these studies suggest that the EU will alter the way Basque authorities exercise political power.

One way the EU may undermine regional power follows from the choices member states have made about the EU's institutional design. Even though there are many policy areas where regional and EU policy competencies overlap, the EU's institutional architecture puts significant limits on the representation of regional interests in EU decisionmaking. It also provides opportunities and justifications for central governments to assume responsibility for competencies that might otherwise belong to regions. Together, these imply an institutional bias in the EU's institutional design against regions and provide a setting in which EU membership may alter the domestic balance of power to the detriment of regions.

In chapters three and four, I examined responses in Spain, and in the EU, to these challenges, particularly whether institutional adaptations allowed autonomous community and central authorities to share power in the formation of the state's EU positions and its representation in EU bodies. I argued that if autonomous communities did not have a meaningful voice in EU matters it would be possible to conclude that transfer of autonomous community competencies to the EU level in the course of integration altered the distribution of power within Spain to the detriment of regions. Overall, the material presented in these chapters shows that the central government was able to dominate the state's EU relations for many years, which limited autonomous community influence over policy with European dimensions. However, the central government gradually overcame its reluctance to share power with autonomous communities, such that there is now much clearer evidence of meaningful autonomous community participation in the formation and representation of state EU decisions.

Domestic institutional reforms established mechanisms for central government and autonomous community cooperation in EU affairs in the state parliament and through the Sectoral Conferences, supplemented by less formal, *ad hoc* cooperation through political parties. The Senate's General Commission for Autonomous Communities has developed a role for itself in the discussion of general issues posed by EU membership, but it does not have a clear or consistent role in the daily negotiation of state EU positions. The parliamentary Mixed Commission for the EU has powers which give it scope for a more meaningful role in the routine negotiation of state EU decisions, and is a body used by certain kinds of territorial actors (including Basque nationalists) to publicise their policy preferences, scrutinise central government EU actions and pressure the central government. However, the very small proportion of autonomous community-designated senators involved in Mixed Commission business has meant it cannot effectively channel autonomous community views into state EU decisions.

The interministerial CARCE and Sectoral Conference system have evolved into fora where autonomous communities and central governments routinely discuss EU issues. In the CARCE, they have negotiated an extensive architecture for autonomous community participation in the formation and execution of EU policy and in the representation of the state in EU bodies. New rules in force since 2005 permitting autonomous community participation in the Council gave the Spanish system of intergovernmental relations a new vitality. Some ten years after its negotiation, there is now clearer evidence that the 1994 Agreement regulating autonomous community participation in EU matters through the Sectoral Conferences is being implemented. There is evidence that a traditional weakness of Spanish intergovernmental relations – collaboration among autonomous communities themselves – is being overcome in the process of preparing for Council participation.

It is less clear that other weaknesses, such as dependence on the political will of central government ministers and the weight of party relationships have been conquered. Regulations and other political practices give central government ministers preeminence in the Sectoral Conferences. Chapter five's study on Basque government efforts to promote the Basque Y HST project in the EU's transEuropean transport networks serves as a reminder that some Sectoral Conferences do not regularly and systematically provide opportunities for autonomous community input. Moreover, conclusions about Sectoral Conferences in general cannot be extended to bilateral bodies: the Basque-State Bilateral Commission for EU Affairs, for instance, only met around half a dozen times in the late 1990s and is currently inactive.

Relations between political parties play a role in state EU decisionmaking. Major steps in the evolution of powersharing arrangements for EU matters have occurred during periods of minority government at the state level, sometimes very clearly at the insistence of minority nationalists. The very informality of party relationships makes it difficult to judge with certainty how prevalent they may be in more routine EU decision processes. Evidence presented in chapters five and six suggest that some form of party links may have played a role in the negotiation of state EU positions affecting Basque interests. Links between PSE-PSOE ministers in the Basque government and party colleagues in the PSOE-led central government were probably one factor that helped them obtain central government support for the inclusion of Basque HST projects in transEuropean transport network plans. The significance of links between the PNV and the PP minority government in the Basque taxation case is less clear. Taxation matters were an explicit part of an agreement for PNV support for investiture of the PP's presidential candidate José María Aznar and set a pattern of prior cooperation between these governing parties in taxation matters. However, the conduct of intergovernmental relations through political parties constitutes a poor substitute for effective formal institutional bodies and procedures. Relations between political parties governing at different territorial levels may serve as an instrument for central government control, and their very informality makes them opaque, potentially discriminatory and contingent.

In addition to domestic arrangements for powersharing, autonomous communities have had access to EU decisionmaking through the CoR since the 1990s, and were slowly granted a role in state EU delegations to Community courts, the Spanish REPER, European Commission advisory committees and finally, the Council. Participation in these bodies does not guarantee autonomous community interests will be taken into account, but it acknowledges that both central government and autonomous community competencies are at stake in the deliberations of EU bodies. Although central government ministers lead state EU delegations, there is scope for autonomous communities to articulate collective views in EU-level debates.

These conclusions justify a revision of my previous work (Bourne 2003), but do not satisfactorily resolve a dispute in existing studies on the effectiveness of the Spanish system of intergovernmental relations in EU decisions. Although others argue that earlier reforms were sufficient to ensure satisfactory participation of autonomous communities in EU decisionmaking

(Börzel 2002: 137 and 147; Cienfuego 1997b: 191–202), I contend that such conclusions can only really be safe after 2004, when Council participation and autonomous community collaboration produced clear evidence that autonomous communities elaborated proposals, and held negotiations with the central government, on EU matters affecting their competencies.

Moreover, certain features of the system of intergovernmental relations described in chapter three raise doubts about the appropriateness of defining current practices as a system of *interterritorial* powersharing in EU matters. As a counterargument to frequent characterisations of the Sectoral Conferences – technically, the pivotal institution of the EU participation system – as irregular, precarious and weak, some have argued that the coincidence of many state and autonomous community interests in EU matters produces little disagreement among them in EU matters. This observation has been a key element of arguments about the effectiveness of the Sectoral Conference system. However, it is possible to argue that where conflicts are rarely apparent – perhaps because party relationships or authentic consensus on many EU issues obstructs the articulation of distinctive territorial interests – the conflict resolution element of interterritorial powersharing is missing. This difficulty seems to underpin many disagreements about the efficacy of the Spanish system of intergovernmental relations in EU matters.

More importantly, at this stage in the development of the Spanish system for EU decisionmaking, it makes conclusions about the general impact of the EU on the territorial distribution of power difficult to formulate. There is now a sophisticated institutional architecture for, and clearer evidence of, cooperation between autonomous communities and central authorities in EU decisionmaking. This suggests that adaptations within Spain respond to, and probably 'correct', imbalances posed by the EU's institutional bias against regions. However, it is less clear that many autonomous communities have sufficiently clear or distinctive interests that can find a verifiable 'meaningful input' in state EU decision processes. The lack of detailed documentary evidence – such as verbatim reports – on the conduct of Sectoral Conference meetings makes it difficult for researchers to develop more sophisticated conclusions on this point. It also suggests that questions posed in the book's theoretical framework about the impact of the EU on the territorial balance of power may be best posed where territorial differences are more clearly defined.

In contrast to conclusions that the EU may undermine regional power, some suggest that membership provides new opportunities for regional empowerment through complex, multidimensional alliance strategies. Chapter five explored this possibility in a study of Basque government campaigns to incorporate the Basque Y, a priority HST project, into transEuropean transport network blueprints. The study provided evidence of complex, transnational alliance strategies targeting other EU regions, the Spanish central government and supranational bodies. The Basque government joined forces with other European regions – especially neighbouring Aquitaine – to build an Atlantic Arc regions' lobby which sought to influence relevant EU decisions. With other Atlantic Arc regions, the Basque government used meetings, contacts and links with EU bodies like the EP, European Commission and the CoR to promote their objectives, even if some of these efforts (relating to the CoR, for instance) were rather halfhearted. EU bodies gave some support to Atlantic Arc and Basque government objectives; support which mostly took the form of passive acceptance of compatible preferences expressed by member state governments on transEuropean transport routes or promotion of very general statements alerting policymakers to the need to take peripheral regions into account.

These findings support observations that the EU has evolved into a multilevel polity (Marks *et al.* 1996; Hooghe and Marks 2001; John 1996; Peterson and Bomberg 1998). Central governments were clearly only one among a variety of political actors contesting decisions. Subnational actors operated at both national and EU levels. Transnational linkages developed between actors located in, and representing, different territorial levels – relationships particularly in evidence in the support networks developed by Atlantic Arc regions. Complex interrelationships in domestic politics extended beyond the nation state, including those among members of the same political party and personal links with individual EU actors like European Commission regional policy director-general, Eneko Landaburu.

Nevertheless, it is difficult to argue that this constitutes evidence of a multilevel process of interest aggregation, where regions stand alongside supranational and central state authorities as influential actors in EU decisionmaking. Despite their complex alliance strategy, Basque authorities relied on central government support for inclusion of the Basque Y in transEuropean transport network blueprints. Once member state governments agreed the basic contours of these blueprints, other EU bodies could not – or did not – really question them in any fundamental way. Once central government support was assured, the Basque government mostly mobilised links with EU bodies and Atlantic Arc regions to keep the project on the political agenda. In this context, domestic processes of interest aggregation were more salient.

A final argument about the EU and regions explored in the book is that supranational institutions may promote ideas that enhance the status of regions as authoritative decisionmakers. This is an argument largely developed from observations about EU regional policy. In chapter six's study of normative preferences and doctrine promoted by supranational actors, very different conclusions emerged. After a series of EU challenges to politically sensitive Basque taxation powers, European Commission and ECJ officials defended positions which would ultimately reduce the scope of Basque taxation prerogatives. These positions were founded on a concern that disputed Basque taxation measures compromised common market goals. Clearly, supranational authorities' actions to promote EU objectives may ultimately lead them to favour reducing the scope of regional powers if they seem incompatible with broader goals of integration. Recent developments show an evolution in ECJ thinking, but it remains to be seen how this will apply to the Basque case.

The study on Basque taxation does not necessarily undermine arguments about supranational support for enhanced regional involvement in EU decisionmaking drawn from observations about other policy areas and it does not necessarily imply that supranational actors want to reduce the powers of EU regions in general. But it does serve as a counterpoint to arguments which see supranational actors as natural allies of EU regions. Moreover, with the preceding study of the Basque HST campaign, chapter six's study identifies a number of obstacles to alliances between regional and supranational authorities. When responding to Basque EU campaigns, supranational authorities are not subject to the same political ties, electoral imperatives and 'historical baggage' as Spanish central governments. EU authorities, for instance, did not have the same stake in the historic compromise between Basque and central authorities that underpins the Basque taxation regime. Such detachment reduces the political costs of taking a position which could go against the preferences of Basque authorities or reduce the scope of Basque powers.

Overall, the book's conclusions do not fully confirm expectations existing studies raise about the contradictory or ambiguous relationship between European integration and regional power. In the cases examined here, there was plenty of evidence of Basque government efforts to find EU allies, but none confirming that these alliances were a source of empowerment for Basque authorities. Rather there was evidence that domestic processes of interest aggregation were more important, a conclusion which lends support to the argument that the EU has 'no effect' on relational sources of regional power. Moreover, in the cases examined here, there was more evidence to support the conclusion that European integration undermined Basque political power. Although there have been significant improvements in construction and operation of institutional arrangements for autonomous community participation in the elaboration and representation of state interests in the EU, fundamental problems have meant that over the longer term, central government authorities have dominated the state's EU involvement, even where autonomous community powers are involved. Far from consistently supporting the position of regional authorities, supranational authorities took positions which could reduce the scope of Basque powers in the politically sensitive field of taxation. These findings confirm the utility of the theoretical approach outlined in chapter two. The breadth of propositions examined allows the researcher to capture much more of the complexity of the relationship between European integration and regional governance. At the same time, it helps to reduce – though not completely eliminate – ambiguity about the nature of that relationship.

Examining other aspects of Basque experiences of European integration may raise different conclusions. Alliances with supranational actors may have been more fruitful in other Basque government EU campaigns, although other studies I have conduced (Bourne 2001), or am aware of (Morcillo 2006), do have not yet shown this to be so. A detailed examination of Basque involvement in the implementation of EU policy, including EU regional policy, may reveal other kinds of political relationships or more subtle alterations in Basque government influence or power resources (Smyrl 1997; Hooghe 1996). Evidence from studies on 'partnership' in the implementation of EU regional policy in Spain during the 1990s, however, suggests potential for regional empowerment through such measures may be difficult to detect (Morata and Muñoz 1996; Bache and Jones 2000). A strength of the theoretical approach developed in the research is that new propositions about the impact of the EU on regional power can be easily incorporated, regardless of variation in analytical focus or methodological approach.

I do not argue that this study sustains conclusions about the implications of EU membership for regional and federal states more generally. It provides a first case study and a theoretical framework which could be used in further comparative studies. To my knowledge a study incorporating the range of research questions I posed here has not been undertaken. However, other studies on regional experiences of the EU suggest employing such an approach would be useful. There have been many studies of institutional adaptations made in different federal and regionalised states to the challenges EU membership raises in relation to the territorial distribution of power (Peréz Tremps et al. 1998; Börzel 2002; Jeffery 1997; Hrbek 1999; Hooghe 1995a; Kerremans and Beyers 1996; Beyers, Delreux and Steensels 2004). These have identified different systems by which regions and central state authorities may share power in EU decisionmaking. The German model is predominantly parliamentary, with regional (Länder) governments represented in the upper house of the state parliament (Bundesrat) jointly determining – sometimes binding – positions on EU matters. The Belgian model, by contrast, centres on frequent intergovernmental encounters among representatives of federal, regional and community governments. Comparison of the effectiveness of these systems of powersharing across different states reveals that some systems, particularly those in federal states, are more robust than others (Pérez Tremps et al. 1998; Morcillo 2006; but see Börzel 2002 for alternative view on Germany and Spain). It is, therefore, to be expected that future studies may not necessarily support this study's conclusions about the effect of European integration on the domestic territorial distribution of power in Spain, at least not to the same degree.

On the other hand, the actions of EU regions, including those from member states with more effective systems for powersharing in EU decisions, continue to demonstrate dissatisfaction with their role in EU politics. Many EU regions mobilized during recent debates producing the Constitutional

Treaty. There was no clear regions' agenda and regional preferences could vary quite considerably (Keating 2004; Bourne 2006). But many regions demonstrated dissatisfaction with responses to address the EU's impact on regional governance made so far. These ranged from legislative regions' criticisms that the CoR did not 'match expectations', calls for a strengthened role for regions in ECJ proceedings and calls for more controls against EU incursions into regional competencies through more effective enforcement of 'subsidiarity' or a clearer 'catalogue' of EU competencies (Keating 2004; Bourne 2006; Verges, 2003; Swenden 2004; Jeffery 2004; see also 2001, 2002 and 2003 declarations by regions with legislative powers, www.regleg.org, accessed 20 July 2006).

There is some empirical evidence that alliances between regions and EU authorities have been more fruitful in other cases. This evidence has identified the European Commission's regional policy directorate-general as an ally of EU regions, a relationship which has involved European Commission support for regions on issues where their central governments have taken opposing views (McAleavey and Mitchell 1994: 237–48; John 1996: 293–313). This is a possibility that could be explored further, even if evidence of collaboration producing meaningful or significant change has been rather thin. And finally, studies of ECJ actions affecting regions suggest this is a potentially insightful, but underresearched area of study (Sobrido Prieto 2003). Since the 1950s, the ECJ has been asked to rule on dozens of cases affecting the competencies and actions of regional, local and municipal authorities from many member states. This not only provides a large body of material which could be analysed to discover broader trends in ECJ rulings. It provides material to be analysed within the context of many individual regions' relations with the EU. Clearly there is much to be done to fully appreciate the impact of the EU on regional power.

The EU, conflict and cooperation in Basque politics

One final research question, particularly relevant to understanding the impact of the EU on nationalist conflict in Spain, was: Has Spain's EU membership been a source of conflict or provided new incentives for cooperation between Basque and central governments? This question was drawn from observations made by Tanja Börzel (2002) and others that the EU creates pressures for regional and central authorities to share power in the state's EU decisions and that these pressures may encourage more cooperative relations between territorial entities. Börzel (2002) argues that the German *Länder* and federal authorities have successfully responded to EU challenges by drawing on their traditional political culture of 'cooperative federalism' and designed new rules that further institutionalise this cooperative culture in the field of European affairs. Similarly, Bart Kerremans and Jan Beyers (1996)

argue that the Belgian response to EU challenges was to establish powersharing institutions that built on Belgian traditions of consensus politics and
consociationalism. Indeed Kerremans and Beyers argue that in the Belgian
case, regional, community and central authorities now accept that for EU
affairs the 'concept of autonomy is meaningless' and that '[b]oth sides are
now condemned to work together if they want to gain something within the
EU Councils' (1996: 54). For the case of Spain, Börzel argues that once
autonomous communities 'learnt' that they could not 'redress the institutional balance of power' through their limited direct access to EU
decisionmakers, they turned their back on the traditional political culture of
competitive regionalism and 'embraced a cooperative strategy' in the domestic arena (2002: 5–6). Material presented in this book provides evidence
lending some support to the argument that the EU provides incentives for
cooperation among central and Basque authorities, even if it has not fundamentally transformed this difficult relationship.

There is now ample evidence of cooperation between Basque and central
governments in EU decisionmaking. With other autonomous communities,
Basque authorities have voluntarily signed up to many of the dozen or so
agreements reached with the central government in the CARCE establishing
institutions for autonomous community involvement in EU decisions (see
Table 3.3). The elaboration of this architecture over the last decade or so has
resolved some important differences between Basque and central governments. Indeed, basic elements of the model for autonomous community
participation in EU decisions elaborated by the Basque government in the
1990s are now in place, at least formally. There are differences still to be
resolved and current arrangements do not fully conform to Basque preferences, but significant progress has been made. Furthermore, institutions,
procedures and practices regulating autonomous community involvement in
EU decisions provide many settings in which Basque and central authorities
have – often with other autonomous communities – met, discussed and
resolved differences on EU matters. More recently, they have jointly represented the interests of the state in the EU (in Council meetings, for instance).

The Basque government has set its own terms for participating in many
of these institutions and procedures, often adopting a dual strategy. It has
symbolically registered discontent with some of these arrangements by refusing to sign regulatory agreements it considered unsatisfactory or by formally
boycotting sessions of bodies like the CARCE before 1995, or the Senate's
General Commission for Autonomous Communities to this day. On the
other hand, it has often made use of the institutional machinery it shunned,
either through the actions of its 'agents' – Basque nationalist representatives
in the Spanish parliament, for instance – or by involving itself in bodies like
the CARCE and Sectoral Conferences as if it had indeed endorsed the agreements regulating their activities.

Some have argued that Basque government involvement in the institutional arrangements that do exist, despite their misgivings, is evidence that the exigencies of EU policymaking make it difficult for Basque authorities to avoid at least a basic level of cooperation with the central government (Börzel 2002; Roig 2002). My own research provides further evidence to support this claim. In each of the EU campaigns studied, Basque government strategies focused on soliciting support from both EU-level actors and the Spanish central government. As we have seen, Basque efforts to see its HST objectives incorporated into transEuropean transport networks relied heavily on central government support given the predominance of member state agreements in the relevant decision processes. In the campaign to defend the Basque taxation regime in the ECJ preliminary ruling dispute Basque authorities had to work with state representatives to achieve their goals. This instance of cooperation was particularly remarkable given the intensity of domestic disputes about the Basque taxation regime and the more general level of tension in relations between the PP, governing in Madrid, and Basque nationalist parties running Basque institutions.

In contrast to claims that conflict between central and autonomous community governments in EU matters is rare, the book provides ample evidence of disputes and disagreements between Basque and central governments. Material interests have sometimes been at stake, such as differing preferences on the priority of Basque HST plans over those in the Mediterranean Arc. Such disputes are the staple fare of territorial relations in federal and regionalised states. In the Basque case, however, disputes relating to EU matters have often been fused with disputes about two more fundamental issues in Basque relations with state authorities.

The first of these has been wrangling over the permissible scope of Basque autonomy. Since democratisation, Basque nationalists have sought the most extensive form of selfgovernment possible, whether this took the form of maximum development of the 1981 Statute of Gernika, or negotiation of a new political framework for Basque relations with the Spanish state. The desire for maximum autonomy extends to Basque government activity beyond the state and a presence in the EU. This preference is something that responds to a complex combination of factors, including Basque nationalist traditions of principled support for European integration, the goal of building a distinctive Basque profile in international politics, and a pragmatic adaptation to the internationalisation of decisions affecting many Basque competencies.

Basque nationalists have long wanted more scope for an autonomous role in EU decisionmaking than subsequent central governments have been willing to concede. For many years central authorities jealously guarded their exclusive competence in 'international relations' and sought to restrict the exercise of Basque autonomy to the territorial boundaries of the autonomous community. The dispute reached such proportions that it was referred to the Spanish Constitutional Court for resolution. There has been a partial resolu-

tion of this issue. The Court's landmark judgement 165/1994 not only authorised a new platform for autonomous action in the EU – an official Basque
government delegation in Brussels – it also undercut arguments fundamentally restricting the conduct of autonomous community activities 'beyond the
state'. The creation of the CoR in 1994, a body whose foundation the Spanish
central government actively promoted during Maastricht Treaty negotiations,
provided another platform for a formal and autonomous role for Basque
authorities in EU policymaking, although this has never been sufficient to
fulfil Basque aspirations. Even after the Constitutional Court's judgement
165/1994, which paved the way for greater autonomous Basque involvement
in the EU, and subsequent treaty reforms expanding the role of the CoR, the
issue is still on the agenda. Basque authorities continue to campaign for a
more extensive, more autonomous role in the ECJ. Basque calls for regional
constituencies to replace current arrangements for a single, statewide electoral constituency for EP elections can also be read as a call for greater
autonomous involvement in the EU; it is likely to bolster the number of
Basque nationalists winning seats in the EP and, thus, the number of
members from the ruling political parties of Basque government institutions
able to transmit its views in EP deliberations.

Basque EU campaigns studied in the book provide evidence that calls for
an autonomous role in the EU were not just fruit of a politically or symbolically relevant desire for a semi-autonomous foreign policy role. They could be
a response to problematic relations between Basque and central governments,
even in cases where cooperation with central authorities became important.
Domestic disputes over Basque taxation measures, for instance, raised
concerns, especially among Basque nationalists, about the conviction with
which central government representatives would defend the modern incarna-
tion of Basque 'historic rights'. Basque authorities therefore developed a
strategy supplementing cooperation with the central government, with separate consciousness-raising activities in Brussels to 'explain' the Economic
Agreement. Similarly, strategies targeting EU actors in Basque campaigns to
influence transEuropean transport network decisions were at least partly a
response to the fact that Basque and state authorities pursued different priorities in these matters.

A second set of issues arose over the construction of instruments allowing central and Basque authorities to share power in EU decisionmaking.
Basque and subsequent central governments have not only had different preferences on what form instruments for powersharing should take. Many of the
new institutions developed were created in, and helped perpetuate, an atmosphere of suspicion and distrust between Basque and central authorities.
Differences over the design of instruments for powersharing in EU decisionmaking have not been trivial. They have formed an important part of deeply
controversial debates in Spain between minority nationalist and statewide
parties about the *hecho diferencial* – essentially debates about the most appro-

priate way of recognising the sociocultural and political distinctions of the Basque Country, Catalonia and Galicia in state institutions and structures. Differences on this question have filtered through to debates about the reform of the Senate, about the balance between bilateral and multilateral mechanisms for cooperation and, at some points, debates on membership of the CoR or arrangements for autonomous community participation in the Council.

Furthermore, differences between Basque and central governments on the design and scope of instruments for powersharing in EU decisions have often revealed high levels of suspicion and distrust. The Basque government harboured suspicions that central government preferences for maintaining the pivotal role of the (hitherto problematic) CARCE and Sectoral Conference system were manoeuvres to avoid authentic powersharing in EU decisions. Delays over the formal constitution of the Basque-state Bilateral Commission for EU affairs had a similar effect, prompting a Basque government boycott of the CARCE for many years. Central government rejections of Basque demands for participation in the Council, and obstruction during negotiation of procedures to implement Council participation once agreed in principle, brought accusations that successive central governments sought to 'empty out', or 'take back', autonomy gains made in the postFranco devolution settlement by limiting Basque involvement in EU decisions affecting their competencies. For its part, dispute over autonomous community participation in state EU delegations (particularly in the Council) revealed central government reservations about whether autonomous communities – particularly those governed by minority nationalists – could be 'trusted' to defend state interests over their own.

In short, Spain's EU membership may have provided incentives for cooperation among Basque and central authorities, but European dimensions of Basque selfgovernment have merged with broader disputes in Spanish territorial relations, disputes including questions about the permissible scope of, and appropriate institutional forms for, Basque autonomy, as well as questions about the place of Basque institutions within the Spanish state and appropriate means for recognising Basque difference.

The book's conclusions do not close debate about the impact of the EU on Basque politics. Nevertheless, it does identify something of what is at stake in the changing context of postwar European politics. Devolution in Spain – and indeed elsewhere in Europe – has been an instrument for political accommodation which will probably continue to evolve. Devolution can help soothe political tensions by addressing key issues at the heart of nationalist conflicts. European integration clearly presents many challenges and opportunities which may affect the utility of devolution as an instrument for achieving such ends.

REFERENCES

Agirreazkuenaga, I. (2001), 'Educación y lengua: reflexiones jurídicas sobre el modelo vasco', *Revista vasca de administración pública*, 61:3, 129–42.

Aguilera de Prat, C. R. (2001), 'Los Socialistas ante los pactos de gobernabilidad de 1993 y 1996', *Revista de estudios políticos*, 3, 9–43.

Ahedo Gurrutxaga, I. (2004), *Pasado y presente del nacionalismo en Iparralde*, Bilbao, Fundación Manu Robles –Arangiz Institutua.

Aizpeolea, L. R. 'Zapatero sube mas de un 50% su oferta inicial para la financiación sanitaria', *El País* (10 September 2005), p. 17.

Aizpeolea, L. R. 'Los acuerdos de una cita histórica', *El País* (29 October 2004), p. 21.

Aizpeolea, L. R. 'Rechazada la enmienda gallega para lograr presencia autonómica en la UE', *El País* (26 January 2002), p. 18.

Aizpeolea, L. R. 'Montoro rechaza la oferta del Gobierno vasco de aplazar la discusión sobre la UE', *El País* (31 December 2001), p. 13.

Aizpeolea, L. R. 'El Gobierno entierra la aspiración autonómica de tener voz en la UE', *El País* (14 December 2001), p. 24.

Aizpeolea, L. R. 'La exigencia de Euskadi a tener presencia en la UE bloquea el acuerdo sobre su financiación', *El País* (30 November 2001), p. 23.

Aizpeolea, L. R. 'Ibarretxe supedita el pacto sobre el modelo de financiación a que Euskadi tenga voz en la UE', *El País* (17 May 2001), p. 13.

Aizpeolea, L. R. 'El Gobierno negocia con Vitoria para retirar sus recursos sobre el Concierto vasco', *El País Digital* (4 January 2000).

Aizpeolea, L. R. and Damborenea, P. G. 'El Gobierno vasco acuerda con Hacienda el Concierto tras retirar su petición sobre la UE', *El País* (21 February 2002), p. 14.

Aja, E. (2003), *El estado autonómico: Federalismo y hechos diferenciales*, Madrid, Alianza Editorial.

Albertí Rovira, E. (1998), 'La posición de las Comunidades Autónomas en la fase ascendente de la formación del derecho comunitario europeo', in Pérez Tremps, P. (ed.) *La participación europea y la acción exterior de las Comunidades Autónomas*, Barcelona, Generalitat de Catalunya, Institut d'Estudis Autonòmics.

Alonso Arce, I. (2005), 'Una sentencia inoportuna y desafortunada', *Forum Fiscal de Bizkaia*, 55:090, 17–28.

Alonso Arce, I. (2004), 'La transparencia fiscal internacional y las vicisitudes en torno al Concierto Económico', *Forum Fiscal de Bizkaia*, 45:090, 17–23.

Álvarez, M. 'El PNV pretende que el Concierto permita a la Hacienda vasca relación directa con la UE', *El Correo* (18 December 1999), p. 46.

Álvarez, M. 'Empresarios e instituciones apuestan por cerrar filas en defensa del Concierto', *El Correo* (4 May 1999), p. 42.

Álvarez, M. 'Con los recursos no cabe negociación política', *El Correo* (3 March 1999), p. 38.

Anderson, J. (1990), 'Skeptical reflections on a Europe of the regions: Britain, Germany and the ERDF', *Journal of Public Policy*, 10:4, 417–47.

Angulo, C. 'El Gobierno vasco planteará al central un pacto para definir el alcance del Concierto', *El País* (3 March 1999), p. 1.

Antolín San Martín, E. (2001), 'Consejero de Transportes y Obras Públicas (1987–1989)', in Bizkarguenaga Atutxa, I. (ed.) *Historia del Gobierno vasco contada por sus consejeros 1980–1998*, Oñati, Instituto Vasco de Administración Pública.

Armentia Basterra, J. and Barrasa Sobrón, A. (2001), 'El pacto fiscal y su incidencia en el próximo Concierto Económico', *Forum Fiscal de Bizkaia*, 15:002, 13–19.

Arroyo, F. 'El AVE a Lleida viajará a 250 kilómetros por hora dentro de 15 días', *El País* (5 May 2006), p. 33.

Artis, M. and Lee, N. (eds.) (1997), *The Economics of the European Union: Policy and Analysis*, Oxford, Oxford University Press.

Aspinwall, M. D. and Schneider, G. (2000), 'Same menu, separate tables: The institutionalist turn in political science', *European Journal of Political Research*, 38:1, 1–36.

Atlantic Arc Commission (2005), *Annuaire Commission Arc Atlantique*, Bordeaux.

Ayala, A. 'El Constitucional reconoce la legalidad de la oficina del Gobierno vasco en Bruselas', *El Correo* (31 May 1994), p. 14.

Ayala, A. 'El PNV confirma al PSE que solo habrá pacto de coalición si el Gobierno central acepta y garantiza sus reivindicaciones', *El Correo* (14 November 1990), p. 10.

Bache, I. (1999), 'The extended gatekeeper: Central government and the implementation of EC regional policy in the UK', *Journal of European Public Policy*, 6:1, 28–45.

Bache, I. (1998), *Politics of European Union Regional Policy: Multilevel Governance or Flexible Gatekeeping?*, Sheffield, Sheffield Academic Press.

Bache, I. and Jones, R. (2000), 'Has EU regional policy empowered the regions? A study of Spain and the UK', *Regional and Federal Studies*, 10:3, 1–20.

Bachrach, P. and Baratz, M. (1970), *Power and Poverty: Theory and Practice*, New York, Oxford University Press.

Barón, C. 'El Gabinete del Gobierno vasco para la Comunidad Europea ampliará sus actividades', *El Correo* (10 February 1987), p. 29

Benzo Sainz, I. (1993), *Régimen de distribución de competencias entre el Estado y las Comunidades Autónomas*, Madrid, Ministerio para las Administraciones Públicas.

Bergara, J. (2001), 'Consejero de Transportes y Obras Públicas (1991–1995)', in I. Bizkarguenaga Atutxa, *Historia del Gobierno vasco contada por sus consejeros 1980–1998*, Oñati, Instituto Vasco de Administración Pública.

Bergara, J. 'El Eje Atlántico', *El Correo* (20 February 1989), p. 23.

Beyers, J., Delreux, T. and Steensels, C. (2004), 'The Europeanisation of intergovernmental cooperation and conflict resolution in Belgium: The case of agriculture', in Bourne, A. (ed.), *The EU and Territorial Politics within Member States*, Leiden, Brill.

Biglino Campos, P. (ed.) (2003), *La política europea de las Comunidades Autónomas y su control parlamentario*, Valencia, Institut de Dret Públic, tirant lo blanch.

Bomberg, E. and Peterson, J. (1998), 'European Union decision-making: The role of subnational autorities', *Political Studies*, 46, 219–35.

Börzel, T. A. (2002), *States and Regions in the European Union: Institutional Adaptation in Germany and Spain*, Cambridge, Cambridge University Press.

Bourne, A. (2006), 'Bringing Europe closer to the citizen? Regions, stateless nations and the European Convention', *Regional and Federal Studies*, 15:1, 1–20.

Bourne, A. (2004), 'European integration and conflict resolution in the Basque Country, Northern Ireland and Cyprus', in Bourne, A. (ed.), *The EU and Territorial Politics within Member States: Conflict or Cooperation?*, Leiden, Brill.

Bourne, A. (2003), 'The impact of European integration on regional power', *Journal of Common Market Studies*, 41:4, 597–620.

Bourne, A. (2001), *The Basque Country and the Politics of Territory in the European Union*, unpublished PhD thesis, University of Bristol.

Bullain López, I. (1998), 'Autonomy and the European Union', in Suksi, M. (ed.), *Autonomy: Applications and Implications*, Netherlands, Kluwer Law International.

Bullain López, I. (1990), *Las regiones autónomas de la Comunidad Europea y su participación en el proceso de integración*, Oñati, Instituto Vasco de Administración Pública.

Bullman, U. (1997), 'The politics of the third level', *Regional and Federal Studies*, 6:2, 3–19.

Bustos Gisbert, R. (1996), *Relaciones internacionales y Comunidades Autónomas*, Madrid, Centro de Estudios Constitucionales.

Calonge Velásquez, A. and Sanz Rubiales, I. (2000), *El Comité de las Regiones: Análisis de una ¿futura institución?*, Granada, Comares.

Calvo García-Tornel, F. and López Ruiz, J. M. G. (1998), 'El arco mediterráneo como espacio de futuro', in Mella Márquez, J. M. (ed.), *Economía y política regional en España ante la Europa del siglo XXI*, Madrid, Ediciones Akal.

Caro Baroja, J. (1985), *El Laberinto Vasco*, San Sebastián, Editorial Txertoa.

Carr, R. and Fusi, J. P. (1981), *Spain: Dictatorship to Democracy*, London, Harper Collins.

Carrera Hernández, F. J. (1994), 'La oficina de la Comunidad Autónoma Vasca en Bruselas', *Comunidad Europea*, Basque Country, Aranzadi Editorial.

Castells Arteche, J. M (1997a), 'Integración de vasconia en el estado español', in Jáuregui Bereciartu, G., Castells Arteche, J. M. and Iriondo, X., *La institucionalización jurídica y política de vasconia*, Oñati, Instituto Vasco de Administración Pública.

Castro Ruano J. L. and Ugalde Zubiri, A. (2004), *La acción exterior del País Vasco (1980–2003)*, Oñati, Instituto Vasco de Administración Pública.

Cheshire, P. (1995), 'European integration and regional responses', in Rhodes, M. (ed.), *The Regions and the New Europe*, Manchester, Manchester University Press.

Christiansen, T. (1999), 'Territorial politics in the European Union', *Journal of European Public Policy*, 6:2, 349–57.

Christiansen, T. (1996), 'Second thoughts on Europe's "third level": The European Union's Committee of the Regions', *Publius: The Journal of Federalism*, 26:1, 93–116.

Cienfuegos Mateo, M. (2001), 'Las cortes españolas ante la integración europea', in C. Closa (ed.), *La europeización del sistema político español*, Madrid, Istmo.

Cienfuegos Mateo, M. (1997a), 'La Comisión Mixta para la Unión Europea: análisis y balance de una década de actividad en el seguimiento de los asuntos comunitarios', *Gaceta jurídica y de la competencia de la Comunidad Europea*, D-27, 7–69.

Cienfuegos Mateo, M (1997b), 'La intervención de las Comunidades Autónomas en cuestiones relativas a las Comunidades Europeas a través de la Comisión General de las Comunidades Autónomas y la Conferencia para asuntos relacionados con las Comunidades Europeas', *Autonomías*, 22, 155–204.

Cini, M. and Bourne, A. (2006), *European Union Studies*, Basingstoke, Palgrave Macmillan.

Clark, R. P. (1984), *The Basque Insurgents: ETA, 1952–1980*, Madison, University of Wisconsin Press.

Committee of the Regions (CoR) (2004), *A Political Forum 1994–2004: Consultative Work, Members' Attendance*, Luxembourg, Office for Official Publications of the European Communities.

Connor, W. (1972), 'Nation-building or nation-destroying', *World Politics*, 24:3, 319–55.

Conversi, D. (1997), *The Basques, the Catalans and Spain: Alternative Routes to Nationalist Mobilisation*, London, Hurst & Company.

Corcuera Atienza, J. (1991), *Política y derecho. La construcción de la autonomía vasca*, Madrid, Centro de Estudios Constitucionales.

Cue, C. E. 'Ibarretxe: He venido a ofrecer y pedir respeto para las decisiones de los pueblos', El País (29 October 2004), p. 22.

Damborenea, P. G. and Ortiz de Arri, E. 'La "paz fiscal" sellada entre los Gobiernos central y vasco caduca dentro de dos años', *El País Digital*, (19 January 2000).

Damborenea, P. G. and Ortiz de Arri, E. 'Los gobiernos central y vasco ponen punto final a la "guerra" por los incentivos fiscales', *El País* (18 January 2000).

Davis, T. C. (1997), 'Patterns of identity: Basques and the Basque nation', *Nationalism and*

Ethnic Politics, 3:1, 61–88.

de Esteban, J. (1992), *El estado de la constitución: Diez años de gobierno PSOE,* Madrid, Libertarias.

del Castillo, J., Gómez-Larrañaga, P. and Samano, A. (1992), 'El espacio atlántico: convergencia de periferias. Análisis de su problemática y definición de una estrategia', in Valverde, J., García Delgado, J. L. and Pedreño, A. (eds.), *Ejes territoriales de desarrollo: España en la Europa de los 90,* Madrid, Colegio Economistas Libros.

de la Cierva, R. (1997), *El nacionalismo vasco de Sabino de Arana a Xavier Arzallus,* Madrid, ARC Editores.

de la Granja Sainz, J. L. (2003), *El siglo de Euskadi: El nacionalismo vasco en la España del siglo XX,* Madrid, Editorial Tecnos.

de la Granja Sainz, J. L. (1995), *El nacionalismo vasco: Un siglo de historia,* Madrid, Editorial Tecnos.

Delgado, D. 'Navarra rompe su último vínculo con el Gobierno vasco por su respuesta "ambigua" al atentado', *El Correo* (25 January 2000), p. 12.

Díaz Herrera, J. and Tijeras, R. (1991), *El dinero del poder: La trama económica en la España socialista,* Madrid, Cambio.

Diego Casals, J. L. (1995), 'La experiencia autonómica en el entramado comunitario: Especial referencia al caso vasco', in *Informe Pi i Sunyer sobre las Comunidades Autónomas 1994,* Barcelona, Fundació Carles Pi i Sunyer.

Diego Casals, J. L. (1994), 'La participación de las Comunidades Autónomas en el proceso de adopción de decisiones de la Unión Europea: Un balance y una propuesta', *Revista vasca de administración pública,* 40:2, 149–68.

DiMaggio, P. and Powell, W. (1991), 'Introduction', in Powell, W. and DiMaggio, P. (eds.), *The New Institutionalism in Organizational Analysis,* Chicago, Chicago University Press.

Domínguez Iribarren, F. (2002), 'El enfrentamiento de ETA con la democracia', in Elorza, A., Garmendia, J. M., Jáuregui, G. and Domínguez Iribarren, F., *La historia de ETA,* Madrid, Temas de Hoy.

El Correo, 'Confebask pide que el Concierto Económico quede al margen de las disputas de carácter partidista, (10 December 1999).

El Correo, 'El Comisario de la Competencia asume las tesis de Van Miert contra la fiscalidad vasca' (17 September 1999).

El Correo, 'El lehendakari reclama para el Gobierno vasco la defensa fiscal en la UE' (23 July 1999).

El Correo, 'Los ministros de transportes del sur de Europa crean un grupo de estudio sobre el TAV', (16 July 1990), p. 38.

El Correo, 'Guevara califica de "acto de hostilidad hacia Euskadi" la decisión de dar prioridad a Cataluña en la alta velocidad', (12 January 1989), p. 33.

El Correo Digital, 'Solbes afirma que la sentencia del Tribunal de la UE no afecta a la fiscalidad vasca' (7 September 2006a).

El Correo Digital, 'Ibarretxe cree que deben acabar los ataques "políticos y jurídicos" al Concierto vasco' (7 September 2006b).

El Mundo, 'ETA condiciona el diálogo al derecho de autodeterminación', (16 January 2005), p. 10.

El Mundo, 'Zapatero consigue convertir el medio en mensaje', (29 October 2004), p. 3.

El País, 'Divergencia fiscal europea', (31 May 1999).

El País, 'El Tribunal Superior Vasco anula incentivos fiscales de Guipúzcoa para grandes inversiones', (2 March 1999), p. 57.

European Commission (2001), *European Transport Policy for 2010: Time to Decide,* Luxembourg, Office for Official Publications of the European Communities.

European Commisson (1991), *Europe 2000: Outlook for the development of the*

Community's territory. COM (91) final, Brussels, 7 November.

Evans, A. (2003), 'UK devolution and EU law', *European Law Review*, 28, 475–92.

Expansión, 'El Tribunal Superior Vasco anula las "vacaciones fiscales" por "despropor-cionadas"' (7 October 1999), p. 68.

Fernández, J. (1998), 'La situación del debate de esta cuestión en el estado español', in *La participación de las Comunidades Autónomas en los Consejos de la Unión Europea, jornada celebrada en el Palacio de Artaza, 2 de Julio de 1998*, Oñate, Instituto Vasco de Adminstración Pública.

Fernández Barbadillo, P. and Ruiz Miguel, C. (2003), '¿Aprobaron los vascos la constitución?', *Revista de estudios políticos*, 122, 167–78.

Fernández de Casadevante Romani, C. (2001), *La acción exterior de las Comunidades Autónomas*, Madrid, Editorial Dilex, Universidad Rey Juan Carlos.

Fernández Manjón, D. (2001), *La colaboración en el estado compuesto asimétrico: El caso de España*, Oñati, Instituto Vasco de Administración Pública.

Fernández Monge, J. (1989), *La Comunidad Europea y la Comunidad Autónoma del País Vasco*, Oñate, Instituto Vasco de Administración Pública.

Financial Times, 'Will ye no', (3 February 1995), p. 15.

Fontova, N. 'Ardanza pide la transferencia de las competencias en materia de investigación científica y técnica', *El Correo* (3 October 1990), p. 40

Fontova, N. 'Antolín promete pedir explicaciones a Barrionuevo', *El Correo* (12 January 1989), p. 33.

Fuentes, M. A. 'La Hacienda vasca advierte que se declarará insumisa si se vulnera su soberanía tributaria', *Expansión* (15 January 1999), p. 52.

Galende, J. L. 'Las regiones atlánticas del sur de Europa piden cambios en la red ferroviaria de alta velocidad propuesta por la CE', *El Correo* (28 April 1990), p. 36.

Garamendia Gutiérrez, A. (2002), 'Alcance y evaluación de la cooperación transfronteriza entre Euskadi, Navarra y Aquitania', *Cuadernos Europeos de Deusto*, 26, 73–105.

Gardner, D. 'Poverty trap with an exit: Is EU structural aid a black hole of funding from Brussels, or an effective way of raising incomes?', *Financial Times* (21 June 1994), p. 19.

Gardner, D. 'Spanish official lost for words in Brussels post', *Financial Times* (12 May 1993), p. 2.

Garea, F. 'Zapatero triplica el dinero para Sanidad en una caótica Conferencia de Presidentes', El Mundo (11 September 2005), p. 1.

Garea, F. 'El PP negocia y se acerca al acuerdo, pero intenta tensar las horas previas', *El Mundo* (10 September 2005a), p. 10.

Garea, F. 'Los líderes autonómicos estudiarán hoy en el Senado la solución al déficit de la Sanidad', *El Mundo* (10 September 2005b), p. 10.

Garea, F. 'Cumbre autonómica', *El Mundo* (29 October 2004), p. 8.

Garea, F. 'El PP forzará el debate territorial en la cumbre de presidentes', *El Mundo* (28 October 2004), p. 12.

Gillespie, R. (2000), 'Political polarization in the Basque Country', *Regional and Federal Studies*, 10:1, 112–24.

Gilmour, D. (1985), *Transformation of Spain: From Franco to the Constitutional Monarchy*, London, Quartet Books.

Gobierno Vasco (2005a), *Valoración de los 25 años de autogobierno y propuesta de nuevo estatuto*, Vitoria-Gasteiz.

Gobierno Vasco (2005b), *Estrategia de acción exterior de la Comunidad Autónoma de Euskadi*, Vitoria-Gasteiz.

Gobierno Vasco (2004), *Participación y labor del Gobierno vasco en el Comité de las Regiones*, Vitoria-Gasteiz.

Gobierno Vasco (2003), *Posición del Gobierno vasco sobre el futuro de la Unión Europea*, www.euskadi.net, (accessed November 2004).

Gobierno Vasco (2001), *Plan territorial sectorial de la red ferroviaria en la Comunidad Autónoma del País Vasco*, Vitoria-Gasteiz.

Gobierno Vasco (1999), *Asociaciones de cooperación interregional*, Vitoria-Gasteiz.

Gobierno Vasco (1998), *Participación y labor del Gobierno vasco en el Comité de las Regiones*, Vitoria-Gasteiz.

Gobierno Vasco (1996), *Euskadi ante la reforma de la Unión Europea*, Vitoria-Gasteiz.

Gobierno Vasco (1993), *Informe sobre la participación institucional de Euskadi en la construcción Europea*, Vitoria-Gasteiz.

Gobierno Vasco (1989), *Europa 93: Plan extraordinario del Gobierno vasco y de las Diputaciones forales (1989–1992)*, Vitoria-Gasteiz.

Gobierno Vasco (1988), *Plan económico a medio plazo 1989–1993: Diagnóstico y* prioridades, Vitoria-Gasteiz.

Goldstein, J. and Keohane, R. (eds.) (1993), *Ideas and Foreign Policy: Beliefs, Institutions and Political Change*, Ithaca, Cornell University Press.

Gómez, J. L. (2005), *A vueltas con España: Hablan las diecisiete presidentes*, Madrid, Temas de Hoy.

Gorriaran, R. 'El Gobierno veta la presencia de las autonomías en los consejos de la UE', *El Correo* (4 January 2000), p. 23

Greer, S. (1995), 'Decentralised policing in Spain: The case of the autonomous Basque police', *Policing and Society*, 5, 15–36.

Groom, B. 'Regions may face thin time on smaller slice of the EU pie: Tight pressure on funds could rob deprived areas of priority status', *Financial Times* (1 December 1997), p. 10.

Gunther, R., Montero, J. R. and Botella, J. (2004), *Democracy in Modern Spain*, New Haven, Yale University Press.

Gurruchaga, C. 'Las Cortes reclaman que las autonomías estén en los consejos de la UE', *El Mundo* (5 March 1998), p. 7.

Gurrutxaga Abad, A. (2002), *La mirada difusa: dilemas del nacionalismo*, Irún, Alga Política.

Gutierrez Vicén, C. (1998), 'El Senado', in *Informe Comunidades Autónomas*, Barcelona, Instituto de Derecho Público.

Haas, E. (1970), 'The study of regional integration: Reflections on the joy and anguish of pretheorising', *International Organisation*, 24:4, 607–46.

Haas, E. (1968), *The Uniting of Europe*, Stanford, Stanford University Press.

Haas, E. (1961), 'The uniting of Europe and the uniting of Latin America', *Journal of Common Market Studies*, 5:2, 315–43.

Hall, P. and Taylor, R. (1996), 'Political science and the three new institutionalisms', *Political Studies*, 44, 936–57.

Heller, W. (2002), 'Regional parties and national politics in Europe, Spain's *estado de las autonomías* 1993 to 2000', *Comparative Political Studies*, 35:6, 657–85.

Hoffman, S. (1966), 'Obstinate or obsolete? The fate of the nation state and the case of western Europe', *Daedelus*, 95: 862–915.

Hooghe, L. (ed.) (1996), *Cohesion Policy and European Integration: Building Multilevel Governance*, Oxford, Oxford University Press.

Hooghe, L. (1995a), 'Belgian federalism and the European Community', in Keating, M. and Jones, B. (eds.), *The European Union and the Regions*, Oxford, Clarendon Press.

Hooghe, L. (1995b), 'Subnational mobilisation in the European Union', *West European Politics*, 18:3, 175–98.

Hooghe, L. and Marks, G. (2001), *Multilevel Governance and European Integration*, Lanham, Rowman and Littlefield.

Hrbek, R. (1999), 'Effects of EU integration on German federalism', in Jeffrey, C. (ed.), *Recasting German Federalism: The Legacies of Unification*, London, Pinter.

Ibarretxe, J. J. (1998), 'A la búsqueda de un acuerdo político para esta participación', in *La participación de las Comunidades Autónomas en los Consejos de la Unión Europea, jornada celebrada en el Palacio de Artaza, 2 de Julio de 1998*, Oñati, Instituto Vasco de Adminstración Pública.

Iriondo, X. (1997), 'La práctica de la cooperación descentralizada en Vasconia', in Jáuregui, G., Castells, J. M. and Iriondo, X., *La institucionalización jurídica y política de Vasconia*, San Sebastián-Donostia, Sociedad de Estudios Vascos.

Jáuregui Bereciartu, G. (2002), 'ETA: Orígenes y evolución ideológica y política', in Elorza, A., Garmendia, J. M., Jáuregui, G. and Domínguez Iribarren, F., *La historia de ETA*, Madrid, Temas de Hoy.

Jáuregui Bereciartu, G. (1997), 'La reforma del senado y la participación de las Comunidades Autónomas en la Unión Europea', *Revista vasca de administración pública*, 47:3, 11–33.

Jáuregui Bereciartu, G. (1996), *Entre la tragedia y la esperanza. Vasconia ante el nuevo milenio*, Barcelona, Editorial Ariel.

Jáuregui Bereciartu, G. (1986), *Las Comunidades Autónomas y las relaciones internacionales*, Oñati, Instituto Vasco de Administración Pública.

Jeffery, C. (2004), 'Regions and the EU: Letting them in and leaving them alone', *Federal Trust Online Paper*, 20/04, July.

Jeffery, C. (2002), 'Social and regional interests: ESC and Committee of the Regions', in Peterson, J. and Shackleton, M. (eds.), *The Institutions of the European Union*, Oxford, Oxford University Press.

Jeffrey, C. (2000), 'Subnational mobilisation and European integration: Does it make any difference?', *Journal of Common Market Studies*, 38:1, 1–23.

Jeffrey, C. (1997), 'Farewell the third level? The German Länder and the European policy process', *Regional and Federal Studies*, 6:2, 56–75.

Jeffrey, C. (1995), 'Whither the Committee of the Regions? Reflections on the Committee's "Opinion on the Revision of the Treaty on European Union"', *Regional and Federal Studies*, 5:2, 247–57.

Jiménez Asensio, R. (1999), 'Ordenamiento comunitario y ordenamiento autonómico: algunos problemas en la adaptación del derecho comunitario por los parlamentos autonómicos', *Revista vasca de administración pública*, 53:2, 159–86.

John, P. (1996), 'Centralisation, decentralisation and the European Union: The dynamics of triadic relationships', *Public Administration*, 74, 293–313.

Keating, M. (2004), 'Regions and the Convention on the Future of Europe', *South European Society and Politics*, 9:1, 56–75.

Keating, M. (2001), *Plurinational Democracy: Stateless Nations in a Post-Sovereign Era*, Oxford, Oxford University Press.

Keating, M. (1998a), *The New Regionalism in Western Europe: Territorial Restructuring and Political Change*, Cheltenham, Edward Elgar.

Keating, M. (1998b), 'Is there a regional level of government in Europe?', in Le Gales, P. and Lequesne, C. (eds.), *Regions in Europe*, London, Routledge.

Keating, M. (1996), *Nations Against the State – The New Politics of Nationalism in Quebec, Catalonia and Scotland*, London, Macmillan.

Keating, M. (1988), *State and Regional Nationalism – Territorial Politics and the European State*, London, Harvester Wheatsheaf.

Keating, M. and Jones, B. (eds.) (1995), *The European Union and the Regions*, Oxford, Clarendon Press.

Kerremans, B. and Beyers, J. (1996), 'The Belgian subnational entities in the European Union: Second- or third-level players?', *Regional and Federal Studies*, 6:2, 41–55.

Knill, C. and Lehmkuhl, D. (2000), 'An alternative route of European integration: The Community's rail policy', *West European Politics*, 23:1, 65–88.

Kohler-Koch, B. (1996), 'Catching up with change: The transformation of governance in the European Union', *Journal of European Public Policy*, 3:3, 359–80.

Kolinsky, M. (1984), 'The nation state in Western Europe: Erosion from "above" and "below"', in Massey, D. and Allen, J. (eds.), *Geography Matters: A Reader*, Milton Keynes, Open University.

Landman, T. (2000), *Issues and Methods in Comparative Politics: An Introduction*, London, Routledge.

Lasagabaster Herrarte, I. (1995), 'Relaciones intergubernamentales y federalismo cooperativo', *Revista vasca de administración pública*, 41, 203–20.

Lasagabaster Herrarte, I. and Lazcano Brotóns, I. (2004), 'La convivencia lingüística en los medios de comunicación en Euskal Herria', *Revista vasca de administración pública*, 69:3, 101–49.

La Vanguardia, 'El PP arranca el apoyo del PNV, que votará por primera vez sí en un debate de investidura', (30 April 1996), p. 12.

Le Gales, P. and C. Lequesne (eds.) (1998), *Regions in Europe*, London, Routledge.

Leonardi, R. (ed.) (1993), *The Regions and the European Community: The Regional Response to the Single Market in the Underdeveloped Areas*, London, Frank Cass.

Letamendia Belzunce, F. (ed.) (1998), *Nacionalidades y regiones en la Unión Europea*, Oñati, Instituto Vasco de Administración Pública.

Letamendia Belzunce, F. (1997a), 'Basque nationalism and cross-border co-operation between the southern and northern Basque Countries', *Regional and Federal Studies*, 7:2, 25–41.

Letamendia Belzunce, F. (1997b), 'La autodeterminación en Euskal Herria, actores colectivos, territorialidad y cambio político', in Goméz Uranga, M., Lasagabaster, I., Letamendia, F. and Zallo, R. (eds.), *Un nuevo escenario: Democracia, cultura y cohesión social en Euskal Herria*, Bilbao, Fundación Manu Robles-Arangiz Institutua.

Letamendia Belzunce, F. (1994), *Historia del nacionalismo y de ETA – ETA en el franquismo*, San Sebastián, R&B Ediciones.

Lezana, C. 'Ofensiva vasca', *El Correo* (4 May 1999), p. 42.

Lezana, C. 'Los jueces actúan con criterios políticos contra el Concierto', *El Correo* (7 March 1999), p. 50.

Lezana, C. 'Ibarretxe llama a aunar fuerzas en defensa del concierto ante la UE', *El Correo* (17 December 1998), p. 45.

Lezana, C. 'Es muy probable que Euskadi vea reducida las ayudas comunitarias', *El Correo* (8 November 1998), p. 47.

Lindberg, L. N. and Scheingold, S. A. (1970), *Europe's Would-Be Polity: Patterns of Change in the European Community*, New Jersey, Prentice Hall.

Lindberg, L. N. (1963), *The Political Dynamics of European Economic Integration*, Stanford: Stanford University Press.

Llera Ramo, F. J. (2003), 'La política en Euskadi 1977–1998', in Llera Ramo, F. J., Savater, F., Arregui, J. and Elorza, A., *Nacionalismo y democracia*, Salamanca, Ediciones Universidad Salamanca.

Llera Ramo, F. J. (1999), 'Basque polarisation: Between autonomy and independence', *Nationalism and Ethnic Politics*, 5:3, 101–20.

López Aranguren, E. (2002), *Relaciones intergubernamentales en los estados autonómico y federal: Estudio sobre los Estados Unidos, el estado Español y el País Vasco*, Oñati, Instituto Vasco de Administración Pública.

Loughlin, J. (1998), 'La autonomía en la Europa occidental: Un estudio comparado', in Letamendia, F. (ed.), *Naciones y regiones en la Unión Europea*, Oñati, Instituto Vasco de Administración Pública.

Loughlin, J. (1997), 'Representing regions in Europe: The Committee of the Regions', *Regional and Federal Studies*, 6:2, 147–65.

Loughlin, J. (1996), '"Europe of the Regions" and the federalisation of Europe', *Publius: The Journal of Federalism*, 24:4, 141–62.

Loughlin, J. (1993), 'Federalism, regionalism and European Union', *Politics*, 13:1, 9–16.

Luaces Fernández, J. I. (2004), *Desarrollo policéntrico y transporte intermodal en el eje Atlántico Europeo*, Vitoria-Gasteiz, Servicio Central de Publicaciones del Gobierno Vasco.

Lucas Murillo de la Cueva, E. (2000), *Comunidades Autónomas y política europea*, Oñate, Instituto Vasco de Administración Pública.

Lukes, S. (ed.) (1986), *Power*, Oxford, Basil Blackwell.

Lynch, P. (1996), *Minority Nationalism and European Integration*, Cardiff, University of Wales Press.

Mackie, T. and Marsh, D. (1995), 'The comparative method', in Marsh, D. and Stoker, G. (eds.), *Theory and Methods in Political Science*, London, Macmillan Press.

Magdalena, J. A. (2003), *Ferrocarril y competencias de las Comunidades Autónomas*, Barcelona, Cálamo.

Mangas Martin, A. (1998), 'La participación directa de las Comunidades Autónomas en la actuación comunitaria: fase preparatoria', in Pérez Tremps, P. (ed.), *La participación Europea y la acción exterior de las Comunidades Autónomas*, Barcelona, Generalitat de Catalunya, Institut d'Estudis Autonòmics.

Mangas Martin, A. and Liñán Nogueras, D. J. (2004), *Instituciones y derecho de la Unión Europea*, Madrid, Tecnos.

March, J. and Olsen, J. (1996), 'Institutional perspectives on political institutions', *Governance: An International Journal of Policy and Administration*, 9:3, 247–64.

March, J. and Olsen, J. (1989), *Rediscovering Institutions: The Organisational Bias of Politics*, New York, The Free Press.

Marks, G. (1997), 'An actor-centred approach to multilevel governance', *Regional and Federal Studies*, 6:2, 20–38.

Marks, G. (1996), 'Exploring and explaining variation in EU cohesion policy', in Hooghe, L. (ed.), *Cohesion Policy and European Integration: Building Multilevel Governance*, Oxford, Oxford University Press.

Marks, G. (1992), 'Structural policy in the European Community', in Sbragia, A. (ed.), *Europolitics – Institutions and Policymaking in the 'New' European Community*, Washington DC, Brooklings Institute.

Marks, G. and Hooghe, L. (1996), '"Europe with the regions": Channels of regional representation in the European Union', *Publius: The Journal of Federalism*, 26:1, 73–92.

Marks, G., Hooghe, L. and Blank, K. (1996), 'European integration from the 1980s: State-centric *v.* multi-level governance', *Journal of Common Market Studies*, 34:3, 341–78.

Martínez-Herrera, E. (2002), 'Nationalist extremism and outcomes of state policies in the Basque Country, 1979–2001', *International Journal on Multicultural Societies*, 4:1, 1–22.

Marugán, J. A. 'Euskadi, Rioja, Cantabria, Asturias y Navarra colaborarán para una mayor integración en Europa', *El Correo* (21 July 1990), p. 28.

Marugán, J. A. 'Ardanza pretende impulsar el "eje atlántico" con la firma de un convenio bilateral con Aquitania', *El Correo* (3 October 1989), p. 14.

Marugán, J. A. 'Bandrés: "Quienes mandan son Sevillanos y el tren podría ser un regalo a su pueblo"', *El Correo* (12 February 1989), p. 48.

Matía Portilla, F. J. (2003), 'La participación de las Comunidades Autónomas en los comités ejecutivos dependientes de la Comisión Europea', in Biglino Campos, P. (ed.), *La política europea de las Comunidades Autónomas y su control parlamentario*, Valencia, Institut de Dret Públic, tirant lo blanch.

Mayor Menéndez, P. (1999), 'Marco regulador del transporte ferrocarril', in Montoro Chiner, M. J. (ed.), *Infraestructuras ferroviarias del tercer milenio*, Barcelona, Cedecs Editorial.

Mazey, S. (1995), 'Regional lobbying in the new Europe', in Rhodes, M. (ed.), *The Regions and the New Europe*, Manchester, Manchester University Press.

McAleavey, P. and Mitchell, J. (1994), 'Industrial regions and lobbying in the structural fund reform process', *Journal of Common Market Studies*, 32:2, 237–48.

McCarthy, R. (1997), 'The Committee of the Regions: An advisory body's tortuous path to influence', *Journal of European Public Policy*, 4:3, 439–54.

Mees, L. (2003), *Nationalism, Violence and Democracy*, Basingstoke, Palgrave.

Mees, L. (2001), 'Between votes and bullets: Conflicting ethnic identities in the Basque Country', *Ethnic and Racial Studies*, 24:5, 798–827.

Millan, B. (1997), 'The Committee of the Regions: In at the birth', *Regional and Federal Studies*, 7:1, 5–10.

Ministerio de Administraciones Públicas (MAP) (2006a), *Informe sobre la actividad de las conferencias sectoriales. Año 2006*, Madrid.

Ministerio de Administraciones Públicas (MAP) (2006b), *Informe sobre el cumplimiento de los acuerdos de la Conferencia para Asuntos Relacionados con las Comunidades Europeas, de 9 de diciembre de 2004, referente a la participación de las Comunidades Autónomas en el Consejo de Ministros de la Unión Europea. 2006*, Madrid.

Ministerio de Administraciones Públicas (MAP) (2005), *Informe sobre el cumplimiento de los acuerdos de la Conferencia para Asuntos Relacionados con las Comunidades Europeas, de 9 diciembre de 2004, referente a la participación de las Comunidades Autónomas en el Consejo de Ministros de la Unión Europea*, Madrid.

Ministerio de Administraciones Públicas (MAP) (2004), *Informe sobre las relaciones de colaboración Estado-Comunidades Autónomas 2004*, Madrid.

Ministerio de Administraciones Públicas (MAP) (2002), *Las conferencias sectoriales las comisiones bilaterales de cooperación: Informe anual 2002*, Madrid.

Ministerio de Administraciones Públicas (MAP) (2001a), *Las conferencias sectoriales: Informe anual 1999*, Madrid.

Ministerio de Administraciones Públicas (MAP) (2001b), *Las conferencias sectoriales las comisiones bilaterales de cooperación: Informe anual 2001*, Madrid.

Ministerio de Fomento (2005), *Plan estratégico de infraestructuras y transporte*, Madrid.

Ministerio de Obras Públicas, Transportes y Medio Ambiente (MOPTMA) (1994), *Plan director de infraestructuras, segunda edición*, Madrid.

Ministerio de Transportes, Turismo y Comunicaciones (MTTC) (1987), *Plan de transporte ferroviario*, Madrid.

Ministerio para las Administraciones Públicas (MAP) (1996), *Puesta en práctica de los Acuerdos Autonómicos de 1992 y sus efectos sobre el estado autonómico*, Madrid.

Montero, M. (1998), 'La transición y la autonomía vasca', in Ugarte, J. (ed.), *La transición en el País Vasco y España*, Basque Country, Universidad del País Vasco.

Morata, F. and Muñoz, X. (1996), 'Vying for European Funds: Territorial Restructuring in Spain', in Hooghe, L. (ed.), *Cohesion Policy and European Integration: Building Multilevel Governance*, Cambridge, Cambridge University Press.

Moravcsik, A. (1998), *The Choice for Europe: Social Purpose and State Power from Messina to Maastricht*, London, University College London Press.

Moravcsik, A. (1993), 'Preferences and power in the European Community: A liberal intergovernmentalist approach', *Journal of Common Market Studies*, 34:4, 473–524.

Morcillo, A. *Contentious Regions and Disorganised Federalism: The Impact of Territorial and Minority Interests on EU Decisions*, unpublished PhD Thesis, Humboldt-Universität, Berlin, 2006.

Moreno del Río, C. (2000), *La comunidad enmascarada*, Madrid: Centro de Investigaciones Sociológicas.

Muguruza Arrese, J. (1999), 'Los inventivos fiscales forales ante la jurisdicción Comunitaria: ¿qué ha pasado y qué podría llegar a pasar?', *Forum Fiscal de Bizkaia*, 99:144, 7–12.

Muguruza Arrese, J. (1998), 'El Código Europeo de Conducta Fiscal', *Forum Fiscal de Bizkaia*, 98:207, 3–7.

Newton, M. (1997), *Institutions of Modern Spain*, New York, Cambridge University Press.

Nichol, W. and Salmon, T. (2001), *Understanding the European Union*, Harlow, Longman.

Nuñez Seixas, X. M. (1995), 'Nacionalismos y regionalismos ante la formación y consolidación del estado autonómico español (1975–1995): Una interpretación', in Tusell, J., Marín, J. M., Supúlveda, I., Sueiro, S. and Mateos, A. (eds.), *Historia de la transición y consolidación democrática en España*, Madrid, Universidad Nacional de Educación a Distancia.

Ordóñez Solís, D. (2003), 'Legitimación procesal y equilibrio institucional: el acceso de las regiones a los tribunales comunitarios europeos', *Revista de estudios autonómicos*, 4, 137–72.

Ordóñez Solís, D. (2000), 'Las Cortes Generales y los parlamentos autonómicos en la Unión Europea', *Revista de las cortes generales*, 49, 210–56.

Oregui, P. 'Paz fiscal, pero con diferencias apreciables', *El País* (23 January 2000), p. 24.

Ormazabal, M. 'Transportes ve "muy difícil" que la 'Y' férrea se halle operativa en 2010', *El País* (5 May 2006), p. 40.

Ormazabal, M. 'Ibarretxe: la ilegalización de los incentivos fiscales, "la muerte" del concierto', *Cinco Días* (4 July 1999).

Ortega Santiago, C. (2003), 'El Comité de las Regiones', in Biglino Campos, P. (ed.), *La política europea de las Comunidades Autónomas y su control parlamentario*, Valencia, Institut de Dret Públic, tirant lo blanch.

Ortiz de Arri, E. 'Álava elimina los incentivos fiscales a la inversión anulados por los tribunales', *El País Digital* (31 December 1999).

Ortiz de Arri, E. 'Álava recurrirá el fallo contrario a los incentivos fiscales de 1998', *El País* (9 June 1999), p. 57.

Ortúzar Andéchaga, E., Gómez Campo, E. and Hernández Lafuente, A. (1995), *La participación de las Comunidades Autónomas en los asuntos comunitarios europeos*, Madrid, Ministerio para las Administraciones Públicas.

Ortuzar Arruabarrena, A. (1998), 'La situación del debate de esta cuestión en el estado español', *La participación de las Comunidades Autónomas en los Consejos de la Unión Europea, jornada celebrada en el Palacio de Artaza, 2 de Julio de 1998*, Oñati, Instituto Vasco de Adminstración Pública.

Paniagua Soto, J. L. (1999), '¿Qué senado? Reflexiones en torno a las propuestas de reforma', in Paniagua Soto, J. L. and Monedero, J. C. (eds.), *En torno a la democracia en España: Temas abiertos del sistema político español*, Madrid, Technos.

Parejo Alfonso, L. and Betancor Rodríguez, A. (1996), 'Spanish Autonomous Communities and the Committee of the Regions', in Hesse, J. J. (ed.), *Regions in Europe*, Baden Baden, Nomos Verlagsgesellschaft.

Pariente de la Prada, I. (1994), 'El sistema comunitario de control de las ayudas estatales a empresas: La decisión de la Comisión de las Comunidades Europeas de 10 de mayo de 1993 sobre un sistema de ayudas fiscales a la inversión en el País Vasco', *Revista vasca de administración pública*, 39, 205–32.

Parkinson, M. and Harding, A. (1995), 'European cities toward 2000: entrepreneurialism, competition and social exclusion', in Rhodes, M. (ed.), *The Regions and the New Europe*, Manchester, Manchester University Press.

Partido Socialista Obrero Español (PSOE) (2003), *La España plural: La España constitucional, la España unida, la España en positiva (Declaración de Santillana)*, 30 August.

Pérez Arraiz, J. (1994), *El Concierto Económico: Evolución, características y fundamento de la financiación vasca*, Oñati, Instituto Vasco de Administración Pública.

Pérez González, M., Mariño Menéndez, F. and Aldecoa Kuzarraga, F. (1994), *La acción exterior y Comunitaria de los Länder, Regiones, Cantones y Comunidades Autónomas*,

Oñati, Instituto Vasco de Administración Pública.

Pérez Tremps, P. (1987), *Comunidades Autónomas, Estado y Comunidad Europea*, Madrid, Ministerio de Justicia.

Pérez Tremps, P., Cabellos Espiérrez, M. A. and Roig Molés, E. (1998), *La participación europea y la acción exterior de las Comunidades Autónomas*, Barcelona, Generalitat de Catalunya, Institut D'Estudis Autónomos.

Pescador, F. 'Respaldo de la UE al Concierto', *El Correo Digital*, 7 September 2006.

Pescador, F. 'El sistema fiscal vasco se juega su futuro ante el Tribunal de Justicia de la UE', *El Correo* (4 May 1999), p. 41.

Pescador, F. 'Una ikurriña en Bruselas', *El Correo* (5 February 1996), p. 14.

Pescador, F. 'Barrionuevo defiende en la CE la conexión del TGV con la red europea por La Junquera e Irún', *El Correo* (17 October 1989), p. 34.

Pescador, F. 'La CE duda que Euskadi justifique el tren de alta velocidad directo con Madrid y baraja una conexión por Zaragoza', *El Correo* (12 February 1989), p. 48.

Piedrafita, S., Steinberg, F. and Torreblanca, J. I. (2006), *Veinte años de España en la Unión Europea (1986–2006)*, Madrid, Real Instituto Elcano.

Plataforma Logística Aquitania-Euskadi (2001), *Plan Estratégico, Gobierno Vasco and Conseil Régional Aquitaine*, February.

Pollack, M. (1995), 'Regional actors in an intergovernmental play: The making and implementation of EC structural funds', in Mazey, S. and Rhodes, C. (eds.), *State of the European Union, Building a European Polity*, Boulder, Lynne Reiner.

Putnam, R. (1988), 'Diplomacy and domestic politics: The logic of "two-level" games', *International Organisation*, 42, 427–60.

Radaelli, C. M. (1999), 'Harmful tax competition in the EU: Policy narratives and advocacy coalitions', *Journal of Common Market Studies*, 37:4, 661–82.

Ramírez de Ganuza, C. 'Conferencia de Presidentes: Las comunidades del PP', *El Mundo* (11 September 2005), p. 9.

Ramírez de Ganuza, C. 'Fraga impone en el PP la aceptación del encuentro', *El Mundo* (29 October 2004), p. 10.

Reniu i Vilamala, J. M. (2002), *La formación de gobiernos minoritarios en España 1977–96*, Madrid, Centro de Investigaciones Sociológicas.

Reniu i Vilamala, J. M. (2001), '¿Merece la pena coligarse? La formación de gobiernos minoritarios en España, 1977–96', *Revista española de ciencia política*, 5, 11–142.

Rey Martínez, R. (2003), 'La participación a través del estado: Conferencias sectoriales y Conferencia para Asuntos Relacionados con las Comunidades Europeas', in Biglino Campos, P. (ed.), *La política europea de las Comunidades Autónomas y su control parlamentario*, Valencia, Institut de Dret Públic, tirant lo blanch.

Rhodes, M. (ed.) (1995), *The Regions and the New Europe*, Manchester, Manchester University Press.

Rhodes, R. A. W. and Marsh, D. (1992), 'New directions in the study of policy networks', *European Journal of Political Research*, 21, 181–205.

Rhodes, R. A. W., Bache, I. and George, S. (1996), 'Policy networks and policymaking in the European Union: A critical appraisal', in Hooghe, L. (ed.), *Cohesion Policy and European Integration: Building Multilevel Governance*, Oxford, Oxford University Press.

Rodríguez Curiel, J. W. (2005), 'La autonomía fiscal de las autoridades intraestatales no excluye la calificación de ayuda de Estado (Sentencia del Tribunal Supremo de 9.12.2004), *Gaceta Jurídica de la Unión Europea y de la Competencia*, 236, 84–91.

Roig Molés, E. (2002), *Las Comunidades Autónomas y la posición española en asuntos europeos*, Barcelona, Generalitat de Catalunya, Institut d'Estudis Autonómics.

Roig Molés, E. (2001), 'La Conferencia para Asuntos Relacionados con la Unión Europea', in *Informe Comunidades Autónomas 2000*, Barcelona: Instituto de Derecho Público.

Roig Molés, E. (2000), 'La Conferencia para Asuntos Relacionados con la Unión Europea', in *Informe Comunidades Autónomas 1999*, Barcelona, Instituto de Derecho Público.

Roig Molés, E. (1999a), 'La Conferencia para Asuntos Relacionados con la Unión Europea', in *Informe Comunidades Autónomas 1998*, Barcelona, Instituto de Derecho Público.

Roig Molés, E. (1999b), 'Asimetría y participación autonómica en la formación de la voluntad española en los asuntos de la UE: ¿participación a dos velocidades?', *Revista vasca de administración pública*, 55, 199–225.

Roig Molés, E. (1998), 'La Conferencia para Asuntos Relacionados con la Unión Europea', *Informe Comunidades Autónomas 1997*, Barcelona, Instituto de Derecho Público.

Rojo, M. A. 'El Gobierno vasco negociará el lunes en Madrid el plan ferroviario, que costará 157.000 millones', *El Correo* (23 February 1989), p. 37.

Rokkan, S. and Urwin, D. (eds.) (1982), *The Politics of Territorial Identity*, London, Sage.

Roller, E. (2002), 'Reforming the Spanish senate: Mission impossible?' *West European Politics*, 25:4, 69–92.

Ross, J. (1994), 'High-speed rail: Catalyst for European integration?', *Journal of Common Market Studies*, 32:2, 191–214.

Ruiz de Alegría Rogel, P. L. (2001), '*Consejero* de transportes y obras públicas 1989–1991', in Bizkarguenaga Atutxa, I. (ed.), *Historia del Gobierno vasco contada por sus consejeros 1980–1998*, Oñati, Instituto Vasco de Administración Pública.

St. Clair Bradley, K. (2002), 'The European Court of Justice', in Peterson, J. and Shackleton, M. (eds.), *The Institutions of the European Union*, Oxford, Oxford University Press.

Sánchez, M. 'Conferencia de Presidentes: Las comunidades del PSOE', *El Mundo* (11 September 2005), p. 9.

Sánchez, M. 'Los presidentes del PSOE, cómodos y coincidente', *El Mundo* (29 October 2004), p. 10.

Santamaría, J. M. 'El Gobierno vasco mantendrá abierta su oficina en Bruselas, pero dependerá de una sociedad pública', *El Correo* (29 September 1988), p. 11.

Santos, A. 'El "corredor del Cantábrico" enfrenta al Gobierno central y a las administraciones autonómicas del norte de España', *El Correo* (18 September 1989), p. 28.

Sanz Gandasegui, F. (1998), 'Aspectos prácticos de la participación de las Comunidades Autónomas en el proceso de la construcción europea', in Pérez Tremps, P. (ed.), *La participación europea y la acción exterior de las Comunidades Autónomas*, Barcelona, Generalitat de Catalunya, Institut d'Estudis Autonòmics.

Segovia, C. 'La aplicación del régimen fiscal vasco es un precedente peligroso para la UE', *El Mundo* (15 July 1999), p. 1 and 39.

Segovia, C. 'Exteriores ve "ineficaz" la iniciativa', *El Mundo* (5 March 1998), p. 7.

Sharpe, L. (ed.) (1993), *The Rise of Meso Government in Europe*, London, Sage.

Sinova, J. (1993), *Un millón de votos*, Madrid, Temas de Hoy.

Smyrl, M. (1997), 'Does European Community regional policy empower the regions?', *Governance*, 10:3, 287–309.

Sobrido Prieto, M. (2003), *Las Comunidades Autónomas ante el Tribunal de Justicia y el Tribunal de Primera Instancia de Las Comunidades Europeas*, Valencia, tyrant lo blanch.

Sobrino, J. M. (1998), 'El marco comunitario de la participación de las Comunidades Autónomas en los Consejos de Ministros de la Unión Europea', *La participación de las Comunidades Autónomas en los Consejos de Ministros de la Unión Europea, jornada celebrada en el Palacio de Artaza, 2 de julio de 1998*, Oñati, Instituto Vasco de Administración Pública.

Solé Tura, J. (1985), *Nacionalidades y nacionalismos en España: Autonomías, federalismo y autodeterminación*, Madrid, Alianza Editorial.

Stevens, H. (2004), *Transport Policy in the European Union*, Basingstoke, Palgrave.

Subirats, J. and Gallego, R. (eds.) (2002), *Veinte años de autonomías en España: Leyes, políticas públicas, instituciones y opinión pública,* Madrid, Centro de Investigaciones Sociológicas.

Swenden, W. (2004), 'Is the European Union in need of a competence catalogue? Insights from comparative federalism', *Journal of Common Market Studies,* 42:2, 371–92.

Tamayo Salaberia, V. (1991), *Genesis del Estatuto de Gernika,* Oñati, Instituto Vasco de Administración Pública.

Tellitu, A. 'Ramón Jáuregui adelanta en Burdeos que la CE aprobará a finales de año el trazado ferroviario del "eje atlántico"', *El Correo* (14 October 1989), p. 10.

Tömmel, I. (1998), 'Transformation of governance: The European Commission's strategy for creating a "Europe of the Regions"', *Regional and Federal Studies,* 8:2, 52–80.

Torres Murillo, J. L. 'El Rey Juan Carlos puso la primera traviesa, en el ancho europeo, de la línea férrea de alta velocidad Madrid-Córdoba', *El Correo* (3 October 1989a), p. 32.

Torres Murillo, J. L. 'Barrionuevo resta importancia al conflicto con Vitoria sobre los protocolos', *El Correo* (3 October 1989b), p. 32.

Torres Murillo, J. L. 'El Gobierno central quiso negociar el "contenido" de la oficina', *El Correo* (29 September 1988), p. 11.

Torres Murrillo, J. L. 'El Gobierno vasco negocia con tres ministros en Madrid proyectos de infraestructura para Euskadi', *El Correo* (27 September 1988), p. 31.

Torres Murillo, J. L. 'El Gobierno central recurre la instalación de la oficina vasca en Bruselas por supuesta invasión de competencias', *El Correo* (10 September 1988), p. 11.

Ubarretxena, A. 'La CE reconoce oficialmente su apoyo a las relaciones entre la CAV, Nafarroa y Aquitania', *Deia* (15 May 1993), p. 5.

Vallejo de Olejua, E. 'Sr. Barrionuevo: ¡Es una evidencia!', *El Correo* (25 January 1989), p. 29.

Van Amersfoort, H. and Mansvelt Beck, J. (2000), 'Institutional plurality: a way out of the Basque conflict', *Journal of Ethnic and Migration Studies,* 26:3, 449–67.

Verges Bausili, A. (2003), 'Rethinking methods of dividing and exercising powers in the EU', in Magnette, P., Shaw J., Hoffmann, L. and Verges, A., *The Convention on the Future of Europe: Working Towards an EU Constitution,* London, The Federal Trust.

Warleigh, A. (1999), *The Committee of the Regions: Institutionalising Multilevel Governance?,* London, Kogan Page.

Wiener, A. and Diez, T. (2004), *European Integration Theory,* Oxford, Oxford University Press.

Wise, M. (2000), 'The Atlantic Arc: Transnational European reality or regional mirage?', *Journal of Common Market Studies,* 38:5, 865–90.

Wright, V. (1998), 'Intergovernmental relations and regional government in Europe: A skeptical view', in Le Gales, P. and Lequesne, C. (eds.), *Regions in Europe,* London, Routledge.

Ysàs, P. (1998), 'El proceso hacia el Estado de las Autonomías', in Ugarte, J. (ed.), *La transición en el País Vasco y España, historia y memoria,* Basque Country, Universidad del País Vasco.

Zubiri, I. (2000), *El Sistema de Concierto Económico en el contexto de la Unión Europea,* Bilbao, Círculo de Empresarios Vascos.

Zubirte, I. 'Socialistas vascos y aquitanos estudian en San Sebastián formulas que permitan un desarrollo del "eje atlántico"', *El Correo* (15 April 1989).

Index

Note: page numbers in bold refer to main entries.